THE PROCRASTINATION ECONOMY

The Procrastination Economy

The Big Business of Downtime

Ethan Tussey

NEW YORK UNIVERSITY PRESS

New York

NEW YORK UNIVERSITY PRESS
New York
www.nyupress.org

References to Internet websites (URLs) were accurate at the time of writing. Neither the author nor New York University Press is responsible for URLs that may have expired or changed since the manuscript was prepared.

Library of Congress Cataloging-in-Publication Data
Names: Tussey, Ethan, author.
Title: The procrastination economy : the big business of downtime /
Ethan Tussey.
Description: New York : New York University Press, [2017] |
Includes bibliographical references and index.
Identifiers: LCCN 2017014188 | ISBN 9781479844234 (cl : alk. paper)
Subjects: LCSH: Recreation—Economic aspects. | Work environment. |
Procrastination.
Classification: LCC GV181.3 .T87 2018 | DDC 306.4/8—dc23
LC record available at https://lccn.loc.gov/2017014188

New York University Press books are printed on acid-free paper, and their binding materials are chosen for strength and durability. We strive to use environmentally responsible suppliers and materials to the greatest extent possible in publishing our books.

Manufactured in the United States of America

10 9 8 7 6 5 4 3 2 1

Also available as an ebook

For Becky

CONTENTS

Introduction

During the Second World War, factory owners responding to trends in industrial psychology devoted considerable time to identifying music that could make employees more productive. In 1937, the Industrial Health Research Board of Great Britain conducted a study in which the productivity of confectionary workers was measured against the temporal qualities of six different music genres.[1] The researchers were looking for music that could alleviate the boredom of repetitive factory work and mitigate procrastination. The study showed that workers responded to a program of "familiar" and "simple" dance music that changed styles after no "less than one hour or more than two hours in each spell of work."[2] The study, and others like it, inspired employers, governments, and companies to compose music that could make their employees more productive.[3]

The arrival of transistor radios a few years later gave individuals the ability to change their surroundings through the power of music. It was clear that music had a positive impact on the workplace, but could people be trusted to listen to the "right" kind of music to maximize productivity? In 1965, a *New York Times* editorial decried the noise and distraction that modern technologies had brought to the city and saved particular vitriol for the "cretins" who "lovingly hug their shrieking transistor radios with a look of rapt idiocy."[4] Mobile devices, whether transistor radios or smartphones, can reveal individual will and threaten institutional order because they offer agency in public spaces. Despite this disruptive potential, people find ways of integrating their mobile device use into the rhythms of their workday.

The proliferation of Internet-connected mobile devices amplifies the issues raised by transistor radios. A 2013 *Advertising Age* report showed that people spend more time engaged with personal mobile devices than with any other media screen.[5] According to the study, people most often use their devices to text, email, Internet browse, make calls, listen to music, play with apps, consult maps, and "check in" (sharing their location information).[6] The centrality of these devices in our daily lives has raised concerns that the technology may be contributing to loneliness, arrested development, shortened attention spans, and declines in grammar, memory, and intimacy.[7] These concerns focus on the functionality of the mobile technology and the time spent on the devices. Often missing from stories about mobile devices is the context of use, which media scholars such as Nick Couldry and Anna McCarthy argue is essential to understanding media technologies.[8] A 2015 Pew Research study showed that the top-five places for using smartphones were "at home" (99%), "in transit" (82%), "at work" (69%), "waiting in line" (53%), and "at a community place" (51%).[9] The hours logged on mobile devices may seem egregious, but they become much more understandable when considered as an enhancement of existing behaviors in these specific contexts.

For example, people such as Lee Ann Hiliker of Hobbs Herder Advertising in Santa Ana, California, have organized NCAA tournament office pools since the sporting event expanded to 64 teams in 1985.[10] For Hiliker, the tournament provided a common topic of conversation and a chance to learn more about her coworkers and to brag about her alma mater, the University of Arizona. Office workers such as Hiliker and her colleagues predict the winner of each tournament game, and the entrant with the most correct predictions wins the pool. In 2006, CBS began offering a free streaming video broadcast of its NCAA tournament coverage, which allowed employees to watch games at their desks.[11] The audience research firm Challenger, Gray, and Christmas estimated that the event cost the nation's economy billions of dollars in lost productivity.[12] Major media outlets picked up on this figure and published stories about the dangers of watching the games at work. These alarmist reports ignored the fact that employees discussed the tournament, checked scores, or set up portable televisions to watch the tournament long before streaming video was a part of office culture.[13] Furthermore, the numbers used in the Challenger, Gray, and Christmas estimate are only accurate if every person that reported to be a sports fan in the country decided to watch every second of every game at work.[14] Such a scenario is highly improbable. The outrage and concern over workplace viewing focuses on the disruptive potential of the mobile devices instead of the ways they relate to existing workplace culture.

A similar complaint is levied against the use of mobile devices on the commute. Critiques of mobile devices claim that this technology disconnects individuals from the community.[15] Buskers have sung on public transit to earn money and transform trains into communal concert halls for decades.[16] Public-transit authorities discourage these performances and encourage riders to wear headphones if they want to transform their commute through music. Considering these restrictions, smartphones actually increase options for socializing on public transit by enabling people to engage in conversations remotely and discreetly.

Music has been a part of commutes just as games and puzzles have been a part of waiting rooms prior to the proliferation of mobile devices. In 1996, Eileen McNamara of the *Boston Globe* wrote about the many ways people cope with the tyranny of waiting.[17] Her story described the "waiting room veteran" who returned to the hospital day after day to dote at the side of a coma patient. To pass the time, the veteran invited people to work on puzzles and provided hugs and comfort to those who needed it. Not all waiting rooms come with a kindhearted veteran, but mobile devices provide tools for coping such as abundant games and easy access to people who can give us comfort.

People also turn to media technologies to help them navigate the social dynamics of their homes. For example, Linda Paulson placed a television in her bathroom to create a private sanctuary away from her daily stresses.[18] Paulson's tactics are echoed in research that demonstrates the variety of ways people use media technologies and content to navigate the politics of everyday life.[19] Media technologies can provide a topic of conversation for coworkers, a shared reference can be the currency that solidifies a friendship, and the positioning of screens can invite conversation or repel unwanted interactions.[20] Smartphones and tablets are merely the latest media technologies to help people navigate the politics of public space.

Long before Internet-connected mobile devices became popular, Paulson, Hiliker, commuters, and "waiting room veterans" looked to sporting events, music, games, and television to help them connect with others and assert themselves in their surroundings. The versatility of smartphones, tablets, and laptop computers makes these technologies all-purpose tools for navigating specific contexts such as the living room, the commute, the workplace, and the waiting room. Mobile devices' association with these specific contexts is meaningful as emerging technologies are inextricably linked to their primary contexts of use. The historian Carolyn Marvin explains that the development of the telephone, for example, was shaped by its integration into the home.[21] As the telephone was a technology of the domestic sphere, manufacturers had to address concerns about privacy.[22] Telephone companies addressed these fears by creating private lines and fostering formal etiquette. The film historian Robert Sklar describes a similar relationship between early film theaters, immigrant communities, and the foundations of the movie industry.[23] The same goes for television's rise to popularity, which Lynn Spigel attributes to the television industry's efforts to situate the technology as a part of postwar suburban living rooms.[24] In each of these cases, media technologies develop aesthetics and conventions appropriate to specific spatial contexts.

While mobile technology gives people greater control over their surroundings, it also allows advertisers and media companies into our everyday routines. Media companies attempt to capitalize on our mobile habits and behaviors in particular contexts. The media historian William Boddy explains, "the commercial launch of any new communications technology typically combines a public rehearsal of contested and self-serving fantasies of the new product's domestic consumption with a polemical ontology of its medium and an ideological rationale for its social function."[25] The "rehearsal" and discursive process travels through five stages: "technical invention," "cultural innovation," "legal regulation," "economic distribution," and "social mainstreaming." Boddy's description provides a structure for tracking the progress of mobile devices in the cultural imagination. Mobile devices are currently in the moment of "economic distribution," in which media industries and creative entrepreneurs attempt to develop long-term business models for this nascent technology.[26] According to Boddy's theory, once a viable business model takes hold, it shapes future production and consumer habits.

In 2007, the audience for Internet video matched the corresponding daytime television audience, inspiring entertainment companies to target online viewers.[27] Digital production divisions such as New Line Cinema's "the hub," Sony's "The Station" and "Crackle," and NBC's "Dotcomedy" created content specifically for the online audience. At the same time, the *New York Times* observed that American cubicle dwellers were increasingly choosing to spend their break time watching online videos, playing Flash games, and engaging in social networking instead of hanging out at the watercooler.[28] The market research firm Visible Measures reported spikes in website traffic during the six-hour period from noon Eastern Time to three p.m. Pacific Time, when the audience went online looking for content during lunch breaks.[29] Digital content executives such as NBC's vice president of digital content and development, Carole Angelo, confirmed that studios adjusted their content and their production schedules to match these view-ing behaviors.[30] Targeting a specific audience at a specific time gave industry veterans a familiar template and business model for mobile screens. The proliferation of smartphones intensified the entertainment industries' targeting of the workday online au-dience. A 2015 Pew study indicates that 68% of US adults have a smartphone, including 86% of those ages 18 to 29, and 83% of 30- to 49-year-olds.[31] These are the same populations that are prized by advertisers and entertainment companies. Targeting these people's "in-between" moments became a strategy for creating platforms and services for mobile devices. These efforts have implications for the form and content associated with mobile devices as companies such as NBC create short-form programs for mobile apps such as Snapchat that feature the vertical orientation and aspect ratio of the mobile screen.[32]

I call these efforts to monetize mobile users' in-between mo-ments the *procrastination economy*. This book reveals the procrasti-nation economy by putting mobile devices in historical, industrial, and spatial context. The procrastination economy predates mo-bile devices, but the proliferation of smartphones and tablets has dramatically expanded commercial interest. The procrastination economy is different from leisure time, for which producers can assume that consumers seek entertainment in the comfort of their home, a theater, or a specialized venue. It is different from work time, when people reach for their mobile phones to complete tasks. It is not a "distraction economy" because people actively choose to use their phones to help them navigate their surroundings. Many businesses offer products and services for leisure and work, but thanks to mobile devices, media companies are now targeting our in-between moments to help us kill time. Consumers in the procrastination economy largely accept efforts to monetize their mobile habits because in exchange, they receive tools for using cul-ture, information, entertainment, or games to help them navigate a variety of social situations and enhance their mobile conversations.

Media companies, device manufacturers, and software developers are each engaged in commercializing the procrastination economy. In these efforts, they contribute to a common understanding of mobile media usage that privileges the behaviors and habits of the most active and monetizable members of the procrastination economy. Media companies develop distribution technologies and platforms such as the mobile apps for Netflix, YouTube Red, and HBOGo, designed to entice people to subscribe to these services in order to fill their in-between moments with streaming video. Marketers develop strategies to integrate their brands in the social interactions of those who will proselytize for their products via Snapchat "lenses," emoji keyboards, and GIF generators. Social media platforms such as Facebook and Twitter develop such interfaces as News Feed and Moments to simplify mobile navigation and make it easier to see advertisements when people communicate with friends during breaks in the day. Apple and Samsung develop hardware and software on their mobile devices, such as Background Playback, to ensure that people can use their Apple Music, Spotify, or Tidal music subscriptions while they multitask in their in-between moments. Whether through content, marketing, or functionality, media companies are monetizing the procrastination economy by focusing on the habits of mobile users that are most amenable to subscription services, micropayments, and marketing.

Industry Studies + Site-Specific Analysis + Software Studies

Researching the procrastination economy requires an understanding of how people use mobile devices in particular contexts. Lynn Spigel and Anna McCarthy have demonstrated methods for analyzing media technologies in context.[33] Both scholars publish research that defines media in relation to the strategies of media corporations, the capabilities of media technologies, and people's use of media within particular contexts. McCarthy advocates for a site-specific approach that provides scholars with stable footing for understanding how spatial dynamics influence public reception. Spigel similarly considers the politics of space as a lens for documenting the domestication of emerging technology, but she combines this analysis with discourse analysis of articles from industry trade publications and the popular press. Following these approaches, this book defines the procrastination economy by examining the rhetoric, regulations, and programming that create the institutional logic of four unique spaces: work, the commute, the waiting room, and the "connected" living room. In addition, each chapter of the book provides accounts of user activity within these spaces on the basis of ethnographic analysis of particular sites and evidence of user-generated content within these sites.

The site-specific research presented in this book pairs with analysis of the software and hardware that make the procrastination economy possible. The field of new media theory provides a research tradition to explain how certain technological affordances relate to patterns of use and the establishment of power relations between consumers and producers.[34] The technological affordances of mobile media devices are determined by the fundamentals of digital technology, the infrastructure that enables communication, the software that shapes the user experience, and the hardware that people hold in their hands. New media scholars such as Alexander Galloway and Lev Manovich have argued that lines of code and the language of digital technology itself have ideological restrictions that favor certain uses over others, including database logic, customization, and personalization.[35] Others, such as Yochai Benkler and Pierre Levy, see the decentralized online network of digital communication as one that favors democracy and collaboration and that challenges the economic position of traditional media companies.[36] Beyond hardware, a layer of software provides a frame for accessing and distributing thoughts and ideas. Scholarship by Ian Bogost and Jose Van Dijck point to the ways in which software enables certain uses of mobile devices and describes those uses' attending ideologies.[37] At their most reductive, these new media theories tend toward technological determinism. Combining these theories with context-based analysis of economic forces leads to a nuanced depiction of the procrastination economy.

In addition, each chapter provides an analysis of the media industries that create the content and services of the procrastination economy. Drawing from the field of media industries studies, the research in these chapters examines industry trade discourse, distribution contracts, and production cultures as evidence of the ways creative workers understand the mobile audience and the mobile "day part." Media industries studies as defined by the work of Alisa Perren, Jennifer Holt, Vicki Mayer, and John T. Caldwell argues that looking at self-reflexive discourse within the media industries provides traces of the creative process and assumptions about media consumers.[38] Adopting these methodologies requires discourse analysis, analysis of technology trade shows, and an understanding of the business models and challenges facing content production, distribution, and exhibition. Accordingly, the research in this book incorporates industry trade publications as well as interviews with media industries workers that focus on the procrastination economy. A consideration of culture of the media industries provides insights into which affordances of mobile technology are nurtured and adopted and which are muted. The use of a media industries approach is particularly important as producers are experiencing a changing relationship with the audience thanks to digital technologies. As media companies arrive at an understanding about the mobile audience, they set the parameters and expectations for their engagement with the audience. Applying media industries approaches to the study of the procrastination economy reveals how media companies come to understand the mobile audience.

Through these approaches, this book argues that mobile media devices are at the forefront of the power struggle between a digitally empowered audience and the media conglomerates that seek to harness and commercialize online behavior. There is a tendency for scholars to describe the emerging online entertainment market either as an opportunity for audiences to wrest control from traditional distributors or as a moment when international conglomerates colonize mobile screens and provide users with a false sense of empowerment.[39] Key to the debate is the question of who benefits from the ways the Internet facilitates the flow of culture and information across the globe. Scholars such as Yochai Benkler see the decentralized nature of digital technology and the culture of collaboration that has defined online interaction as a sign that digital technology will foster bottom-up "folk" culture, free from the institutional influences that have made other mass media so manipulative.[40] Other scholars such as Manuel Castells look at digital technology in terms of economic realities and conclude that the culture of the Internet is actually fostering neoliberal principles that ultimately serve the media conglomerates.[41]

The public use of mobile devices is ideal for examining the political potential of a new technology. Mobile usage in public space is a moment when people use technology to navigate the private/public divide through the products and services of the procrastination economy.[42] I do not accept the dichotomy that sometimes splits cultural studies from political economic analysis; rather, I embrace the spatial approach that brings together the macro-analysis of the media industries and micro-analysis of cultural objects in specific contexts. The procrastination economy reveals conflict between audiences' desire for greater control over content and the industries' attempts to restrict control and maintain or establish revenue streams.[43] The friction points in these negotiations have material influence on the use of culture in our daily lives. Analyzing these points, such as access to content on mobile devices or the quality of a streaming video clip, exposes the media industries' challenges as they attempt to integrate digital entertainment into their existing media operations. Analyzing the actions of the mobile media audience, entertainment studios, digital distribution divisions, television producers, and web companies provides a way of understanding the creation and consumption of online media culture. The research presented in this book shows that certain audiences and industries have more influence over our understanding of mobile media culture than others do but that the meaning of mobile media culture is ever changing as the technologies and businesses of the procrastination economy continue to evolve.

The site-specific analysis in the following chapters focuses on the in-between spaces separating private and public life. The theorist Marc Augé calls these spaces "non-places" and claims they are important sites for understanding modern identity.[44] According to Augé, the modern global citizen feels most at home in these non-places because they are similarly designed no matter where one is in the world. Adriana de Souza e Silva argues that using a mobile device in these non-places makes them a "hybrid space," at once virtual and corporeal.[45] Still more abstract is Mackenzie Wark's concept of "telesthesia," which suggests that our sense of location is mediated through the global flows of media; thus, these non-spaces only become specific through the ways they are represented by the media content that people can access in them.[46] For example, the sound studies scholar Michael Bull points to the ways people use mobile devices to bring definition to these non-spaces through their customizable playlists, which turns a "cold" non-place into a familiar "warm space."[47] Across each of these theories is an insistence that in the era of mobile media, our devices define our experience of space. Indeed, in an increasingly globalized world, mobile media devices may be the key technology that helps one navigate and bring order to these spaces.

The Procrastination Economy at Work, on the Commute, in the Waiting Room, and through the "Connected" Living Room

Each chapter of the book provides an example of how a particular in-between space is constructed by the procrastination economy, together with an example of how audiences use their mobile devices to engage with this construct. These spatial politics are central to entertainment companies considering mobile devices as a key site of commerce and marketing. The media franchises that accommodate the politics of space will be more useful to their audiences and thus more successful.

Chapter 1 argues that the procrastination economy has fostered a mobile day part that assists media companies as they program and distribute content to mobile audiences. Film and television studios, mobile carriers, and software developers use this procrastination economy to monetize the in-between moments of the workday. While mobile devices have become essential to the entertainment industries as vehicles of promotion, branding, distribution, and engagement, audiences use smartphones, tablets, laptops, and wearable technology to wield the culture and conversation of the procrastination economy as a tool for navigating public space. Drawing from media industries studies, cultural studies, and new media theory, this chapter shows that mobile devices are enhancing and amplifying certain mobile users' behaviors and privileging them as the preferred mobile audience. The economic effort to monetize the ways a mobile audience spends their in-between moments has significant repercussions for the possibilities of the mobile Internet.

Chapter 2 examines the procrastination economy of the workplace. Composed of several case studies including a look at the Fox Sports web series *Lunch with Benefits* and three examples of workplace audiences, the chapter reveals how the entertainment industry targets the workplace as a way of promoting television programs and film franchises. Through interviews and observations of a production culture of the procrastination economy, it is clear that television networks intentionally program snackable content, positioning it as an entertaining alternative to the drudgery of modern work. Though media snacking is intended to carry audiences from one conglomerate-owned media platform to the more substantial (and lucrative) offerings on television and movie screens, the procrastination economy actually affords workers enough freedom to add new and interesting, if perhaps unintended, uses for this content. Watercooler gossip, office camaraderie, and mood management are a few of the ways workers use these snacks to creatively engage with one another and foster community.

Chapter 3 examines the procrastination economy of the commute as defined by "smart" car technology, outdoor advertising companies, audio-streaming platforms, and public-transit agencies. The media companies targeting the commute present in-between moments as a time for commerce and personal leisure. At the same time, networked mobile devices offer a means of communication that has previously been impossible on the commute. Contrary to concerns about individualism and increased disconnection with public space, this chapter argues that mobile devices have actually increased social opportunities in spaces in which people were previous disinclined to be social. Evidence of this communication is drawn from a study of the mobile media habits of MARTA (Metro Atlanta Rail Transit Authority) commuters. Over 200 participants shared their opinions and provided evidence of their mobile device use on their commute. The results show that the commute has become a key site for social maintenance and offers people digital tools for enhancing conversations with friends and family.

Chapter 4 considers the procrastination economy of the waiting room. The act of waiting is a moment when people are confronted with their economic and social standing. Those who are made to wait are subject to the schedule of an institution or authority. Mobile devices and the culture of the procrastination economy provide tools for navigating this feeling of powerlessness. Through interviews with Turner Private Networks, the division of Time Warner that programs content for CNN Airport and other waiting rooms, the chapter reveals how companies have approached the waiting room audience for over three decades. Previous research on airports and waiting rooms done by Anna McCarthy provides a template for this chapter and the theory that accompanies it.[48] An analysis of the mobile gaming industry and its users adds to these historical accounts and the interviews with Turner. Examining the fans of "casual games," the chapter shows that mobile technologies allow people in waiting rooms a sense of empowerment and agency. The games and their fans provide evidence of the ways waiting room audiences use culture to navigate their spatial dynamics, their relationship to a media franchise, and their own position in public space.

Chapter 5 looks at the "connected" living room as a space of multiple screens. The evolution of "second screen" apps and "smart" TVs is presented as evidence of efforts to monetize the audience's attention as our eyes drift from the television screen. An examination of the relationship between the television industry and Twitter provides evidence of the ways the entertainment industry understands the procrastination economy in the living room. While dual-screen efforts to capture attention is concerning, research on cable television owners' desires for mobile functionality shows that people look to their mobile devices as a way of gaining control over the social dynamics of the living room. Considering the history of studies on the living room audience, this chapter shows how mobile devices offer solutions to decades of competition and gender-based inequality regarding control of the television remote.

The conclusion draws from the evidence of the preceding chapters to argue that the procrastination economy is crucial to the development of the "Internet of Things." The Internet of Things refers to a future in which computer technology will network together everyday objects to increase efficiency and productivity. In this formulation, media companies will be further engrained in our everyday lives, and owners of intellectual property will find new ways of managing their brands across media platforms. The evidence throughout this book offers a warning to this efficiency discourse. The procrastination economy will continue in an era of ubiquitous computing. This means that attempts to integrate networked technology in everyday routines will require an understanding of how people behave in particular contexts. Through analysis of Pokémon Go, Snapchat, and Samsung's "smart" appliances, the conclusion applies the principles of the procrastination economy to theories about the Internet of Things. Critical to this argument is the idea expressed by Henry Jenkins that a major danger of the convergence era is the "participation gap."[49] The procrastination economy privileges mobile users who know how to use their mobile devices to their advantage. This means that those who understand how to adjust the settings, privacy controls, and push notifications can exert the most control over the technology. Those who struggle to control their devices will face an Internet of Things that automates the experience of navigating a digitally networked world. The development of the procrastination economy participation gap has serious implications for the development of the Internet and the future of the entertainment industry.

The Procrastination Economy considers mobile media culture from the theoretical perspectives of media industries studies, cultural studies, television studies, and new media studies. From these perspectives, I argue that the context of use is critical to understanding mobile media devices and their concomitant culture. By emphasizing social context and media use through various case studies, I debunk oversimplified arguments about mobile technology. This book provides a sense of continuity by showing how mobile technology complements and enhances existing audience behaviors. It also provides a critical history of the development of mobile media as a cultural object. The chapters that follow build on traditions and accepted theoretical arguments in cultural studies and media studies to explain that mobile technology is not so much a revolution as it is an amplification of people's creative uses of culture in everyday life.

1

The Procrastination Economy and the Mobile Day Part

Comedian Louis C.K. often aims his acerbic wit at mobile phones and their users. Expressing concern about the technology, he claims it provides constant distractions that keep people from facing the realities of life: "That's why we text and drive. I look around, pretty much 100 percent of the people driving are texting. And they're killing, everybody's murdering each other with their cars. But people are willing to risk taking a life and ruining their own because they don't want to be alone for a second because it's so hard."[1] C.K.'s humor reflects concerns about media technologies that have occupied scholars for decades. Media and communications technologies change our relationship with the outside world by blurring the division between public and private life. Evaluating the technological affordance of television, Raymond Williams used the concept of "mobile privatization" to describe the ways television enabled people to enter public life from the comfort of their home.[2] In an analysis of portable television, Lynn Spigel flipped Williams's term to "privatized mobility" to describe how mobile devices enable people to bring the comforts of home to public spaces.[3] People enjoy privatized mobility every time they use their mobile devices to access their personal media collections or have a private conversation in public spaces. Critics of mobile devices see these activities as a cocoon that separates people from the outside world.[4]

The fact that mobile devices often act as a barrier to public interaction leads people to see mobile technology as detrimental to empathy and community. The cultural theorist Jonathan Sterne equates mobile devices with increased individualism, as people can use these devices to customize their experience of public spaces.[5] Michael Bull claims that mobile devices create an "audio bubble" that physically separates people from their fellow citizens.[6] A substantial amount of research on mobile devices has focused on the question of the effects of mobile devices on social interactions.[7] Zizi Papacharissi's work sees mobile devices as offering a retreat to a private sphere where people can feel comfortable engaging with public life.[8] For Papacharissi, mobile device use in public space is a political act in which people assert their autonomy by "sustain[ing] existing relationships and creat[ing] new ones."[9] Scott Campbell's research confirms some of Papacharissi's arguments, as he finds that mobile devices offer "network privatism" by supporting strong relationships and hindering weak relationships.[10] Essentially, these devices make it easier to stay connected with our loved ones while also helping us disconnect from our immediate surroundings.

Mobile devices amplify and enhance preexisting behaviors and tactics for navigating public space. If we focus on the procrastination economy, mobile devices are positioned in the appropriate spatial and historical context. Media technologies have long been used to fill our downtime, and modern mobile devices are a part of this history. Only by understanding this history does the procrastination economy emerge as the dominant logic that supports mobile use and the monetization efforts that attempt to profit on those habits. Scholars tend to overlook the contextual factors in favor of an examination of the technological affordances of mobile devices. For example, Campbell contends that mobile devices, smartphones in particular, have affordances that offer "an added layer of flexibility by allowing for flows of information, communication, and content while users are physically in motion and/or carrying out their normal, and not so normal, affairs and activities."[11] Campbell's assessment of the technology is accurate—mobile devices do enable constant connectivity—but this technological affordance does not determine use or explain why people use them in particular contexts. Campbell's concept of "network privatism" suggests that we look to our mobile devices for comfort and familiarity, but the history of the procrastination economy shows that we have always looked to media to fulfill this desire. Contextualizing mobile device use as part of the history of site-specific media more accurately explains how the technology extends social and cultural practices.

The History of the Procrastination Economy

The pervasiveness of personal mobile devices has brought new attention to our everyday routines. Yet, compared to leisure and recreational pursuits, the activities we enjoy when "killing time," multitasking, or procrastinating are often dismissed as ephemera. Cultural critics and academics treat the cinema, television, and video games as art forms worthy of analysis, while procrastination is the domain of efficiency experts, a bad habit to be corrected. Despite the stigma, accounts of mobile media use throughout history reveal the sophisticated ways different technologies have allowed people to weave entertainment properties, telecommunication, and art into their everyday lives. The history of the procrastination economy shows that mobile technologies have always been used for productivity, recreation, and socializing appropriate to particular social and spatial politics. At the same time, marketing and media companies have targeted the procrastination economy in an attempt to monetize these mobile habits. The pursuit of the mobile audience informs the development of products and services. The history of the procrastination economy is one in which people have consistently used mobile technologies to assert their agency in public space, while media companies have supported this desire and privileged those audiences who most often turn to mobile media in their in-between moments.

Books

The history of mobile media culture begins with the first mobile media technology, books. The historian Sydney Shep explains,

"Unlike cave paintings, stelae, totems or monuments, the material form of the book is a fundamentally portable communication technology."[12] In Shep's estimation, the portability of the book enabled globalization; it facilitated the transport of revolutionary ideas and injected media into everyday life.[13] The power of this portable media was also seen as a danger, particularly for women, who were considered weak-willed and susceptible to retreating from reality via reading. Even more distressing to early cultural critics was the concern that people could steal away with a book and, unsupervised, encounter lewd ideas or dangerous notions. These concerns resulted in the banning of books—a practice designed to ensure that any books people privately enjoyed would be wholesome and safe.[14]

The desire to regulate the use of mobile media for the sake of the public good is one that reoccurs throughout the history of mobile media. Censors could control the content of mobile media but not how that content was used. Reading in public spaces presented a number of opportunities for people to navigate the politics of public space. Mary Hammond notes that at the beginning of the nineteenth century, "reading in public spaces such as train carriages serve[d] a number of social functions, from avoiding the gazes of predatory fellow-passengers to advertising one's literary taste."[15] The history of books makes clear that people use mobile technology intentionally to negotiate their relationships to public spaces despite efforts to regulate usage. The act of bringing a book to a public space can be threatening to the status quo because the act of reading signals that a person's attention and engagement is private and not necessarily aligned with the ideology of his or her surroundings.

Amateur Portables Era

The invention of electronic mobile media devices in the 20th century could only intensify the issues raised by books. As early as the 1910s, radio amateurs were converting military wireless radio technology and consumer electronics to create early portable radios.[16] These early "portables" were designed in response to amateur radio contests and were not intended for commercial use.[17] The anthropologist Michael Brian Schiffer explains that though the first portables were popular for outdoor activities, such as Boy Scout retreats, they were primarily a curiosity.[18] Amateur operators dominated the early history of wireless communication. This largely male community of hobbyists influenced early efforts to expand the capabilities of broadcasting. For this group of pioneers, portable radios were more science experiment than a conduit to culture and conversation.

Entertainment and cultural programming were not broadcast until businesses understood the commercial potential of radio. Throughout the 1920s, consumer products companies such as Crosley Musicone, Outing, and Grebe attempted to capitalize on the public's love affair with radio by making portable devices for cars, camping trips, and other summertime activities.[19] The ability to be in public spaces and reach a faraway place fascinated early adopters. From the beginning, the design of mobile devices was conceived with particular public places in mind, namely, on vacation, in the car, and in nature. The technology may not have been reliable, but the brief portable craze of the 1920s provided a glimpse of Americans' desire for mobile entertainment to enhance their experience of public spaces.

Transistor Radio Era

Portable radios became more technologically advanced in the 1930s and 1940s, as the components became smaller, but the devices did not become truly popular until the invention of the transistor in the early 1950s. Transistors replaced the bulkier and more energy-intensive Audion tubes, making portable radios inexpensive and long lasting. The end of the Second World War, the development of America's automobile culture, and the beginnings of teen-focused marketing had a massive effect on mobile media. Portable radios provided people with a sense of independence and control over space, as it enabled people to fill their surroundings with music. The rise of the teen audience changed the music industry, as record labels began making rock 'n' roll music that teens could conceal from their parents via personal headphones.[20] Schiffer writes, "The shirt-pocket portable or, simply, *the transistor* (as it was called then) became a metaphor for freedom and independence; the right to express, in music and in things, the style and tastes of youth."[21] The popularity and utility of the transistor to youth audiences came as a surprise to manufacturers that originally thought these devices would be too expensive for young people and targeted adults instead.[22] Teens' desire for control and the ability to evade adult supervision guided the design of mobile devices. Not only did the needs of the audience dictate the direction of the technology, but the aesthetics of the music adjusted to be more conducive to headphones.[23] Throughout the late 1950s, portable-radio makers such as Zenith directed their advertising to American teens by inserting the devices in teen hangouts like the soda shop.[24] As American radio makers competed with Japanese companies, prices dropped, and portable radios became ubiquitous by the end of the 1960s.[25]

Transistor radios concealed music and allowed listeners to create a "soundscape" to accompany their movements through the world. The composer Murray Schafer initially described soundscapes as an urban-planning concept that can be deployed to institutionalize and organize public space.[26] The mobile device allows the listener to make his or her own soundscape, potentially against institutional design. Mobile devices provide both a customizable and a clandestine audio experience while also giving listeners a sense of control over their surroundings. Shuhei Hosokawa has found that this customization and feeling of autonomy provided by portable radios only increased as mobile devices evolved from transistors to the cassette players of the 1980s.[27] Hosokawa explains that the feeling of autonomy provided by mobile devices is most obviously observed in the way people move through public space. The listener's soundscape can augment his or her bodily experience and can affect the listener's gait and passage through space.[28] Thus, listening to a mobile device provides the user with an enhanced reality and the power to choose a route through everyday life.

Portable TV Era

Portable television devices also provided a similar sense of control and autonomy over public space but with an added visual element. Spigel describes a 1967 Sony advertisement for portable television that compares mobile viewing to the romantic intimacy of the drive-in movie.[29] The Sony ad offered this fantasy as a way of differentiating portable television from its more domesticated older sibling. The appeal and the target demographic are similar to the teen-oriented advertising of the transistor radio era. In both cases, the concept of the portable device as a transgressive technology is foregrounded. Spigel makes the point that the desire for mobility in television was often couched in gendered assumptions.[30] A portable screen meant that people could personalize their viewing, since men and women did not have to watch the same show if they had an additional portable screen. Spigel explains that, contributing to the gender divide, within the rhetoric of the 1960s "New Frontier" political ethos, men were depicted as "sportsmen and adventure seekers."[31] Portable television, and most new media devices, target men as the early adopters, those users willing to test the limits of the technology. This gender split is one that Spigel sees continuing in later mobile technologies such as the home office and the mobile worker.[32] During the 1960s, mobile technology continued to blur the distinctions between public and private through the depiction of gender distinctions that reinforced divisions between public and private spheres.

At the same time, portable television offered the family a way to bring their home with them on the road. Spigel describes the desire in the 1960s to bring the comfortable and family-unifying activities of television viewing on the road.[33] In the 1950s, television addressed the suburban family by offering them a "window on the world," which helped them stay connected to the nation from the comfort of the living room. The portable-television ads of the 1960s advocate leaving the home, enjoying nature, and bringing a piece of home with you. The rhetoric of portable television encouraged a more passive media experience for mobile devices than the one presented by portable radio devices. Mobile television suggested that, instead of using mobile devices to create a soundscape to enhance a public place, you could ignore your surroundings by making any place your living room. Both technologies shared an emphasis on using mobile devices as personal technologies that allowed you to transform your surroundings. Yet they differed in terms of the active versus passive engagement with public space. Listening to a portable radio, a person uses the soundscape as he or she travels through space, sometimes transgressing the restrictions of traffic laws. Watching a portable television, a person is in public space but retreats to a makeshift living room.

Car Phones and Pagers

Mobile phones continued the evolution of mobile devices that blurred distinctions between private and public space. Unlike portable radio or television, these devices facilitate communication between users. Early car phones and pagers offered a way for the outside world to intrude on the private sphere. Mobile phones have long been associated with work; early adopters were mainly taxi drivers, truckers, emergency services, and the military.[34] Other personal mobile communication devices, such as pagers, were associated with particular professions, such as medicine, because these tools allowed busy multitaskers to receive messages without disturbing other daily activities.[35] Bell and AT&T launched the first commercially available car-mounted telephones in 1978. Despite international appeal, there was a strong feeling in the US from engineers, marketers, and managers that these new phones were more viable in cars than as portable phones carried by people. This insistence on car phones over personal mobile devices reflects the cultural attitudes around this technology, the intended audience, the current technological capabilities, and the American preoccupation with automobile travel. Correspondingly, mobile phones became associated with "businessmen" extending their workday, transforming the time spent commuting into productive work time.[36] The mobile phone shifted from being a trapping of the business elite to a status symbol of the wealthy in the late 1980s.[37] Eventually this technology became the tool of many tradespeople traveling from client to client.[38] The expense and limitations of car phones helped to shape their initial usage and cultural association with work. Unsurprisingly, the flexible labor associated with the mobile worker continued to influence the use and design of mobile devices.

Walkman Era

In the 1980s, a new technology surpassed the portable radio in popularity: the mobile cassette player. The most popular model of these was Sony's Walkman. The cultural studies theorists Paul Du Gay, Stuart Hall, Linda Janes, Anders Koed Madsen, Hugh Mackay, and Keith Negus famously used the Sony Walkman to demonstrate the usefulness of applying the circuit of culture methodology to an analysis of a cultural product.[39] Throughout Du Gay et al.'s analysis, there is documentation of Sony's advertising campaigns for the technology. These ads emphasized youth, mobility, and originality; the Walkman represented the cutting-edge of miniaturization technology and 1980s personalization.[40] Sony created numerous versions of the Walkman to attract consumers of various self-definitions.[41] The concept of movement and outdoor use was consistent among all models. An attachable clip allowed a person to fasten the device to his or her waistband, allowing hands-free operation.[42] A solar-powered version of the Walkman gave users the capability of using the device outside the home, away from power sources. The Walkman was a technology of the young and energetic. It was a way for this demographic to choose its own soundscape distinct from the one provided by previous generations. No longer were listeners limited by the reach of their radio tuner. The ability to select music (via audio cassettes) helped these youthful consumers realize this feeling of autonomy. The Walkman heightened the economic divide between people who could afford the technology and harness this control and those who could not. At the same time, these mobile devices ushered in new practices of creative expression such as the mix tape and the audio book.

Handheld Electronic Games

Portable game devices, modern descendants of Jiggle Puzzle BB games and other nonelectronic handheld games, built on the mobile media habits of portable television.[43] Both portable electronic games and portable television demanded more of the user's attention than the headphones of a portable music player did. The gaming devices, however, were more overtly active than television was, which was apparent in the design of the games and in their public use. Toy companies such as Mattel, Milton Bradley, and Coleco enjoyed success in the late 1970s and early 1980s with a line of handheld electronic video games that accounted for $1 billion in annual sales, one-fifth of all toy sales in the US.[44] However, Nintendo's Game Boy was the most successful and sophisticated of the portable game devices. Launched in 1989, the device succeeded largely due to the popularity of the game *Tetris*, a simple game of stacked cubes that the player must fit together as they descend from the top of the screen.[45] *Tetris*'s popularity may derive from its simplicity; because it did not require much player instruction, it was easy to play while waiting in a public space.

Nintendo's Game Boy was a handheld iteration of Nintendo's 1980 platform Game and Watch, which was designed with the needs of the mobile gamer in mind. According to the game studies scholar Samuel Tobin, Nintendo's creative team saw Game and Watch as a way to "mitigate and recast modern urban boredom."[46] The inspiration for the Game and Watch occurred to video game designer Gunpei Yokoi when he observed "tired and bored commuters playing with their calculators."[47] Tobin remarks on the intentionality of the Game Boy design: "the Game Boy not only was well matched to its market, but . . . it also contributed to calling into being the contexts of its play by redefining how people dealt with commuting, standing in line, and passing time in waiting rooms, at the dinner table, in the bedroom, and in the interstices of work and school day."[48] It is clear from this statement that Nintendo was deeply engaged with the context of gameplay, which is a major feature of the procrastination economy that defines later mobile media devices.

Mobile Phone Era

First generation portable phones, affectionately known as "bricks," were neither widely adopted nor paid much attention by American consumers. Second-generation cell phones did resonate with consumers because they offered new textual, informational, and digital ways of talking with others. In the late 1980s and early 1990s, multimedia mobile phones began to reach the marketplace. Unlike portable game devices, the decision to develop additional functionality on mobile phones was less related to the needs of the consumer and more related to the efforts of electronics companies to diversify and compete in a growing marketplace. In accordance with the International Mobile Telecommunications Act of 2000, 3G (third-generation) infrastructure became an industry standard. 3G networks offered expanded bandwidth, which in turn offered the opportunity to enhance the capabilities of mobile phones. Phone companies identified multimedia functionality, such as text messaging, as a way to capitalize on these enhancements. The media and communications scholar Gerard Goggin points out that the phone embodied the digital era's concept of multimedia as it expanded communication from voice to text, image, sound, and touch.[49] Text messaging was an especially popular enhancement, offering a clandestine language between friends that could be hidden from those who were not in the know. As has been the theme with mobile devices, this illicit and titillating usage was particularly attractive to young people, who were among the earliest adopters of text messaging. Texting also became integral to new forms of interactive television, for example, voting via text for a favorite performer on Fox's *American Idol* reality-TV singing competition.

Goggin notes that media coverage about the adoption of mobile phones renewed concerns over the breakdown between public and private spheres.[50] As Larissa Hjorth and Ingrid Richardson note, "the domestic, private, and personal become quite literally mobilised and micro-mediatised via the mobile phone—an intimate 'home-in-the-hand'—effecting at the same time a transformation of experiences of presence, telepresence."[51] In many ways, the mobile phone expands on the concept of "privatized mobility" presented by Spigel by offering a way to speak to the world from the comfort of the mobile-private sphere of the phone.

The history of mobile media demonstrates a consistent pattern in which people use mobile media in social situations to improve their surroundings and assert themselves. Mobile devices provide access to entertainment, information, and communication that can change the physical and social dynamics of public spaces. The cultural theorist Michel de Certeau argues that as the divisions of work and leisure continue to break down, people adopt tactics for operating within the confines of their surroundings.[52] Cognizant of this history and building on the work of Certeau, this book places mobile devices as part of a lineage of devices that have helped people make meaning within the ideological designs of public spaces, institutions, and media companies. The companies and institutions of the procrastination economy prescribe preferred behavior and social order for the use of mobile devices in everyday life. Modern mobile devices offer people new tactics for navigating this social order. The interplay between the monetization strategies of media companies and the creative tactics of mobile users reflects the struggle for control and meaning making that defines modern life.

The Procrastination Economy: Targeting In-Between Moments and Creating a Mobile Day Part

While consumers enjoy the ways that mobile devices enhance socializing and control over physical space, media companies use these same devices to monetize our in-between moments. Entertainment companies are dedicated to getting consumers to answer boredom with their content and services. Industry metrics such as "engagement" and "ratings" measure which products and services do the best job of capturing consumers' time and attention. The broadcast industries (television and radio) provide a template for companies targeting the mobile audience because they pioneered the strategy of "day parts" (for example, morning, daytime, prime time, and late night), which match genres, aesthetics, and formats to the perceived needs of people watching at different parts of the workday.

The use of day-part programming inspired scholars such as Nick Browne to analyze programming lineups as evidence of the ways the television industry constructs an ideal spectator and attracts him or her with an ideological argument about everyday life.[53] For example, the soap opera genre was designed for the afternoon day part in which producers targeted stay-at-home mothers by creating story lines that could accommodate the interruptions of housework.[54] Browne argues that day-part scheduling established television as a cultural institution because it showed that broadcast networks could reflect and reinforce a "socially mediated order of the workday and workweek" and could "mediate between the worlds of work and entertainment."[55] These scheduling strategies framed television as a part of everyday life, with each day part designed to reinforce the divisions between labor and leisure.[56]

The procrastination economy creates a mobile day part around our in-between moments. The content and programming of the procrastination economy similarly mediate the tension between productivity and entertainment by fashioning a subject position for those who are waiting, procrastinating, and/or killing time. Media companies create content, apps, and services based on the idea that we look to our phones to fill liminal moments. Television and film distributors, cable service providers, and streaming media platforms contribute to the procrastination economy by distributing, repackaging, or expanding their existing storyworlds on mobile apps.[57] Social media platforms are also a part of the procrastination economy, as they provide "communitainment," a term developed by Stuart Cunningham and David Craig to describe the entertainment industries' efforts to participate in the activities of digital communities and create media content out of the user-generated creativity and communication on social media platforms.[58] Mobile-device manufactures and video-game developers contribute to the procrastination economy by creating functionality and capabilities appropriate for specific mobile usage contexts. While often a company will announce a mobile strategy that is simply an effort to translate the leisure economy to mobile devices, the procrastination economy applies to efforts to customize content and services for context-specific mobile usage.

Each of the chapters of this book details the ways that media companies are adapting their mobile strategies to focus on particular contexts and audiences. Just as television scholars have analyzed day parts for their underlying ideology, the procrastination economy reveals an industrial belief about the mobile audience.

The companies that contribute to the mobile day part also contribute to definition of the ideal audience of the procrastination economy. The pursuit of this audience informs the functionality, content, and services for mobile devices. The preferred audience of the procrastination economy has much in common with the "commodity audience" described in Eileen Meehan's work on television ratings.[59] In this essay, Meehan analyzes the historical development of television ratings to explain how macroeconomic structures shape decisions about programming and understanding of the audience.[60] Focusing on the macroeconomic analysis provides evidence that the television industry's "forms of measurement are selected on the basis of economic goals, not according to the rules of social science."[61] As with ratings, media industries' efforts to understand the mobile audience are framed by their desire to monetize the procrastination economy. For example, Elizabeth Evans points out that those mobile video games are predominantly funded by the freemium business model, which capitalizes on gamers' impatience.[62] Freemium games allow anyone to play free of charge (or with advertisements) but offer gamers with disposable income the ability to bypass the structured waiting periods within the game. Chapter 4 describes how this economic strategy reflects the media industries' understanding of the procrastination economy of the waiting room. Indeed, each chapter describes how macroeconomic efforts to monetize mobile devices through micropayments, advertising, and subscription services influence media companies' efforts to serve the procrastination economy.

Understanding the macroeconomic realities behind the procrastination economy is crucial, as mobile devices become a dominant conduit to the Internet. The development of the procrastination economy coincides with the commercial turn of the Internet. The media scholar Jonathan Zittrain has argued that the "generative" spirit that defined the early days of the Internet is disappearing as media industries establish digital business models.[63] In the August 2010 issue of *Wired*, editor Chris Anderson and writer Michael Wolff argued that the World Wide Web had finally reached its commercial stage of development. They explain that the rise of mobile computing privileges "semi-closed platforms that use the Internet for transport but not the browser for display," simplifying web navigation and creating convenient delivery systems.[64] The emergence of this more convenient and commercially viable Internet brings with it the standardization of certain norms around Internet use, in this case the privileging of the procrastination economy.

Smartphone Era

The release of the iPhone in 2007 was a landmark moment in the development of the procrastination economy, as it introduced mobile devices as multitasking devices that could assist the busy consumer. An Apple press release the day before the launch of the iPhone touted it as a device that "redefines what users can do on their mobile phones" by combining three products: "a mobile phone, a widescreen iPod and the Internet."[65] While Apple's initial marketing campaign focused on the variety of tasks the iPhone could complete, the second series of advertisements from 2007 featured testimonials from iPhone users.[66] Particularly relevant to the procrastination economy, was an advertisement featuring "Elliot" relaying a story about a time he was attending a dinner and trying to remember the name of his boss's fiancée.[67] In the commercial, Elliot describes how he used his iPhone while waiting for his boss to arrive to search for the name of his fiancée on the Internet. Several other advertisements, including ones featuring entrepreneurs, people settling a bet, Facebook users, and a pilot on a weather delay, situate the phone as a tool for navigating the in-between moments of everyday life.

The capabilities of smartphones affected Internet companies and social media platforms, as they hurried to optimize their sites for mobile use. Facebook has been a popular destination for the mobile audience since the arrival of smartphones, developing a mobile platform in 2006. Later that year, Facebook introduced its News Feed feature that redesigned the functionality of the site to act as a personalized "news aggregator that reports on activity in a user's social network and highlights relevant information about people, activities they have been involved in and other information they have chosen to share."[68] News Feed has been called "the most significant invention in the history of the social web," and this is especially true for the procrastination economy, as it became the de facto design for social networking on mobile devices.[69] Before News Feed, Facebook users actively sought out the status updates of their friends. After the redesign, all status updates were delivered to the user in an automatically updating content stream, which contributed to the procrastination economy in two important ways. First, it effectively changed the business model on social media sites from page views to advertising-sponsored social interaction.[70] Second, simplifying the navigation of Facebook made the platform a reliable mobile app for checking in with friends during the in-between moments of the day. Advertisers could now target those in-between moments and make their appeals context specific. While the redesign initially inspired outrage, it did not affect users' enthusiasm for Facebook, as it has consistently been a top-used mobile app.[71] In addition, the interface design and advertising business model became standard strategies for defining and reaching the mobile audience.

As Internet platforms optimized their sites for mobile devices, film studios, television networks, and brand managers began to see smartphones as a new screen for their intellectual property. For example, Warner Bros. Home Entertainment group created a special division for digital distribution in 2007.[72] Warner Bros. Home Entertainment is tasked with packaged media (DVDs and Blu-rays), electronic sell-through (on-demand and downloadable files), and designing digital platforms and tools (games and social media promotions) to support its media properties. In 2011, the division purchased Flixster, the company that owns the movie-review site Rotten Tomatoes.[73] Warner's digital team designed a mobile app using Flixster's branding and database of reviews. The app provided users with access to digital copies of their collection, reviews of films, management of their Netflix queue, and discovery tools that helped mobile customers find movie tickets and information. Chuck Tryon describes the app as an attempt to offer consumers "platform mobility," or access to their media collection from any device.[74] Whether through the Flixster app or in Warner Bros. experiments on Facebook,[75] iTunes,[76] or BitTorrent,[77] the consistent relationship the company cultivated with the digital audience was the promise that they would be able to watch film and television on the go. The focus on mobile access to content emerged from an effort to apply the strategies of home entertainment to the mobile audience.[78] While these digital distribution efforts often ignore context-specific use, media companies also produce a number of paratexts and ephemeral media such as promotional clips, branded apps, emoji keyboards, and GIF generators that are more conducive to the specifics of the procrastination economy. No matter the intention, these products and services are the services people use during their in-between moments.

The procrastination economy has flourished in the era of smartphones and Internet-connected mobile devices because these technologies blur the lines between work and leisure. Tryon's concept of "platform mobility" and Lynn Spigel and Max Dawson's description of "flexible leisure" describe industry efforts to position mobile media as an all-you-can-eat buffet at which consumers can help themselves at any time or place.[79] Contrastingly, the procrastination economy details the entertainment industries' efforts to entice the mobile audience to fill their downtime with context specific "snackable" content and social media conversation. To continue with the metaphor, the products and services of the procrastination economy are the media equivalent of the snack-food industry.

Spigel and Dawson see the "'social arrhythmia' of the new 24/7/365 post-industrial information economy" as inciting television networks to give up on their familiar day parts and strategic targeting of audiences on the basis of the eight-hour workday.[80] While there have been changes to the workday and increased demands on consumers' attention, entertainment companies still attempt to define the context of the mobile spectator. Whereas Spigel and Dawson see "flexible leisure" as the logic behind on-demand content, a closer look at the media industries' efforts reveals that day-part programming is alive and well. The procrastination economy is filled with examples of content and services purposefully designed to target the media snacking habits of people at work, in the waiting room, during the commute, and in the "connected" living room. On-demand services give consumers some control over how and when they use content, but media companies still make decisions about curation and accessibility. The chapters that follow demonstrate how digital platforms deploy strategies based on beliefs about consumers' behavior in particular spatial contexts. As a result, mobile devices are defined by the logics of the procrastination economy.

2

The Workplace

Snacks and Flows

The midday spike in Web traffic is not a new phenomenon, but media companies have started responding
in a meaningful way over the last year. They are creating new shows, timing the posts to coincide with hun-
ger pangs. And they are rejiggering the way they sell
advertising online, recognizing that noontime programs can command a premium.
—Brian Stetler, "Noontime Web Video Revitalizes
Lunch at Desk," *New York Times*, January 5, 2008

As the Internet became a common workplace tool in the 1990s,
the *New York Times*, like the majority of news outlets, circulated
stories about the dangers of "cyberslacking," which included such
observations as "surfing the Net, it seems, can make the desktop
computer anything but an employee productivity tool."[1] The anxiety over digital distractions supports a cottage industry of digital
management manuals designed to help employers and employees
resist the temptation to click. An Amazon.com search for "productivity" returns reams of manuals and management guides that
provide strategies for combatting this annoying "illness."[2] Stories
about Internet use at work reflect larger concerns about the way
mobile devices and Internet access in general steal time from
more productive tasks. Despite these concerns, several studies
have shown that "media snacking" can be restorative and actually
increase productivity and creativity.[3]

Given research that shows that digital procrastination "may act as 'digital watercooler'—enhancing workers' productivity and effectiveness," it is important to understand how these media snacks are made and for whom.[4] *Wired* contributor Nancy Miller describes the concept of "snackable" media as the dominant mode of media engagement in the digital era: "Today, media snacking is a way of life. In the morning, we check news and tap out emails on our laptops. At work, we graze all day on videos and blogs. Back home, the giant HDTV is for 10-course feasting—say, an entire season of *24*. In between are the morsels that fill those whenever minutes, as your mobile phone carrier calls them: a 30-second game on your Nintendo DS, a 60-second webisode on your cell, and a three-minute podcast on your MP3 player."[5] The relationship between "snacking" and "feasting" described by Miller also describes the hopes of media companies, that viewers will use their break times as appetizers—teasers for the "main course" of prime-time television or new film releases. Despite the designs of the procrastination economy, snacking can be more than just an amuse-bouche; it can be an indulgence and a rebellion as well. Digital content designed for the workplace is sustenance that helps certain people cope with the demands of their workday.

The workplace has always been an important location for social interaction; digital technologies make these activities more visible. Media studies scholars have encouraged a nuanced approach, producing research that considers social context as a contributing factor to cultural understanding. Much of this analysis takes social factors such as gender and class into account, although few scholars have examined specific sites such as the workplace.[6] Digital content—whether in the form of movies, sporting events, social media feeds, television shows, websites, or games—provides a foundation for discussion around the virtual watercooler, break room, or lunch table. These discussions are part of the rhythms of the workday, bringing levity and camaraderie that help a place of employment feel like a community. In addition, media content can act as a common language for dealing with the local politics of the office or the larger politics of the nation.

In this chapter, I argue that the procrastination economy gives certain workers the ability to manage their workday with "media snacks." Certain snacks correspond with the time of day or the work activity. The procrastination economy provides an endless variety of media snacks to ensure people can find the flavor, texture, and indulgence appropriate to their circumstances. Media companies support this workday media snacking in an effort to build programming flow, labor flow, and platform flow that can carry audiences and industry workers from one franchise, service, and product to another. While there are many types of media snacks available to the workplace audience, the media industries privileges those audience members who are most interested in checking in, catching up, and commenting on the latest headlines dominating cultural conversation. While audiences are free to use their mobile devices to spend their lunch breaks texting and catching up with loved ones, there is a consistent effort by media companies to entice the workplace audience to spend "snack time" with their intellectual property.

The Value of Snacking: Analysis of the Workplace Audience

Research on workplace procrastination shows that certain kinds of media snacks are more likely to support productivity than other kinds of media snacks.[7] In addition, gender, relationship status, personality type, and workload contribute to the frequency and effects of media snacking.[8] These studies demonstrate that snacking is related to a variety of contextual and social issues. Marshall McLuhan famously described media technology as "extensions of ourselves," arguing, "the personal and social consequences of any medium—that is, of any extension of ourselves—result from the new scale that is introduced into our affairs by each extension of ourselves, or by any new technology."[9] While McLuhan has been criticized for his tendency toward technological determinism, he aptly describes the way media technologies amplify "the scale and form of human association and action."[10] For example, workers already use media content in their work lives during break times and in conversation with coworkers. Mobile devices are tools for expanding this activity because they can include more participants and provide dynamic digital content that stimulates discussion. As digital technology and the ability to record usage of it proliferate, audience practices that were long ignored by entertainment companies begin to reveal themselves.

Mobile devices have enhanced media snacking at the workplace in two key ways: via mobility and choice. The fact that mobile devices are portable means that people can now do their media snacking in a variety of situations. This snacking is not limited to the break room but can happen at any time people need assistance from their mobile devices. Not only does this portability increase the utility of media snacking, but the access to a variety of content means that people can select the best snack for the occasion. Some situations call for audiocentric snacking, others require a short video, and sometimes people like to gather to watch a whole episode of a show. While mobile devices expand the possibilities for snacking, the use of mobile devices is still determined by routines. Multiple studies have shown that media snacking occurs within the flow of routines and becomes habitual, making it predictable and planned in relation to social factors.[11] The types of media snacking relate to the social dynamics of the workplace and the routines of the workday. Mobile devices are a tool that enables workers to optimize their snacking for particular circumstances.

Evidence of the ways mobile devices enhance media snacking comes from ethnographic observations of three workplaces. From this analysis, it becomes clear that mobile devices are a crucial outlet for employees to stave off boredom, interact with colleagues, and assert their identities as informed consumers and citizens. Media-snacking practices can be categorized in three distinct periods: morning, lunch, and afternoon break times. Different technologies, digital platforms, and modes of viewing correspond to these snack breaks. Taken together, the way workers use their mobile devices demonstrates how workdays are built around a system of rewards and coping mechanisms that propel assignments toward completion, sustain connections between coworkers, and assuage the stresses of modern labor practices. The procrastination economy does not have to be a drag on the economy. Mobile devices help employees craft a more comfortable work environment. In this manner, workplace media habits are not much different from other workplace coping activities such as trading gossip around the watercooler. The procrastination economy is not a new threat to worker productivity but merely an enhanced version of snacking and coffee breaks that helps employees refocus and reward themselves for the completion of tasks.

Workers in monotonous jobs with repetitive tasks and low stakes in the success of the company are most likely to crave media snacks.[12] This category of worker was readily available in the workplaces of two computer businesses in the Santa Barbara and Goleta area of central California and a large call center in New York City. The first company, Ameravant, is a website-production company that services businesses in the downtown Santa Barbara area of central California. Ameravant helps companies increase their online web presence and maximize their search-engine relevance. The entire company is composed of six programmers who all work in the same room at different desks with multiple computers running on each desk. Ameravant's offices are located in the owner's house, with each of the programmers organized in corners of the living room. The kitchen and living room are available to all employees, so meetings—both between coworkers and with clients— happen in the kitchen. The programmers work in the living room, and the owner's office is in his bedroom. The atmosphere is relaxed but busy, since each programmer is responsible for maintaining multiple websites.

The second company, Latitude 34, is situated in a strip mall in downtown Goleta, California. Employees provide IT support for a variety of Santa Barbara companies. The company's office has a more traditional office feel than Ameravant's offices do. Latitude 34 is also family owned and employs seven workers. The office has an open floor plan with a variety of workstations used for computer maintenance. The employees arrive in the morning to contact customers and get a sense of the workload for the day. Most of the employees spend a great deal of time driving to client locations to repair computers. The moments when everyone is in the office are lively and full of conversation and collaboration.

The third workplace is the call center for a national distance-learning company.[13] The offices feature multiple rows of cubicles with employees sitting at terminals dedicated to specific types of calls. This office is enormous and feels much less congenial than the other two smaller offices do. Despite the impersonal "cube farm" environment, there is a lot of collaboration between coworkers and a general atmosphere of enthusiasm. Compared to Ameravant's and Latitude 34's employees, the call center employees have less direct supervision (though their computers are monitored by a program) and are more responsible for their own workload. Workload is determined by the volume of calls and emails fielded by each division. The sales teams, whose job it is to send out calls, are by far the busiest employees; the online tech-support team is the most relaxed group, since their work does not involve having to respond instantly to a caller's questions.

The Morning Routine

Employees at each of these offices began their workdays with an invigorating media snack that helped them prepare for the day. As soon as computers were operational, employees logged in to email, instant-messaging services, and Facebook, immersing themselves in that day's workload and social world. To assist in the preparations for the day, employees in each of the locations set up personal mobile devices (tablets, laptop computers, and mobile phones) to act as second screens. One employee described his second screen as his "distraction computer," which he used to separate his personal media from his work screen. The term "distraction computer" suggests that he sees his personal media as detrimental to his productivity, and so he segregates his media snacks from his primary work screen in order to keep them from drawing his attention from his work. The media snacks on these mobile devices primarily featured audio content including music, podcasts, and talk radio. The sound from these audio snacks blocked out office noise and helped employees focus on their individual tasks. Rather than causing work distraction, mobile audio devices actually gave workers tools to manage existing distractions through customizable offerings.

The use of sound to manage distraction has been a popular practice in work environments long before the advent of mobile devices. Streaming audio services can be considered modern incarnations of field songs sung by agricultural workers or radio broadcasts piped into factories by business owners in the 1940s.[14] Employers have long believed that music improves workers' productivity by creating a soundtrack that fades into the background and becomes a kind of white noise, masking the sounds of other activities.[15] Silence is nearly impossible to attain in the workplace, so the radio, and now mobile devices, offers a controllable and consistent source of noise that assists employees' focus on the completion of their work. Studies have found that employees who listen to music during repetitive tasks or during work preparation show increased productivity.[16] Employees in all the workplaces I visited certainly believed that music enjoyed via a personal mobile device helped them prepare for their workday. Furthermore, they appreciated the ability and freedom to self-manage their focus by creating a comfortable white noise.

The music industry has carved a niche for itself in the procrastination economy through the development of user-friendly, customizable digital platforms. The subscription-based music service Spotify offers a variety of focus-boosting playlists for the workplace featuring music that fades into the background and blocks distracting noises. Spotify users can also create their own playlists, which workers frequently label with names that evoke a specific workplace context. For example, Spotify features playlists called "Workday Pop," "Workday Lounge," "Workday Soul," "Your Coffee Break," "The Office Mix," "The Office Stereo," "Jazzy at Work," and "Rock at Work." The playlists of Spotify users Sarah-Louise Thexton, who has a playlist called "Safe for Work (Pop)," ihascube, who has a playlist called "Work Music (Clean)," and Lisa Roach, who has a list called "Work Playlist," as well as hundreds like them, reflect the workers' understanding that there is particular music that is appropriate for the workplace.[17] Spotify and its users make playlists for the rhythms of the workplace and censor their music tastes to be appropriate for public listening.

The ability to manage distractions is especially important in shared workspaces, where, at any given time, multiple workers may be talking on the phone with clients or discussing work with colleagues. The call center, with its rows of people talking on the phone, was a prime example of digital content being used to manage distraction: employees switched from phone headsets, used during phone calls, to headphones, used while working out problems on their computers. In the small offices of Ameravant, the customer service manager often met with clients in a room adjoining the computer programmers' workspace. Much to the programmers' chagrin, the door that separated the two rooms was frequently left open. Even after sitting in the office for only a few days, the customer-service pitch quickly became repetitive. The employees used their mobile devices to combat this distraction. Some workers sought refuge in their iTunes library; others listened to streaming music services and podcasts. These technologies are similar to personal radios because they allow employees to select a particular genre of music, an album, or a playlist. Employees can further customize their "white noise" by choosing forms of audio beyond music. For example, one of the employees toggled between NPR podcasts, previously viewed episodes of favorite television shows, and movies. He explained that accessing a variety of media was essential to his productivity.

Often the employee's choice of digital content depended on whether he or she was using headphones or listening through speakers. Michael Bull has written about his concern over the use of headphones and portable media devices, claiming that these devices put people in their own "private bubble" and cut them off from their surroundings, as "sound enables users to manage and orchestrate their spaces of habituation in a manner that conforms to their desires. The sound of the personal stereo is direct, with headphones placed directly over the ears of the user, thereby over-laying the random sounds of the environment passed through with privatized sounds."[18] One employee remarked that his choice of music depends on who is in the room. When a fellow programmer with a shared sensibility is working near him, he puts on a song they both enjoy, and this provides a consistent background beat. If there are not multiple people in the office to share the music, he is more likely to put on his headphones and listen to a podcast related to his interests. In this instance, the ability to customize and stream music through digital services encourages a connection be-tween coworkers; when working solo, the programmer uses sound to alleviate his isolation.

The ability to personalize a workday soundtrack is one of the ways mobile devices have enhanced everyday office practices. Before the Internet, the options for "white noise" were limited to media that were playable on a personal stereo. Smartphones and other mobile devices enable catalogs of content to travel with an employee into the workplace. Barbara Klinger, drawing on the work of Roger Silverstone, has argued that the proliferation of home entertainment products has expanded the role of media texts within our daily lives.[19] Though she mainly focuses on home viewing, she describes repeat viewing of media texts as part of an intense process of personalization in which a text can help "confirm individual identity."[20] The workplace is another venue where people are actively engaged in this identity exploration, and digital content's inherent portability and customizability supports that practice.[21] A favorite film or television show may contain dialog or a soundtrack that is reaffirming to an employee, but, being sufficiently familiar, it does not distract from work-related tasks. These media snacks become a form of audio pleasure that serve multiple purposes: they provide pleasant background noise, allow employees to assert control over their workday, and give employees a way to express their identities through their media consumption choices.

Lunch

Musical media snacks help concentration and motivate employees to start the day, but by lunchtime, employees are hungry for more relaxing and communal media snacks. Mobile devices offer mobility and community that surpasses the offerings of traditional break rooms and the limitations of modern labor schedules. Employees within the service industry do not leave for lunch together because someone is required to stay and answer phones or continue working. (The Latitude 34 offices were an exception to this; employees were often out on service calls during the lunch hour and could stop for food as they went from assignment to assignment.) The inability to go to lunch as a group and the pressure to finish work tasks within a strict timetable encourage many employees to eat lunch at their desks, whether lunch is brought from home or purchased outside the office and brought back. Cultural critics have debated the merits of "desk-eating"; some claim that leaving the office during lunch is an important restorative act, while others argue that the demands of the modern workday and family life have made a leisurely lunch impossible.[22] Consuming digital content while desk-dining constitutes a compromise: employees get a short break from the workday but also have the convenience of staying at the desk, ready to respond should a problem arise.

Lunchtime relaxation has been a part of the procrastination economy ever since employees lobbied for break-room televisions in the 1950s. Mobile devices improve on break-room televisions by enabling on-demand viewing and mobility. Anna McCarthy describes the way much "site-specific" media, like break-room televisions, are typically controlled by employers and not by visitors, customers, or employees.[23] She argues that group viewing in such places as taverns is largely about the institutional expectations of public viewing. For example, the viewing of sports in bars is partly a response to the social understanding of public viewing as a separate space for male audiences away from the more feminized space of the home.[24] Workplace viewing transcends these boundaries, bringing fan communities together around shared interests, instead of forcing a confrontation over office hierarchy and remote-control privileges.

Mobile devices make "break rooms" mobile, as they allow employees to customize their relaxation and their viewing partners. While this mobility points to the isolation that some people see as the downfall of mobile privatization, the effect is context specific. Not all companies have break rooms, and not all break rooms are inviting places of camaraderie. Anna-Lisa Linden and Maria Nyberg describe the office break room as a place of self-presentation in which diverse ethnicities and social classes collide and draw conclusions about their coworkers' personal lives.[25] Mobile devices help workers navigate this social anxiety while allowing them to get the relaxing benefits of the break room. Indeed, break rooms are defined by constraints, from the time one has to prepare one's lunch to the options on the break-room television to the company one keeps while having one's lunch.

Mobile devices exponentially expand an employee's options for lunchtime viewing and give the individual control over the viewing experience. If a group of employees wants to discuss something that happened in a recent TV episode, they can watch (or rewatch) together, pausing and rewinding to allow for conversation without missing any of the action. This enhanced group-viewing experience increases the likelihood of creating workplace-based fan communities. A group of coworkers at Ameravant, watching *The Daily Show* during lunch, paused the show when a joke about current events elicited a laugh from one person and confusion from another. The coworkers kept the program paused while they discussed the political events referenced in the joke. In this instance, the show was more than just a lunchtime distraction; it was part of a social meaning-making and community-building process. The ability to control the on-demand content through the rewind and pause functionality provided a sense of control in a context that is typically defined by constraints.

Unlike other types of fan viewing, in which people come together organically over a shared interest, a workplace contains people with widely varying tastes and interests. Dorothy Hobson has written about the importance of workplace fan communities as a crucial site for the meaning-making process that accompanies television viewing.[26] Her analysis shows that many community-viewing practices, such as bonding and catching up, also occurred around the office watercooler, well before the advent of digital technology. Media devices make it easier to find something to discuss that has office-wide appeal and is available on demand for lunchtime viewing. In this way, workplace viewing resembles the practices of family viewing, in which different members of the family establish hierarchies of taste and negotiate to determine what is viewed.[27] Workplace fan communities are also similar to a high school lunchroom: different cliques break off and assemble to discuss or, in the case of digital content, engage in a shared interest.

Office-based fan communities are context based; shared interests reveal themselves through office interaction with digital media.

The selection of *The Daily Show* as a shared community text reveals how context-based fandom operates. According to audience statistics, *The Daily Show* appeals to young, educated, and technologically savvy viewers.[28] The 20-something programmers at Ameravant fit this profile. The show's humor, running time, and "online/anytime" availability made it a good fit for the context of the Ameravant office. Many of the workers at Ameravant shared political leanings that matched those expressed on *The Daily Show*. They also shared a desire to watch a show each day that lasted the length of a lunch break. By contrast, workers at the call center were much less likely to watch digital content together at lunchtime. The diversity of perspectives in the call center, the variety of lunchtimes, and the high turnover of employees made the environment more isolated. Yet they could still look to social media platforms to find community during lunch time. A Pew study found that social media services are most often accessed at work during break times.[29] In all cases, lunchtime media snacking involved streaming-media platforms and a desire for community and socializing.

While mobile devices offer control over how employees enjoy their media snacks, the variety of options, including live streaming events, influenced when employees at the three companies took their lunches. Several of the employees planned their lunchtime around real-time news and sports programs. One employee enjoyed taking part in live chats hosted by the media personality Joe Rogan, a comedian and UFC announcer. This employee timed his lunch break to coincide with the airing of the live chat. Sports personalities and sporting events are particularly popular digital content in the workplace, since sporting events occur throughout the day across the globe. During the 2008 Olympics, Nielsen reported that 20% of the "active at work audience" viewed events during the workday.[30] Similarly, the 2006 FIFA World Cup drew nearly four billion page views during its day game broadcasts of the global soccer tournament.[31] Sports leagues and television networks hungry for larger audiences (and therefore larger advertising revenues) have made deals with European football leagues, which have matches that begin during the morning and afternoon during US workdays.[32] These streaming-media deals create the midday media snacks that workplace audiences build their days around.

These examples of lunchtime viewing show how mobile devices expand the options and mobility of the benefits of the office break room. Missing the previous evening's "must-see TV" used to exclude an employee from office conversations; with so much content available on-demand and from streaming platforms, work colleagues can catch each other up on the shows they collectively enjoy. Mobile devices also allow those who may not connect with their colleagues with a way to connect with people outside the office. These devices enable these workers to avoid the social politics of the break room while still enjoying the benefits of relaxation in the middle of the day. The streaming services and social media platforms provide the media snacks that people want during lunchtime.

Break Time

Media snacks help employees focus to begin the day and provide relief in the middle of the day, but they can also act as rewards for completing a task. A number of employees at the three companies explained that they set goals for themselves to finish a task within a given timeframe, and if they met this goal, they rewarded themselves with a media snack, such as a few YouTube videos, before starting another assignment. Management in some workplaces contributes to this work-and-reward system. For example, the management of the call center incentivized its employees by adjusting the network firewall as an incentive for employees who met particular production quotas. The call center's firewall allowed employees to browse the Internet for non-work-related sites for a set amount of time throughout the day. If an employee completed a high volume of calls during a set time, then the firewall restrictions were relaxed and allowed the employee more time to visit non-work-related sites. Research on cyberslacking prohibitions, such as firewalls and monitoring software, shows that these measures reduce media snacking.[33] These kinds of restrictions can also reduce employees' morale and foster a sense of surveillance and distrust.[34] While this management implemented a reward system focused on the firewall on employees' desktop computers, workers often ignored these restrictions by using their mobile devices to give themselves a media-snacking reward system.

Yvonne Jewkes's research on prison inmates shows that when media access is used as a reward, it helps to normalize the rules and regulations of the institution.[35] As with any incentive system, the group that controls the object of desire, such as access to media content, can require certain behaviors from the people who want the object. The research on prisoners also shows that media content is essential to a person's perception of him- or herself. Jewkes argues that within strict institutions, media content provides people with essential tools to reclaim their identities, mark time, and generally survive day-to-day stresses. Hopefully, most work environments are not as damaging to personal agency as prison is, although the restriction of media content in some workplaces may be similar. Unlike in prison, mobile-device viewing in the workplace, during break times, can be a negotiation between employee and employer. The employee agrees to abide by the structures of professionalism in exchange for some measure of freedom to engage in media consumption and, therefore, personal expression during his or her managed break times.

Break times are self-selected or scheduled moments during the day when employees are permitted to divert their minds from work to topics of their own interest. Despite the lack of federally mandated break times, several state governments and various unions have successfully instituted compensated break times for workers. These regulating bodies have argued that break times perform an important stress-relieving function.[36] Researchers at the University of Melbourne demonstrated that employees who spent break time online were more productive than were employees who spent their break offline.[37] Study coauthor Brent Coker explains that "short and unobtrusive breaks, such as a quick surf of the Internet, enables the mind to rest itself, leading to a higher total net concentration for a day's work, and as a result, increased productivity."[38] Another study by researchers at the University of Singapore compared media snacking to a "coffee or snack break," as it provided pleasure and rejuvenation to employees.[39] These findings show that media snacking is as restorative as other break time activities are.

Much like lunchtime media snacking, employees in the three companies were strategic in their planning of their media snack breaks. One employee would check to see what his favorite online personalities had scheduled during the day and would plan his break times accordingly. He used Twitter, for example, to see if a comedian would be hosting a live chat or to see if a new episode of a favorite web series would be posted. If there was no time-sensitive digital content, break times were filled with casual web surfing in short breaks throughout the day. Employees at the call center often returned to social media sites throughout the day, sometimes as frequently as every 20 minutes, to see if any new updates had been posted. These employees claimed that their total visits to these sites spread throughout the day totaled the 15–20 minutes they were allowed for daily break time. By spacing out the media snacking at regular intervals, the employees gave themselves a number of rewards throughout the day. As one employee explained, "You can't keep constantly working, nonstop, on work like this. You gotta take breaks."[40] The association between the type of work, in this case computer coding, and the need for media snacking has appeared in additional research on workplace Internet use.[41] The repetitiveness and monotony of certain types of modern work make employees look for media snacks as a reward for completing tasks.

Break times are not just for personal restoration; they are also opportunities to socialize with coworkers. The symbol of workplace socializing is the watercooler, a place to discuss the previous weekend's happenings and gossip about office politics. The association between watercoolers and workplace socializing is so strong that HBO created an entire advertising campaign with the premise that its shows were watercooler worthy.[42] The campaign reflected the way coworkers discuss a previous night's television programs. Digital technology has enhanced watercooler media discussions by providing tools for facilitating conversation. Before on-demand viewing and mobile devices, watercooler conversation depended on all participants having watched a particular program on a particular night; nowadays, when someone misses a memorable moment in a show, he or she can access it via digital resources. If television plays a central role as society's common language, as television scholars have argued, digital media take things a step further by providing an easy way for fans to reminisce about a favorite movie or show, research a rumor, or create new fans by converting the uninitiated around a mobile device.[43] Because digital content is more easily accessible than broadcast content is, nearly everyone in the office can participate in the watercooler conversation. In this way, the conversation becomes more inclusive, more diverse, and richer as a result.

The desire to discuss common interests during break time was broadly evident during my workplace visits. A colleague-to-colleague conversation about a video game or a YouTube video would often be overheard by other coworkers and would suddenly grow into several employees gathered together around a mobile device, where they would watch (or rewatch) the media object en masse. A prime example of this phenomenon occurred in the Latitude 34 offices. One day during observation, several of the employees decided to incorporate movie and television dialog into their regular conversations. At one point during a conversation involving lines from *South Park*, the employees repeatedly described the work they were collaborating on as "super cereal." (This phrase is a reference to the *South Park* episode "ManBearPig.") One of the employees was not familiar with that episode, so another employee described the episode and then frantically searched the web for a clip in which the characters used the joke phrase.

Not only is this kind of media snacking restorative, but like a break at the office watercooler, it offers an opportunity for socializing and reinforcing relationships. Cultural references are a way of distinguishing between groups of insiders and outsiders. John Fiske has written about the way slang terms and cultural references operate as a form of cultural capital that separates those who belong from those who do not.[44] As seen in the preceding example, mobile devices help bridge these boundaries. Instead of excluding people who may be unfamiliar with a text, web-based content expands inclusivity by providing quick access to information about the references people use. By uniting people in this way, media snacking has proven to be an important tool in the development of fan networks. As Manuel Castells has noted, digital technology allows groups at work with shared interests to gather around the cultural events they find meaningful and not the ones that broadcast networks dictate.[45] This community building culminates in such activities as workplace fantasy-sports leagues, group viewing parties, and the circulation of viral videos.

The media snacking observed throughout the offices I visited was notable for the ways it enhanced preexisting procrastination such as coffee breaks, lunch breaks, and snack breaks. Evidence of this media snacking reflected many of the results of larger studies conducted in the field of organization and management studies that show media snacking, in moderation, has restorative capabilities. In addition, this snacking fits within rhythms of the workday. Mobile devices enable on-demand access to digital content, which enables employees to take control of their media snacking and fit preferred types of media snacks to the appropriate types of day. Mobile devices allow employees to customize their snacking and enhance the benefits of restorative break times by providing access to the snacks they enjoy most. The versatility of mobile devices also enables employees to manage their own media snacking in relation to the specific content offerings on the web on a given day. Media companies contribute to the schedule of media snacking, as they target the procrastination economy with a variety of media snacks.

"Lunchtime Is the New Prime Time": The Procrastination Economy at Work

Media companies are just as strategic creating media snacks as employees are in assigning them to particular parts of the workday. The history of web production reveals that the creation of media snacks is heavily influenced by the established media industries. Aymar Jean Christian explains that the financial realities of web production only allow "testing the medium from its margins."[46] The lack of sizable revenue in the procrastination economy means that the media snacks designed for the workplace are also designed to support and promote established media industries such as film and television productions. Media companies produce and distribute media snacks as appetizers meant to entice the workplace audience to integrate their intellectual property into their everyday routines and conversations. Media snacks provide brand maintenance and labor training through cross-platform flow, programming flow, and labor flow from mobile devices to film and television properties.

Fox Sports' *Lunch with Benefits* programming schedule provides an example of this production strategy for the procrastination economy. *Lunch with Benefits* featured a collection of web series produced for the workplace audience that were designed to engage sports fans on the Monday after a busy sports weekend and encourage them to check in with Fox Sports properties as they prepared for the next weekend's games. Each day of the week featured a new episode of a web series. Each web series was a different genre and style, covering the spectrum from interview talk shows to scripted workplace comedy to comedy clip show to sports strategy show. Each day at noon, the web series of the day would be featured on the MSN.com landing page and on the various Fox Sports apps. Monday's *The After Party with Jay Glazer* and Tuesday's *Coach Speak with Brian Billick* were both shows dedicated to providing wrap-up and analysis of the previous weekend's football games. *The College Experiment* and *Cubed* aired on Wednesday and Thursday to provide humorous commentary about the sports world. Friday's *The Inside Call* previewed upcoming games and featured the hosts of Fox's NFL Sunday TV show preparing for the weekend's broadcast. Each webisode lasted about half an hour and had its own sponsor.

Lunch with Benefits ended production after a three-year run, beginning with heavy promotion in 2009 and ending as a featured section of the Fox Sports app that launched in 2012. Though the series did not last long, the programming logic and labor practices associated with it are often replicated by digital departments across the media industries. The enthusiastic launch of *Lunch with Benefits* and the effort to connect traditional production practices and digital distribution are emblematic of a pervasive desire that shapes the culture of the procrastination economy.

The Fox Sports press release launching *Lunch with Benefits* positioned it as the flagship creation of the newly created Fox Sports Digital Entertainment division. The new unit was charged with making "lunchtime the new primetime" by offering the workplace audience a weekday web series programming block.[47] The announcement's use of the term "primetime" is indicative of how Fox Sports understood digital content and the importance of establishing a digital day part. This terminology and strategy connected the procrastination economy with traditional television production. The story of Fox Sports Digital Entertainment is emblematic of many efforts to create content for the procrastination economy. Specifically targeting the workplace audience, the network reused processes and insight gained from years creating television programming in its effort to provide snackable content that could elevate the conglomerate's brands and franchises.

Lunch with Benefits is one of the earliest efforts to monetize the mobile-media procrastination economy. Its history of successes and failures reveals the self-reflexive process of media companies as they worked out what was appropriate for the mobile audience. Like the development of other day parts across media history, the workplace day part developed a "common sense" idea of programming that balanced revenue expectations, programming aesthetic, and a concept of the audience. Media industries scholars have problematized these "common sense" assumptions by analyzing production cultures and interrogating the belief systems that structure creative work to uncover ideology and, in this case, the values of the procrastination economy.[48] The production culture of *Lunch with Benefits* shows this process of arriving at a "common sense" that inspired Internet programming that could fit neatly within different industrial flows, including programming flow, platform flow, and labor flow.

Analyzing *Lunch with Benefits* as an example of the production culture of the procrastination economy, I engaged in ethnographic observation of the offices, sets, and workplaces of the Fox Sports production during its initial season in December 2009. From this on-set analysis, I am able to, as Paul Willis argues, "theorize from the ground up" and determine how beliefs about the online audience, digital production, and career advancement shape the production and establish standards that reaffirm traditional business practices at Fox Sports.[49] I do not pretend to be able to understand the creative workers' culture better than they do themselves, but through observation and analysis of industry trade publications, I present an argument about the production culture that informed these early efforts to cultivate a workplace audience.

Media Snacks and Programming Flow

The *Lunch with Benefits* web series struggled to gain sponsors for all of its programming because online advertising for streaming media was still in its infancy in 2009. Despite the lack of revenue, Fox Sports committed to producing five 20- to 30-minute web episodes a week. A 2015 *Hollywood Reporter* investigation revealed that it costs $3.5 million to produce one episode of television.[50] The time and money that go into television production is recouped several times over if the series succeeds, earns larger advertising fees, and is eventually sold or leased out to streaming sites, home-video shelves, and syndication deals.[51] The more distribution windows a program can be spread across, the more value it has. Higher-value shows receive larger budgets.[52] The content made for the procrastination economy typically costs around $5,000 per episode to produce and usually earns little revenue.[53] Low potential revenue means that projects such as *Lunch with Benefits* are designed to support their conglomerate partners by reminding the workplace audience of Fox Sports television properties. Digital programming such as *Lunch with Benefits* was marketed as bonus content for advertisers during the television up-fronts (an annual television-industry event in which US networks introduce their fall programming lineups to advertisers).[54] Advertisers are told that if they purchase time on Fox television channels, they will get not only broadcast exposure but support from the company's digital properties.[55] The synergistic relationship between *Lunch with Benefits* and Fox Sports television programming shapes the media snacks produced for the procrastination economy.

The cast and crew of *Lunch with Benefits* understood that their job was to bring viewers to Fox Sports properties both on the web and on television. This strategy was accomplished through cross-promotions both on television and online. Fox broadcasts of NFL and college football games included graphic interstitials that encouraged audiences to check out *Lunch with Benefits* throughout the workweek. *Lunch with Benefits* returned the favor by creating content that promoted upcoming games. The television scholar Jennifer Gillan calls this kind of promotional content "anticipatory media," arguing that it extends television flow across digital platforms by focusing the digital production on analysis, questions, and predictions of what will happen next in an ongoing television narrative.[56] Sports programming is not always thought of as a continuing narrative, but a football season provides five months of weekly programming. *Lunch with Benefits* supported the story lines of the NFL and college football seasons by creating anticipation for upcoming games. Not only did the cross-platform flow strategy place the procrastination economy in the realm of promotional ephemera, but it also had a censoring effect on the digital productions of *Lunch with Benefits*. Producers from *The College Experiment* explained that their writers had to adjust the crass humor and overt sexuality on the show because Fox Sports' NCAA partners did not want to be associated with this potentially offensive content.[57] Additionally, they explained that in order to get Fox Sports' Internet partner, MSN.com, to feature their content on the landing page, they had to find content that would appeal to a broad audience. The demands of serving their workplace audience, their television partners, and their web partners made a target difficult for the digital team to hit. These constraints produced media snacks defined by the logics of anticipatory media and the negotiation of synergistic partnerships.

Lunch with Benefits' cozy relationship with Fox Sports' television partners did help the series book marketable guests. In 2009, the New Orleans Saints were the NFL's best team, going undefeated up to that point in the season. *Lunch with Benefits* featured a video interview with Saints linebacker Jonathan Vilma, which was picked up by MSN.com for "center placement" on the popular online platform.[58] The clip attracted a large audience, and traffic statistics suggested that a portion of that audience returned to *Lunch with Benefits* throughout the week to watch the rest of its offerings.[59] The producers explained that while they were unlikely to get center placement on MSN.com for all of their content, featuring a newsmaker that related to Fox's NFL programming was a strategy that had worked in the past. Other types of content that could achieve *Lunch with Benefits* center placement included clips of spectacular plays, scandalous headlines, and breaking news—all high-interest, snackable content that is assumed to be ideal for the lunchtime audience as well as supportive to Fox Sports' television partners.

These examples of promotional flow situate *Lunch with Benefits* as a bridge, transporting viewers from the closing credits of one program to the opening titles of the next broadcast. *Lunch with Benefits* picks up where the games end, providing football fans with information, analysis, and replays that create anticipation for next week. Sports programming is especially conducive to the media-snacking promotional flow. As Victoria E. Johnson points out, sports programming is "predisposed to being parsed out in small 'bytes' of information or highlights and news alerts best suited for miniaturized technologies and a la carte delivery."[60] Johnson identifies a natural connection between sports and mobile content because highlights from games can be unbundled from their original context and turned into media snacks.[61] The inherent snackability of sports highlights allows the *Lunch with Benefits* producers to draw connections between sports aesthetics, the workplace audience, and the logic of media snacking that justifies the programming-flow strategy.

Sports programming may be ideal for this programming-flow strategy, but scripted television shows also employ these methods. During an interview with Fox's senior vice president of marketing, Steven Melnick, the programming-flow strategy was cited as a principle that producers use for creating snackable digital con-

tent on YouTube, MySpace, and Twitter.[62] Melnick's team managed
the Twitter feed for the CBS sitcom *How I Met Your Mother* by
selecting clips, creating websites, and managing Twitter feeds for
the show's characters. During and directly after episodes of *How I
Met Your Mother*, a member of the writing staff would tweet as the
popular character Barney, extending the story of the episode and
providing the character with a digital presence.[63] During the week
leading up to an episode, Barney and the show's other character-
based Twitter feeds would comment on current events in their
character's comedic style. As a new episode approached, Twitter
accounts for all of the *How I Met Your Mother* characters would
tweet reminders that the show would be airing that evening. Each
of these promotional tweets was posted during work hours (typically during lunchtime) and reminded the workplace audiences
of the TV schedule for the evening. According to Melnick, digital divisions follow this schedule because "right now the web and
streaming revenues aren't there, but the marketing is, and so it has
the ability to discuss with consumers directly the things they like
about the show."[64] Melnick's comments reflect a common sensibility within the creative community that the procrastination economy is useful for rallying viewers but not for generating revenue.
Using the procrastination economy in this way keeps the audience
invested in more lucrative traditional media texts. Engaging with
fans online throughout the workweek has turned the workplace
into an interactive marketing venue with benefits for producers
and fans alike.

One genre of television that has wholeheartedly embraced
workplace programming flow is late-night talk shows. Late-night
television programs such as *The Tonight Show*, *Late Night*, *Jimmy
Kimmel Live*, *The Daily Show*, *Saturday Night Live*, *Conan*, and
others have been a staple of network broadcasting since the earliest
days of television. Talented comedians would sum up the previous
day's events with wit and humor and send people to sleep with a
smile on their face—an old-fashioned idea of broadcasting. Yet the

topical comedic commentary on these shows and their short segments are similar to the sports highlight clips used by *Lunch with
Benefits*, making late-night shows ideal for the procrastination
economy.[65] Late-night shows have proven to be popular on digital platforms particularly with younger viewers.[66] Conan O'Brien's
late-night show on the basic-cable network TBS does not compete
in the ratings race against broadcast-network late-night shows, but
it often surpasses them in digital metrics.[67] The ability to cultivate
a workplace following contributes to the brand of the network and
is becoming a significant marker of late-night success. The focus
on the workplace audience and cross-promotional flow affects the
style and casting of late-night shows. Jimmy Fallon's success in late
night is largely attributed to his ability to craft sketches that translate to workplace viewing.[68] The departure of Jon Stewart from
Comedy Central's *The Daily Show* was seen as an opportunity to
welcome a younger, more Internet-savvy host that could capitalize
on the procrastination economy.[69]

John T. Caldwell has termed this promotional strategy "second-
shift media aesthetics," as the audience is encouraged to follow the
story across a variety of platforms.[70] Using an example of stunt
programming from NBC's *Homicide: Life on the Streets*, Caldwell
describes how digital content channels television viewers across
screens, increasing the amount of effort the audience has to ex-
pend to keep up with favorite television shows.[71] This process
exposes the audience to new interactive experiences while keeping it tied to familiar advertising business models. Elana Levine
explains that this is the strategy employed by soap operas in the
postnetwork era.[72] As soap opera ratings dipped, producers began
to cultivate online games and exclusive content to attract viewers
back to the daytime broadcasts. Levine says that this accomplishes
two things: it provides additional online advertising revenue, and
it promotes the daily episodes. As more shows use the Internet to
shore up flagging ratings, the procrastination economy day part
becomes an essential component of the broadcast day. It reminds

viewers of the more lucrative television content while simultaneously advancing the series' storytelling goals and growing the
audience.

In addition to the "second-shift" approach to generating revenue for the parent conglomerate, *Lunch with Benefits*' producers
also employ another familiar programming strategy, termed "flow"
by the cultural theorist Raymond Williams. "Flow" describes the
way in which commercial television encourages viewers to watch
an endless stream of content.[73] Flow is possible in television because, unlike film or literature, there is no end to content; there are
only transitions from programs to commercials to new programs.
John Ellis and Jane Feuer have refined Williams's concept of flow
by pointing out that television programming is made up of segments that are tied together to cater to certain audiences.[74] Media
theorists describe television as a medium of inherently distracted
viewing because television is watched in the home; therefore,
activity in the kitchen, for example, can draw viewers' attention
away from the screen in the living room. The mobile audience has
been similarly described, since people frequently use their devices
in public spaces for media snacks. Shared characteristics between
the distracted viewing or snackable media for television and for
online workplace audiences encourage digital producers to adopt
aesthetic strategies similar to those employed in television production.[75] In this way, the producers of *Lunch with Benefits* are jus-
tified in their use of attention-grabbing short-form to half-hour
content in the workplace because it fits the expectations of multitasking and media snacking in the workplace. It is the kind of
common sense that justifies the thrifty approach to programming
for the procrastination economy. Similar scheduling strategies
have framed television as a part of everyday life, with each day
part designed to address different audience needs and contexts.[76]
The procrastination economy replicates this programming strategy
by moving audiences through the programming schedule and establishing a social order for the workday.

Media Snacks and Platform Flow

The programming-flow strategy developed out of the procrastina-tion economy's lack of advertising revenue. This fact caused media companies to see the workplace audience and mobile devices as promotional tools for television and film properties. Though the promotional goals are central, media companies also treat the pro-crastination economy as a low-stakes proving ground for television content. Digital divisions of multimedia conglomerates run like small-scale television studios. The constraints of the television business model influence the content created for the procrastina-tion economy. The structure and business model of *Lunch with Benefits* follow these guidelines in a few clear ways: by focusing on a target demographic of 18- to 49-year-old men, by attracting sponsors, and by replicating the familiar genres of talk shows (*The After Party with Jay Glazer*), workplace comedies (*Cubed*), sports news and analysis (*Coach Speak*), clip shows (*The College Experi-ment*), and behind-the-scenes features (*Inside Call*). These shows' success depends on building a relationship with the audience and the sponsors that can translate to television.

Lunch with Benefits producer Judy Hoang Boyd says that the ultimate goal of the shows is building an audience that will be at-tractive to advertisers. She calls web content a "test spot" that can prove that a show is "ready to be moved onto cable."[77] The goal of developing digital programming that can translate to televi-sion is instructive for how the producers of *Lunch with Benefits* understood their jobs. While they were tasked with creating pro-gramming for the workplace audience, they understood this audi-ence in the same entertainment- and leisure-oriented position of the traditional television audience. With reference to the media snacking of the office workers in the first part of this chapter, the *Lunch with Benefits* understanding of the audience only served the lunchtime-viewing media snacking that people craved. The pro-ducers of *Lunch with Benefits* recognized that the online workplace audience was different and experimented with aesthetics and tone to reflect this difference, but ultimately they dismissed other forms of media snacking in the pursuit of content that could achieve cross-platform flow.

The history of the *Lunch with Benefits* web series *The College Experiment* is an example of how the production team struggled to manage cross-platform flow. From September 14, 2009, to September 8, 2011, *The College Experiment* emulated the clip-show format popularized by *The Soup* (E!) and *Tosh.o* (Comedy Central) by showing and commenting on clips from the past week's sports broadcasts. The humor in these shows derives from the snarky commentary provided by comedian hosts, who poke fun at people in the clips. The crew described the show as the most "irreverent" offering of *Lunch with Benefits*, "a sort of *The Daily Show* of sports."[78] The atmosphere on set was very loose, with the comedian host, writers, and producers all pitching different ideas for jokes that could accompany the clips they had chosen to lampoon. For Boyd, irreverent comedy meant developing something "you can't find on TV" but not so controversial that it repels sponsors.[79] The lack of censorship online would seem to provide *The College Experiment* with more freedom than its television counterparts, but the need to adhere to television standards limited the type of content the producers could pursue.

Negotiating issues of censorship and standards of decency is a constant dilemma for producers of online content such as *Lunch with Benefits*. Digital creative workers realize that web-based programming offers more freedom to push the envelope, but the desire to migrate the show from the web to television acts as a governor. In 2009, *Lunch with Benefits* was still trying to find its voice and balance the freedom of the Internet with the business standards of television. When asked about what types of content worked well online, the producers stated that they relied on old formulas such as "sex sells" and using controversy to capture attention, but these strategies are not neatly transferrable to producing content for a wider television audience.[80] The *Lunch with Benefits* producers learned this lesson on their first day of programming, when an episode of *Cubed*, which featured female nudity and a conversation disparaging women's athletics, was pulled after being chastised by Fox Sports' Internet partner, MSN.com.[81] Fox Sports chairman David Hill called the incident "creative hiccups," and Boyd chalked it up to overeagerness to capture attention in the crowded online market.[82] *Lunch with Benefits* continued to offer risqué content, such as a weekly pillow fight between two bikini-clad models, but a line of decency had been drawn that put this web content in line with cable-television standards.

Despite the first-season troubles of *The College Experiment*, the show continued to feature politically incorrect humor and failed to find the balance between TV and web standards of decency. In the show's second season, Fox Sports began rebroadcasting episodes of the web series on its alternative sports TV network, Fuel TV (now Fox Sports 2), effectively intensifying the application of traditional decency standards. In an early second-season episode, a comedian interviewed Asian students at the University of Southern California and mocked their accents. The segment caught the attention of a University of Colorado ethnic studies professor, Darryl Maeda, and the *Colorado Daily Camera*, which criticized the show for being highly offensive and racist.[83] This type of humor might have passed for acceptable in the corners of the Internet but was judged completely unacceptable when exposed to a broader TV audience. The show was eventually canceled for being racially offensive.[84] The producers of *Lunch with Benefits* failed to consider how their corporate parents would react to charges of offensive or controversial content. In discussing the cancellation of the show, a Fox Sports Networks spokesperson said that the video was "clearly offensive and inconsistent with the standards Fox Sports believes in."[85] The decency standards upheld by Fox Sports television do not match those of the Internet. *The College Experiment* seemed doomed from the beginning, as producers repeatedly attempted to create humor that could live on two platforms: the Wild West of the Internet and the more polite sports network owned by News Corporation.

Although *The College Experiment* failed to transfer from web series to cable television, there are many examples of series that began in the procrastination economy and were picked up by television networks. *Quarterlife* was a famous early example that had its origins in the Hollywood writer's strike of 2007–2008 but failed to maintain its grass-roots momentum.[86] HBO has developed a reputation for translating digital content into television series, beginning with *Funny or Die* and *Web Therapy* and continuing with *High Maintenance*.[87] The Comedy Central hits *Broad City* and *Drunk History* began as web series but became critically acclaimed shows on the network.[88] Writing about this trend, Nick Marx argues that media companies' failure to create their own web platforms and profits leads them to look for series with established followings that they could purchase.[89] Due to small budgets and the nature of the online audience, these web series are typically short-form entertainments that complement media snacking. Media companies identify the snacks that people like the most and then try to develop those shows into full-fledged television series. In this way, the procrastination economy and the workplace audience act as an incubator for new television series.

Media Snacks and Labor Flow

Media companies look to the procrastination economy for new content and new talent. It is helpful to think of the procrastination economy as analogous to the B-movie system of the classical Hollywood era, the studio-produced television of the 1950s, and Roger Corman's B-movies of the 1970s. Each of these lower-prestige industries supported more prestigious entertainment markets by providing inexpensive content and training creative workers.[90] Historically, these "support" industries have low artistic status, second-class budgets, and "make-do" labor practices. This hierarchy is yet another traditional structure informing the way entertainment companies treat and think about mobile content. The production of *Lunch with Benefits* emphasized that television production skills were the key to creating successful digital content. This defensive logic insists that television production skills will be relevant in the digital era and that those who succeed on digital platforms can succeed on television. The procrastination economy therefore acts as a labor flow for media producers and talent to prove themselves and climb the corporate ladder.

The implications of this labor-flow strategy are clear in the initial press release for *Lunch with Benefits*, which emphasized the relationship between digital production and television talent. Fox Sports chairman and executive producer David Hill launched *Lunch with Benefits* with the assertion that digital content is best understood and programmed by television veterans, stating, "Original programming on the Internet is set to explode as the web transitions from being controlled by engineers to being run by producers, much the same way television did in the 1950s."[91] Hill's statement is remarkable in two ways: First, it exposes an industry-wide belief that the storytellers and programmers in the field of television are the natural heirs to the Internet. Second, it suggests that certain programming strategies and business models are necessary in order to transform the Internet into a viable entertainment industry. The discourse surrounding *Lunch with Benefits* reflects a belief that if talent can be successful on mobile screens, it will be successful on television screens, and vice versa.

The success of the journalist and television personality Jay Glazer is an example of how the procrastination economy facilitates labor flow. Glazer was the host of the *Lunch with Benefits* web series *The After Party*. The show was shot on set with a traditional studio camera setup, with Glazer interviewing call-in guests. When asked to name something that made *The After Party* distinctly "web content," the producers pointed to the web-camera aesthetic achieved by their use of Skype for interviews. Boyd claims that this made the series seem more intimate and replicated the one-to-one conversation that many people experience on their mobile screens.[92] Other than this aesthetic detail, *The After Party* had the same overall look and feel as any studio-based sports talk show.

Glazer is a star within sports journalism, bolstered by his ability to break stories ahead of the competition. He developed cozy relationships with football players thanks to his interview style and shared interest in weight training and mixed martial arts (MMA). His interest in MMA fighting made him popular with both fans and colleagues and resulted in an additional *Lunch with Benefits* show, titled *MMAthletics*.[93] Glazer followed a path from sports journalism to television hosting that had been blazed by contributors to *The Sports Reporters* (ESPN), *Pardon the Interruption* (ESPN), and *Around the Horn* (ESPN). Fox Sports has developed Glazer's trajectory along similar lines, using his web series to see if his journalistic chops translated to on-screen charisma. Fox insists that Glazer's web-based endeavors do not interfere with his main job as a journalist but are rather an effort to capitalize on his popularity and develop his talent. Fox presents Internet labor as a side project, as secondary to "legitimate" pursuits, while simultaneously benefiting from the web traffic that Glazer generates for the online platform.

On-screen talent are not the only ones that are successfully leveraging their efforts on *Lunch with Benefits* into more prestigious opportunities in television. Producer Bill Richards had proven himself as a rising star with Fox Sports by successfully working on Fox's NASCAR prerace show, *Fox NASCAR Sunday*, and producing segments with the comedian Frank Caliendo for *Fox NFL Sunday*. In 2009, Richards was responsible for producing *Cubed*, a scripted workplace comedy airing on the Thursday slot for *Lunch with Benefits*. The show successfully reaired on Fox's television network Fuel TV, earning Richards a promotion to the director of the show *Fox NFL Sunday*. Describing the promotion, Fox Sports

Media Group president and co-COO Eric Shanks cited Richards's ability to "maintain the highest production standards."[94] Richards, like Glazer, did not transition from web series to television because he created the most popular content on the web; he made it because he met the benchmarks of the industry for creating a commercially viable and digital property (or studio show).

Throughout the first decade of the 21st century, the procrastination economy was a training ground for editors, comedians, writers, and actors seeking the attention of media conglomerates by demonstrating the ability to create high-traffic digital content that operates within industry standards of decency. The story of Robert Ryang, a film editor, is one of the first examples of a below-the-line worker riding the success of digital content to greater opportunity in the entertainment industry. Ryang won an Association of Independent Creative Editors (AICE) contest with his reedited trailer for the movie *The Shining*.[95] The contest's challenge was to create a video that changed the genre of a classic film. Ryang reimagined *The Shining* as a romantic comedy and named it *Shining*. The video quickly circulated around the web and became one of the *New York Times* top-12 viral videos to define the genre. This example shows the extent to which procrastination economy content is often driven by the media industries' desire to use web platforms as inexpensive proving grounds for emerging talent. Web series may offer new avenues to the industry, but the common sense about what will appeal to a wide audience persists.

Appetizer or Indulgence

It is clear from analyzing the *Lunch with Benefits* production culture that there is a connection between creative labor, programming strategies, budgets, and digital aesthetics. Through the creation of digital departments and digital programming, Fox Sports is standardizing digital content to serve a workplace constituency looking for leisurely snackable media. Not only does this standardization help media companies define digital production in relation to existing entertainment-industry practices, but it also builds an apprenticeship system in which new talent can rise through the ranks and be tested in the procrastination economy. The economic realities determine the types of media snacks that these companies produce. Instead of cultivating an aesthetic that is distinctly digital, Fox Sports produces ephemeral promotional paratexts that are meant to turn workplace viewing into a day part within programming flow, platform flow, and labor flow.

Beliefs about the relationship between short-form content, digital platforms, and labor practices have become the common knowledge of the entertainment industry. Producers make claims that certain content is inherently "digital." Gail Berman provides an example of this assumption when discussing her plans to create digital content for her series *The Cape*: "It is not a case that we propose to go with a television show because we think that it will fit well on the web. It is much different. There are components of *The Cape* that could live very well online. We come up with millions of ideas for digital because the audience for the show is living in this space. It is going to be a 'now' audience, a family audience, a young audience."[96] Peter Levinsohn, the president of new media and digital distribution at Fox, oversees the creation and distribution of digital content and shares Berman's assumptions about digital content. He points out that "when you think about content that has been successful on the Internet, it is content that has been produced with arcs that are relatively short, 5–8 minutes long, that have the ability to integrate brands into them that have some kind of mythology. Think [about] *The Blair Witch Project* or so many others that strike a chord within the culture."[97] Berman's belief that a show has "components" that will "live very well online" not only suggests that there are aesthetic components that are suited to digital platforms but assumes that there are production standards and labor practices specific to digital platforms as well. These executives' statements about digital technologies factor into decisions about corporate priorities and budgets; this thinking may explain the low-budget/low-prestige production practices that define digital production.

These assumptions about digital content and labor are closely related to issues of cultural status. Pierre Bourdieu argues that fields such as those in the entertainment industry develop specific dispositions and practices based on the exchange of capital within that field.[98] In the entertainment industry, this process occurs across a variety of markers: budgets, job titles, and genres. According to Bourdieu, a field is "established between practices and a situation," the meaning of which is produced by "the habitus through categories of perception and appreciation that are themselves produced by an observable social condition."[99] In other words, the distinctions between cultural fields, film versus television or television versus digital media, is socially produced and reinforced by production standards and economic realities. Digital production has a low cultural status because programming efforts such as *Lunch with Benefits* adopt low production standards and merely act in a supplementary capacity to the higher-status content offerings of other Fox properties. This low cultural status does not mean that the procrastination economy is unimportant to media conglomerates, but resource allocations such as talent development and promotion are adjusted according to digital content's perceived cultural value to its corporate overlords.

The procrastination economy positions digital content as the "minor leagues" and television shows as the "major leagues." While this relationship conveniently provides an understanding of digital content's position in the media-industries hierarchy, it prevents the genre from establishing a larger cultural presence. The *Lunch with Benefits* crew believed that "making do," capitalizing on the DIY aesthetics, promoting other Fox properties, and proving themselves in the procrastination economy would pay off in upward professional mobility. These beliefs reiterate digital content's secondary status below television and film. An entertainment medium's cultural value is determined by its economic and social impact. Digital content has neither of these. Television has long been considered an inferior art form to film because of a similar (perceived) low status, as indicated by such phrases for the medium and its viewers as "boob tube," "couch potato," and "idiot box." The academic community has challenged this hierarchy, but television's low cultural status persists. Digital content suffers from similar labels. The prevailing images of the mobile audience are the multitasking slacker, the childish dreamer, and the sophomoric clown; all of these characters are reinforced by the procrastination economy's production practices and industrial beliefs.

The workplace audience is encouraged to maintain their fandom by checking in with digital content throughout the workweek. Joe Turow describes the significance of this promotional strategy in his book *Niche Envy* by explaining that the relationship between the consumer and programmers changed significantly in the digital era.[100] Turow notes, "retailers and their suppliers are learning to use the Internet, interactive television, mobile telephones, and other consumer-driven interactive technologies to find new customers, gather information on new and old ones, and reach out to consumers with advertisements and content rewards that are increasingly tailored to what [consumer] databases know."[101] Turow argues that digital technology encourages advertisers and programmers to go after consumers who are most likely to spend money; this more valuable group becomes the privileged audience for digital content. Those who give more time to the media brand through the procrastination economy get a more customized experience. Salaried office workers with desk jobs constitute the lunchtime Internet crowd; this affluent demographic is certainly an attractive advertising target, one with the flexible time to engage the procrastination economy, and consequently, they are the ones that this mobile content privileges.

Not surprisingly, the workplace audience does not follow lockstep with the programming strategies set up by the media industries. Digital content may be designed as touch points and appetizers that engage users with media brands and foster cross-platform synergy, but the unpredictability of any individual person's workday calls for flexible uses of digital content. Mobile devices themselves offer workers control over their surroundings, their fandom, and their communication with friends, family, and the larger public. Although the procrastination economy offers snacks, workplace audiences show a fascinating ability to imbue these morsels with meaning that goes far beyond corporate marketing. Perhaps as digital revenue sources develop, a greater variety of media snacks will be produced by the entertainment industries. Until then, the workplace audience will find creative ways to make do with content to help them navigate the social and spatial realities of their workplaces.

Workplace audience practices are one more example of how fan communities use popular culture in more sophisticated ways than their status suggests. The work of Henry Jenkins, Constance Penley, Matt Hills, Dorothy Hobson, and Will Brooker (among many others) explains how these creative consumption practices complicate claims that media texts manipulate their audiences.[102] A person's creative use of a text is proof of how frequently a consumer who seems most in the thrall of a commercial object is actively negotiating his or her relationship to the text. Workplace audiences also negotiate this relationship but in a more politically motivated way: fans use media in the workplace to assert their positions within the work ecosystem. The use of work tools for leisure purposes is not a new phenomenon; Michel de Certeau described employees repurposing the tools of work for their own needs throughout the history of labor. He calls this practice "la perruque," a way for employees to "steal" time from their employer and co-opt the tools of labor for their own means.[103] Certeau contends that an employee engages in these activities to "confirm (with pleasure) his own solidarity with workers or his family through spending his time in this way."[104] Information technology greatly increases the customizability of "la perruque," as modern-day tools of labor provide a quick and easy access to a wide variety of personal pleasures. In the workplaces I visited, my observations made it evident how "la perruque" is waged in the modern workplace.

3

The Commute

"Smart" Cars and Tweets from Trains

Many American car owners have an affective relationship with their automobiles; the car is "closely integrated into daily or weekly routines and comes to support feelings associated with taking care of loved ones, as well as a sense of liberation."[1] In *American Graffiti* (1973), George Lucas uses the automobile and the car stereo as essential signifiers of American independence and autonomy. Cars separate and protect us from the outside world; they also give us control over how we negotiate public spaces. One of the most common uses of the car, at least in American cities, is the daily commute to and from the workplace. Networked mobile devices and "smart" cars have changed our relationship to automobiles, transforming travel time between work and home into a key site of the procrastination economy. Using mobile media during the commute empowers users to assert their independence from the crowd *and* to connect with friends and family.

Mobile devices and headphones provide commuters on public transit with a similar ability to separate themselves from their immediate surroundings. The Internet connectivity on these devices allows commuters to interact while keeping to themselves on public transit. Scott Campbell calls this "network privatism" and situates it as a dominant behavior in the era of mobile devices.[2] Thus, the commute is no longer the epitome of dislocation but rather a site of engagement with friends, family members, and larger cultural conversations. Mimi Sherry and John Urry point out that mobile devices are complicit in expanding work hours:

increased connectivity to work functions (such as email) has led to "flex-time" schedules that allow people to work anytime, anywhere. The downside of this greater flexibility is that it also keeps people tethered more closely to the demands of the workplace.[3] Indeed, a court within the European Union ruled that the commute should be counted as part of the workday.[4] While mobile phones facilitate more onerous work conditions and intrusive commercialism, they also provide the means for managing those conditions and staying connected to the world on the commute.[5]

While mobile phones bring work and socializing to the commute, the procrastination economy also provides entertainment options. The products and services of the procrastination economy are designed to counteract modern labor and social pressure to make every moment productive. For many people, the commute is a useful site of productivity that helps free up time for leisure at home. Still, for others, the domestic sphere has similar labor requirements, making the commute one of the only places for personal time. The procrastination economy provides digital content for the commuter that emphasizes the value of personal time while also promoting subscription services that make a leisurely commute possible. Streaming services, music services, and data packages all operate on a subscription model that encourages commuters to entertain themselves through their mobile devices.

Entertainment companies may present the commute as a space for leisurely procrastination, but unreliable cellular service and the length of commutes make some subscription services useless. Commuters surveyed in this chapter primarily used their commute as a time for network privatism.[6] People's desire to chat with loved ones on the commute suggests that the economic motivations of the procrastination economy are at odds with the desires of the commuting audience. This chapter argues that the procrastination economy of the commute is defined by subscription services that offer leisure and communication apps that make the ride to and from work a social occasion. The promise of subscription revenues accounts for the dominant aesthetic in the procrastination economy of the commute, but emerging social media apps may offer an alternative economic incentive.

Subscription Services and Platform Mobility: The Procrastination Economy of the Commute

Commuters have long been a target of the advertising and entertainment industries, but the appearance of mobile devices has brought subscription services to this part of the procrastination economy.[7] These subscription services, such as Netflix, YouTube Red, HBO Now, SeeSo, Amazon Prime Video, and Spotify, offer commuters mobile apps that allow them to reconstitute the viewing experience of the living room in train cars and passenger seats.[8] The television scholar Chuck Tryon argues that entertainment companies market these subscription services through "platform mobility" and the promise that a mobile device can transform an individual's surroundings.[9] These subscription services provide on-demand access to media collections, but the mobile apps that deliver the content rarely account for the specifics of public viewing. Anna McCarthy has shown that television screens bring an "elsewhere" to the specific politics of a space; however, the mobile platforms of the procrastination economy do little to distinguish the commuting audience from the at-home audience.[10] Ignoring these different contexts of use, media companies provide a continuous stream of content that replicates traditional passive viewing practices across mobile platforms in the quest to deliver a personalized media experience to the commuter.[11] Specific locations such as the freeway, the subway car, the bus, or the automobile are governed by strategies of control and institutional ideologies. Screens—whether television or mobile devices—can either fortify these strategies or provide audiences with tools for negotiating these spaces and subverting space-specific ideologies. Commute-ready content produced by the culture industries often reinforces

the strategies of particular spaces, in this case ensuring that commuters keep to themselves in their own audio bubbles.[12] In fact,
the subscription services of the procrastination economy assist in
pacifying commuters to ensure orderly travel. While there is nothing wrong with arriving quietly at one's destination, the emphasis
on platform mobility and subscription services ignores other possibilities for the procrastination economy.

The subscription companies have good reason to assume that
people want a leisurely solitary commute; after all, mobile screens
are small and come equipped with individual headphones, suggesting that people want a solitary audio-visual experience during
the commute. Michael Bull's analysis of mobile devices claims that
the practice of customizing playlists, using headphones, and separating oneself from the public engenders individualism and commercialism.[13] Tryon and Bull arrive at similar conclusions about
media companies' intentions vis-à-vis the devices they create and
the content they produce.[14] The subscription services of the procrastination economy foster individualism.

The streaming-media company Netflix is a premium member
of the commuter procrastination economy. Netflix's marketing
and promotional materials provide insight into how the company
identifies the commuter audience's needs. The production culture
scholar John T. Caldwell refers to these industrial and promotional documents as "deep texts" that can be mined for symbolic
meaning.[15] In February 2013, Netflix announced that it would
be creating its own awards, "The Flixies," to recognize the programs its subscribers most liked to watch. The categories of these
awards reflected the different viewing audiences Netflix identified as unique to its subscribers, including "Best Hangover Cure,"
"Best PMS Drama," "Best Tantrum Tamer," "Best Marathon TV
Show," "Best Guilty Pleasure," "Best Bromance," and "Commute
Shrtnr."[16] Among the nominated content in the commuter category were stand-up comedy specials, animated shorts, music documentaries, sketch-comedy series, reality series, documentaries,

and a food show.[17] Industry awards (such as the Flixies) and the accompanying promotional discourse illustrate common logics within the media industries. Netflix's creation of award categories and the selection of texts for those categories demonstrate the company's belief that the context of the commute correlates to particular types of entertainment—in this case, audiocentric, half-hour, light, informative, and comedic content. The list of commute-appropriate content does not include any "quality" drama shows or premium content that are commonly celebrated in other awards shows. According to Flixies promotional documents, Netflix imagines commuters as looking for something relaxing on the trip between work and home.

The functionality of the Netflix mobile app provides an additional strategy for using the subscription service. In 2011, Apple released an update for their iOS operating system that enabled "background playback" on iPhones and iPads. Essentially, this feature allowed users to stream content in the background, enabling them to engage with multiple tasks or activities while listening to streamed media. Apps such as uListen, SuperTube, and Viral provide this functionality to numerous devices that do not have the option built in, including those that run on the Android operating system. In addition, there are numerous user tutorials online explaining how to run audio on a device while the screen is off. Following the trend, the social networking platform Twitter updated its software to allow users to listen to videos while they scroll through their feed.[18] These audio-only efforts reflect the commuter audience's desire to multitask: to listen to a video's soundtrack while engaging in other activities. Netflix's "Commute Shrtnr" category similarly emphasized audiocentric content. Commuters have long gravitated to music for the pleasant background noise. Mobile devices are extending this capability by allowing commuters to listen to just the audio tracks of popular videos. In 2013, Netflix CEO Reed Hastings announced the decision to develop comedy specials as an attempt to serve "fans of this much loved and often under-distributed genre," citing their "broad appeal."[19] In 2016, Netflix secured comedy specials from Jerry Seinfeld and Chris Rock in deals worth $140 million while also producing 25 comedy specials (five times as many as it had three years prior).[20] Netflix's investment in comedy specials is one clear indicator of the company's strategy to capitalize on consumers' habits. Additionally, YouTube launched a subscription service in 2015 called YouTube Red that offered ad-free streaming media and background playback.[21] YouTube had originally made this functionality available for all its videos, but at the time of the launch of the subscription service, it was deemed such an enticing feature for the procrastination economy that it was put behind a pay wall.

Aesthetically, these audiocentric streaming services have much in common with another form of subscription-based digital media, podcasts. Podcasts are audiocentric long-form programs that provide listeners with stories, reports, interviews, and informal conversation between hosts. They are very nearly the ideal form of culture for the commute, as they are plentiful, typically free (with advertising), and run for between 30 minutes and an hour. Research by Steven McClung and Kristine Johnson found that podcast listeners look to this content for social connection.[22] Thus, like radio programs before them, podcasts inspire large followings and participation, as fans send in questions, attend live podcast recordings, and document the history and ephemera of the show on websites.[23] Podcasts are not directly interactive conversations, but they do have an intimacy that feels similar to listening in on a conversation of friends or a confessional.[24] Unlike radio, podcasts cater to a wide variety of niche interests and communities, even replicating ethnically specific social spaces.[25] Podcasts' popularity can reach such a significant level that some become major conduits to the public. For example, Hollywood press tours and even President Barack Obama used podcasts to reach people who do not watch the traditional news outlets.[26] Podcasting as a form owes much of its success to its portability, which has helped it become extremely popular with commuters.

Evidence from the earliest podcasts in the middle of the first decade of the 21st century reveals the potential of this form in the procrastination economy. The first major hit in podcasting was *The Ricky Gervais Show*, distributed by Positive Internet and Guardian Unlimited.[27] It was immediately apparent that podcasts were a cousin or even child of radio; the stars of *The Ricky Gervais Show* had previously worked together in radio.[28] Other radio programs soon released podcast adaptations of their shows, with few differences between the podcast version of the shows and the broadcast version (except for different sponsors and fewer commercials). Throughout the early 2000s, podcasts developed beyond rebroadcast radio programs by embracing a more intimate discussion format with longer running times. The 2009 debut of *WTF with Marc Maron* represents an important milestone in podcast history: Maron's autobiographical interview format and his ability to attract sponsors became a model for success in the procrastination economy.[29] Podcasts became even more popular in 2014 with the advent of *Serial*, a true-crime anthology featuring the story of Adnan Syed.[30] *Serial* brought so much public scrutiny to Syed's case that an appeals process was initiated on Syed's behalf.[31] Richard Berry describes *Serial* as benefiting from the shift from iPods to networked smartphones, which brought in new demographics to the genre and essentially provided the capabilities for it to expand beyond a niche audience.[32] As the popularity of podcasts has grown, podcast networks have begun to form, with the goals of helping listeners discover new shows and offering archived and premium content via subscription deals.[33] Even though all podcasts share an audiocentric style of delivery, there are a burgeoning number of genres available, including serialized storytelling, interview shows, and conversations between journalists.

Like many aspects of the procrastination economy, the development of podcasts is parallel to the history of television, which also began as an adaptation of radio. Television also developed stars and networks over time, finally establishing an association with an audience segment. Podcasting has become so associated with commuters that streaming-audio services such as Spotify and Pandora primarily stream music but also offer podcasts.[34] Audiocentric content such as podcasts and Netflix's comedy specials fit the needs of the multitasking commuter audience. Television historians such as Lynn Spigel have revealed the industrial logic that leads to television programmers developing daytime genres for the homemaker audience.[35] Daytime shows often featured audiocentric aesthetics, including repetition of plot points, to help a distracted, multitasking audience follow the story.[36] The aesthetics of podcasts and audiocentric video programs function in a similar fashion by giving commuters the ability to listen, work, and travel simultaneously. Indeed, Spotify long argued that it was a company solely focused on music but has recently embraced alternative audio and video forms including audio books, stand-up comedy, and spoken-word recordings to better cater to the procrastination economy.[37]

Selling to Busy Commuters

The strategies for enticing commuters to use subscription services are built on the established marketing appeals of outdoor advertisers. Outdoor advertisers have offered commuters a fantasy of leisure and escapism for decades. Advertising companies such as Outfront Media (formerly CBS Outdoor), Clear Channel Outdoor, JC Decaux, and Lamar Advertising bring marketing messages to commuter rails, buses, and billboards. Gas Station TV, a division of Turner Private Networks, programs content for gas-station pumps that commuters might watch during a commuting pit stop. Since the 1920s, these advertising endeavors have attempted to monetize the commute by playing on the stress and anxiety of travel. In advertisers' packaging and programming for this audience, they have developed a set of strategies for defining the mind-set of the commuter that influences the current subscription services of the procrastination economy.

Once commuters began using mobile devices, these companies began characterizing commuters as multitaskers with busy schedules. As demonstrated earlier, the multitasking of commuters is reflected in the features of mobile apps, such as background playback. Outdoor advertisers' marketing materials are preoccupied with the fractured attention of the commuter. This is not surprising given that the primary goal of advertisers is to capture the attention, however fleeting, of the mobile-device-wielding commuter. Outfront Media is almost defensive about the industry as it touts its continued relevance in the age of mobile devices, stating that its products are the best investment in marketing because people still pass by billboards and outdoor advertisements even if they no longer watch traditional television and listen to traditional radio.[38] In public-relations materials, advertisers describe commuters as busy professionals charging through the workday in the pursuit of money that they will spend shopping online during the commute home. These fantasy commuters are so engaged that they need to recharge their phones while they commute. These descriptions fit neatly within the ethos of the neoliberal global economy, in which people are expected to use their devices to be productive and efficient at all hours of the day and night or, in the case of commuters, on the way to work, at work, and on the way home from work. This understanding of the commuter audience plays into the marketing messages and the products of the procrastination economy, which foreground multitasking and commuters' desire for relief from their busy schedules.

Advertisers' assumptions about the busy commuter audience are displayed plainly in the business-to-business marketing materials of these companies. Outfront Media claims that the best way to capture the attention of these distracted commuters is through the aesthetic philosophy that "less is better." This strategy is based on the notion that the commuter is moving through a space when in transit and only has time for a glance at an advertisement.[39] The result is advertising that either "position" a product or "sell" a product but never attempt both.[40] According to Outfront, ads must deliver one message in "a big and bold way" because audiences are reading from a distance and do not have time to scan several lines of text. The company claims that "research shows" humor helps but only if it is simple.[41] It is hard not to see marketing anxiety woven throughout these promotional promises. Digital technology has complicated the advertising business, and Outfront is confronting that changing landscape with specific recommendations for an audience that it imagines as harried commuters. Mobile advertisers and app designers are reacting to this same anxiety, as people are just as likely to be shifting attention from their mobile screen as they would a billboard.

Anxiety is also apparent through Outfront's variety of attempts to integrate signage and mobile devices. The company offers its clients signage that works with mobile devices via augmented reality programs, QR codes, proximity beacons, and visual search features.[42] These features seem to violate the "less is better" philosophy, but Outfront Media insists that outside-the-home media and mobile devices are "natural partners." To this end, companies are creating "smart" bus shelters that offer commuters Wi-Fi hotspots, USB charging stations, and transit information.[43] Mobile devices are being used as a way to draw the consumer into the advertisement, whether to recharge devices or to engage them in commerce while commuting. One of the most revealing assumptions about the modern commuter is Outfront's claim that commuters want the option to shop while traveling. Outfront tells its clients that people's "lives become busier and everything is done on-the-go," including shopping.[44] Outfront accommodates this behavior by posting advertisements featuring products that people can purchase by tapping on the corresponding QR code.

Pacifying the Commuter

Whereas marketers see the commute as a place of multitasking productivity, municipalities and public-transit authorities design mobile apps that attempt to calm the anxious traveler. Transit authorities throughout the nation create public-service campaigns to inform and unite their commuters under a "code of conduct" that outlines appropriate etiquette and citizenship. The digital offerings of these institutions can be as utilitarian as interactive maps and schedules of the commuter rail and bus lines and as prescriptive as surveillance apps. Atlanta, Boston, and San Francisco hired the Elerts Corporation to create a mobile app dedicated to promoting safety and surveillance. The app, called See and Say, instructs users to discreetly record and report any suspicious activity witnessed during their commute. The app even disables the camera flash on smartphones so that the individual under surveillance will not detect the documentation. Additionally, the app allows commuters to send messages to transit authorities even when cellular service is unreliable: the app saves messages and sends them automatically when cellular connectivity is renewed.

It is remarkable that the only official apps offered by these transit authorities foreground expedient travel and surveillance. Both of these functions attempt to calm commuters by giving them a tool for monitoring and reporting on their fellow citizens. These apps depict commuters as antisocial and suspicious. Often, campaigns to enhance cellular reception on public transit and to expand Wi-Fi capabilities are presented through the rhetoric of public safety rather than facilitating social connection.[45] The municipalities' contributions to the procrastination economy foster a sense of individualism, competition, and distrust—all qualities that are attributed to the inherent problems of mobile devices. Yet the versatility of smartphones allows users to counter the atmosphere of surveillance encouraged by municipalities. Entrepreneurs, start-up companies, brand managers, and everyday citizens create mobile apps that foster social interaction in public spaces. One of these alternative apps, iFlirtero, is designed to help people discreetly flirt with others on commuter trains.[46] Several iPhone games allow players to challenge each other while commuting.[47] Examples such as this, and countless others, demonstrate that commuters are interested in connecting with each other and their surroundings, despite the fact that the public-transit authority depicts the commuter as antisocial and anxious.

Smart Cars as Mobile Phones

The frustrations and anxiety of the commute also appear in the appeal to drivers of smart cars. Smart-car producers create products and functionality for the procrastination economy that depict commuters as thirsty for customization and independence. The term "smart car" is applied to automobiles with Internet-connected display panels. The functionality offered by smart cars, such as hands-free telephony, GPS, streaming media, and weather reports, is tailored for white-collar workers and professions who routinely spend a lot of time in the car.[48] The business community has historically been the target demographic for these types of cars.[49] Here again, the connected commute is designed for the "productive" worker who feels obligated to continue the workday while sitting in traffic between home and office. The focus on the business community is especially clear given the high cost of smart-car Internet-data subscription packages. The only people likely to pay these fees are those for whom the service is essential to their jobs or whose employers provide the service.[50]

Both Apple's CarPlay and Android's Audio convert cars into customizable media and communications tool controlled by mobile devices.[51] These services offer streaming audio, voice command, apps, voice recognition, and texting. Each of these options makes multitasking easier, as a driver can toggle between conversations with coworkers and listening to music.[52] Outfitted with such a device, the car becomes a mobile device itself with the dashboard operating like an iPhone touchscreen.[53] CarPlay was originally launched in collaboration with the luxury car brand Ferrari, reinforcing the assumption that this segment of the procrastination economy is reserved for the upper echelon of white-collar professionals.[54] It is clear that smart cars offer capabilities that feed into the individualism, competition, and commercialism feared by the critics of modernity. At the same time, smart technology brings a social element to the automobile that was previously impossible.

A Procrastination Economy Designed for Anxious, Busy Multitaskers

The smart-car industries' understanding of the procrastination economy is especially relevant given developments in driverless car technology. Driverless car initiatives have become a key goal for technology companies and car manufacturers.[55] As this technology develops, the principles of the procrastination economy and companies' understanding of anxious, busy, multitasking commuters will drive functionality and technology. Content companies, advertisers, governments, software companies, car manufactures, and others inform the procrastination economy of the commute. Consistent across these groups is the insistence that commuters are anxious and looking to their mobile devices for relief and multitasking. The products and services of the procrastination economy offer commuters subscription services to help them relax and multitask as well as surveillance technologies for calming their anxiety. As the strategies of billboard advertising and the proliferation of "See and Say" surveillance apps and "smart" car technology illustrate, a variety of business and public-transit authorities contribute to this understanding of commuters and the products of the procrastination economy. While these products and services may help commuters in need of relief or looking for a way to multitask, they ignore the constituencies that see their commute as a time for socializing with friends and family.

Quality Time via Text Messaging: Communicating on the Commute

The depiction of the commuter articulated through the functionality and products of the procrastination economy is of an anxious and busy worker in need of multitasking and relief. This depiction makes sense, as the companies operating in the procrastination economy offer subscription services that can be enjoyed while multitasking and provide leisure materials such as music, film, and television through platform mobility. Many commuters avail themselves of these services, but the commute is also a place for the kind of communication that Scott Campbell calls "network privatism."[56] Commuters see the drive as a time to check in with loved ones in order to catch up and make plans. The mobile device's ability to offer social interactions on the train is one of the major ways the technology has changed the experience of commuting. The commute is a key site for socializing, as it allows people a moment to discuss the issues of the day, check in on the public sphere, and engage with culture. The commute enables people to use their mobile devices in the way Zizi Papacharissi describes: as a comfortable place to engage with public life.[57]

The research on commuters' mobile habits presented in this chapter reveals a disconnection between the realities of the commute and the depiction of anxious, multitasking commuters presented by media companies and municipalities. The commute is often unconducive to the fantasy presented by "platform mobility," that mobile devices will provide the escapist leisure of the living rooms. For one, the commute-based telecommunications infrastructure makes using streaming subscription services unreliable. Second, the idea of passive leisure on the commute runs counter to the realities of the surroundings. People are strategic with their mobile devices in public space. Texting while on public transit or calling loved ones in the car provides social connection, but it can also be done discreetly and intermittently while commuters monitor their travel. Media companies looking at the social activities of the commute have begun to develop products and services to capitalize and enhance this practice, but these efforts are minuscule compared to products that associate subscription services with the procrastination economy. The evidence presented in this chapter shows that functionality of mobile applications for the commute reflects the economic opportunity of types of commuters rather than the technological affordance of mobile devices.

The economic motivations driving the procrastination economy foster the belief that mobile devices increase individualism and disconnection. Subscription services are connected to individual consumers, and when used on the commute, they provide a private viewing screen for disconnecting from one's surroundings. This functionality allows critiques to place mobile devices as part of the lineage of technology designed to help people disconnect from the anxieties of modern life. Early 20th-century theorists described modern city life as an audio-visual assault.[58] In an effort to cope with the onslaught of noise, advertisements, and human movement, people dissociate with their surroundings. According to the technologist Mariam Simun, one way people detach is by using portable, personal music devices; these allow people to withdraw from their surroundings physically, not just metaphorically, via a mask of polite indifference.[59] Mobile audio devices, portable games, reading material, broadcast radio, and smart cars are all cultural objects that can assist commuters in the effort to manage their interactions in public space. This anxiety has been growing throughout the modern age; theorists such as Margaret Morse have identified various scenarios in which public and private collide. In her essay "An Ontology of Everyday Distraction," Morse challenges the work of Michel de Certeau and argues that freeways, cars, and malls have adopted the economics of distraction and leisure, turning previously open spaces into closed non-spaces defined by their standardization and homogeneity.[60] In these non-spaces, people travel distractedly and half aware, following a routine, displaced from reality. Morse worries that people prefer this fugue state, organized on consumer logic, to the messy realities of their surroundings.[61]

Both Morse and Certeau considered the privatization of public space prior to the pervasive adoption of networked mobile devices. Work by the sound studies scholars Michael Bull and Stephen Groening describes the design of mobile devices and software applications as fostering the individualism and distraction that Morse lamented.[62] Yet the actual behaviors of the mobile audience reveal a much more engaged populace. The question is whether mobile devices' technological affordances have revitalized public life or whether the economics of distraction described by Morse have become fully realized in the mobile procrastination economy. Trend research suggests that the former scenario is happening: people are moving out of suburbs and back into the cities; car ownership is on the decline, as young people increasingly choose mass transit for both ecological and financial benefits.[63] These same young professionals are rejecting traditional television options, looking instead to on-demand entertainment and procrastination economy content. It is possible that the ontology Morse described is outdated or, at the very least, evolving to take full advantage of mobile devices' empowering capabilities.

But how does this empowerment function during the commute? Samuel Thulin and Shuhei Hosokawa provide evidence that commuters, even when using mobile devices, can never truly disengage with their surroundings because the outside world always intrudes on the sonic experience.[64] Beyond this practical critique, the technological capabilities of mobile phones separate this technology from previous portable leisure culture. The commute, as Groening points out, has been "romanticized" as "a refuge from work and the hyperstimulus of the urban environment," but it is

no longer just a moment of passive relaxation; it is an opportunity for connection.[65] Morse once deemed socializing during the
commute as "impossible"; mobile technology has made commuter
socialization not only possible but extremely popular as well.[66] It
is true, as these critics have argued, that the commute is defined
by many of the products of the procrastination economy as a time
for relaxation. Now, however, relaxation can include social interactions, not just with the comfortable "others" of Raymond Williams's "private shell" but also with the challenging, opinionated
conversations often found on social media sites.[67]

Commuters, whether on the train or in the car, face an environment that promotes disconnection and alienation. Mobile devices recast the commute as an opportune setting for connecting
with others and engaging with the world. Commuters' desires for
communication are clear in the results of a 200-person survey
of Metropolitan Atlanta Rapid Transit Authority (MARTA) commuters conducted during the fall of 2014. The survey results indicate that social networking, text messaging, and access to the
Internet are all tools that enable commuters to use their rides to
and from work to strengthen their bonds with friends, family, and
the public at large. The complexity and intentionality in many of
the survey respondents' answers contradict charges about mobile
media technology's supposed negative impact on socialization
and empathy.

The development of the commute as an opportunity for socializing is significant, as historically there is little evidence that people ever regularly engaged in conversation with strangers on their
commute. Mobile devices have been found to increase social behavior in a variety of public spaces.[68] Keith Hampton, a professor of
communication and public policy, conducted a study of social interaction in public spaces before and after the arrival of networked
mobile devices. The study compared time-lapse photography from
the 1970s and '80s of public spaces and with recordings of the same
public spaces in 2010. Hampton discovered more social interaction

among groups and between men and women in the photographs from 2010.[69] The research also showed that people typically only use their mobile devices in transitional moments, when they are alone or waiting for someone to arrive. Even in these transitional moments, mobile devices offer a social experience via connecting with others through networked communication. Beyond these observations, Hampton's team found that people on mobile devices would spend more time in public spaces than would those without them.[70] This finding has led Hampton to argue that public Wi-Fi should be factored into the design of any modern public space because of its ability to bring citizens together.

Considering the history of the commute, it is not surprising that mobile devices have provided a path to social interaction that avoids previous prohibitions. Transit authorities have used public-service campaigns to teach commuters proper passenger etiquette. These campaigns condition people to be quiet and keep to themselves during their commute. The "quiet car" is an extreme example of the kind of behavior that transit authorities desire. The quiet car is a separate train or subway car with signs informing passengers that they are to remain extra quiet in order to accommodate riders who are trying to sleep, work, or read.[71] Far before the development of designated quiet cars, transit authorities used public-service campaigns to encourage courtesy, politeness, and manners.[72] Often these campaigns emphasized giving up seats to the elderly and allowing passengers to disembark before new passengers came aboard.[73] In the 1950s, the New York Transit Authority hired television stars to record demographically targeted announcements to teach students, homemakers, and sports fans how to behave on the train.[74] The messages targeting homemakers were particularly revealing of the gender politics of the time, as they announced "a message for housewives": "There is plenty of room on your subways when the rush hour is over. Why not do your traveling then?"[75] In these examples, transit authorities define the appropriate way to be a commuter. These definitions reflect assumptions about social hierarchy and behavioral norms that emphasize quiet and privacy.

Perhaps the most relevant public-service announcement concerning mobile media devices comes from the Japanese National Railway Corporation (JNRC) in the 1950s. Attempting to address cultural traditions that had migrated to train cars, such as the removal of outer clothing on long train rides, the JNRC coordinated a commuter etiquette campaign to inform citizens about behavioral norms on its trains.[76] In addition to reminding passengers to please keep their pants on, authorities attempted to correct the ways commuters were using portable transistor radios on the train by asking passengers to use earphones and turn the volume down. Reports explained that passengers "generally turn up the volume instead of using the individual earphone with which most such receivers are equipped."[77] Mobile media devices are blamed for the way they encourage isolation in public settings, yet it is clear that commuters have been encouraged to keep to themselves since the earliest days of mass transit. Given this history and social conditioning, it is no wonder that many of the products and services of the procrastination economy help commuters keep to themselves.

The ability to connect with others on the commute is especially enticing, considering the intensifying demands of the modern workday. According to studies published in *American Economist* and from the Pew Research Center, Americans work more and vacation less than in the past.[78] The increase in workload is not just a phenomenon among adults. Children and teens also face increasing workloads, as competition for prestigious universities results in more homework, tests, and extracurricular activities.[79] In addition to increasing pressures from work and school, concerns over rising rates of health problems such as obesity and heart disease have brought greater urgency to regular exercise for children and adults.[80] For adults with children, a culture of involved parenting pressures parents to devote more time and attention to child rearing than in the past.[81] The cultural theorist Mira Moshe has argued that the spread of neoliberalism and the development of digital technology have created a "media time squeeze" in which our devices help us handle the increasing demands of modern life.[82] All of these demands eat away at leisure time and social interactions, making our devices conduits to connection and pleasure in the stolen moments of the day, especially on the commute.[83]

Mobile devices are key tools in managing these demands, while they also provide an outlet for engaging with culture, conversation, and relationships. The way in which mobile devices facilitate social interaction is not always apparent from external observations of mobile usage. Yet in a 2015 Pew study on mobile devices, the majority of respondents (78%) explained that they used their mobile devices to maintain friendships and keep in touch with social groups.[84] People see their commute as the appropriate setting for using their mobile devices to connect with others.[85] My survey of public-transit commuters provides more detail on the relationship between mobile device use and the spatial and technological constraints of the commute.[86] Specifically, 68% of respondents explained that they use these devices differently on the train than they do at home. Typically, they used their smartphones more during the commute, which makes sense given the variety of screens and other diversions available in most homes. Respondents also described their activity on the commute as dedicated to short tasks, in contrast to the more sustained forms of engagement performed at home.

To this point, the most popular way to communicate among MARTA riders was via text message. Some critics have decried the rise of text messaging as evidence pointing to the devolution of language. They claim that people are losing empathic ability, a skill that (they claim) only exists in face-to-face exchanges.[87] On the other side, technology theorists refer to text messaging and social network conversations as an "ambient intimacy"—a form of communication that provides an ever-present connection to our loved ones and a running conversation throughout the day.[88] For commuters, the preference for text messaging is based on etiquette and practicality. Over 70% of respondents reported noise reduction as a primary form of etiquette when on the train; carrying on conversations via text messages, as opposed to talking on the phone, reduces noise considerably. In-transit noise reduction as a social rule is supported by a larger sample from a survey conducted by the Pew Center for Internet Research.[89] Beyond etiquette, communication on the commute is constrained by the limitations of the telecommunications infrastructure. Text messaging is the most reliable form of communication during train transit because cellular signals are often inconsistent.

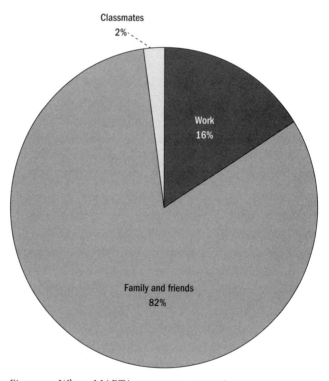

Figure 3.1. Whom MARTA commuters are texting

When people were asked whom they contacted via text while on the train, they overwhelmingly reported talking with family and friends. Over 70% of respondents reported using their devices to connect with others. For young people especially, mobile devices provide a platform for maintaining relationships; more than half of the Pew survey respondents indicated that text messaging, social media interactions, or messaging apps are the primary means of daily connection with their friends.[90] The frequency of socializing on the commute stood in stark contrast to those who used the commute to work. The relatively few respondents who reported

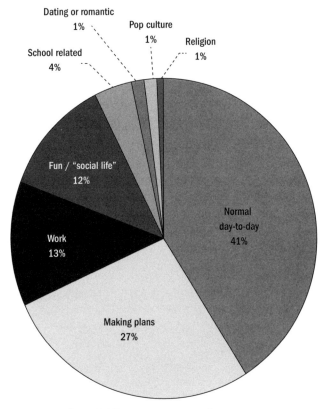

Figure 3.2. What MARTA commuters text about

working (5%) and who presented screenshots of work (3%) on the train shows that most commuters associate their travel with an opportunity for connecting with others and reclaiming leisure time in a busy workday.

In those conversations, respondents reported a variety of topics (see fig. 3.2). Over half of the commute-based conversations were dedicated to checking in with loved ones and discussing everyday life; some conversations even included gossip and romance. From this information, we can see that the commute is a crucial site for relationship maintenance: a time to relay day-to-day business, to

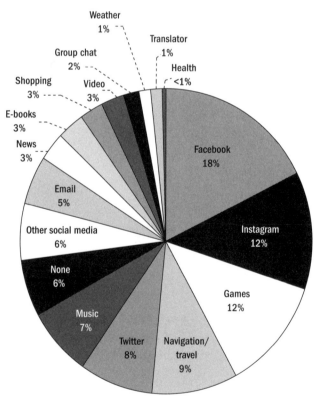

Figure 3.3. App usage by MARTA commuters

make plans for the rest of the day, to connect. Multiple respondents reported sending a "good morning" message to their friends and family in an effort to stay in daily contact. People may not be engaged with their fellow commuters, but they are strengthening their friend and family networks in a world that puts increasing demands on their time.

Among MARTA riders using social media platforms, there was a similar desire to communicate with others. Several respondents reported using social media apps to check in with family and friends

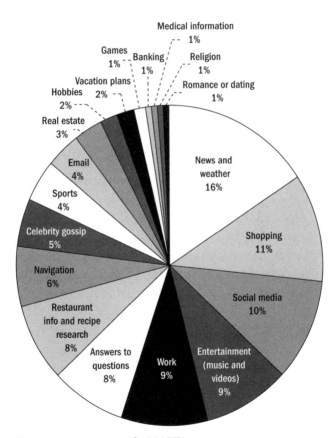

Figure 3.4. Internet usage by MARTA commuters

and to learn about current events. Games were also popular as a way of relaxing, "getting focused," or keeping to oneself while on the train. Often this communication happens alongside other activities, since multitasking is built into mobile devices' DNA. Many respondents reported doing Internet searches while on the train. As you can see from figure 3.4, the types of searches vary widely. The most popular activities all relate to some form of engagement with the outside world, including checking the news, social media, and email and learning about local restaurants. These results confirm advertisers' hopes and fears in equal measure: although respondents reported shopping while on the train, survey results make it clear that MARTA commuters are doing a lot more than just shopping. They are using their mobile devices to engage with the people they love and check in with the public conversations of the day.

Popping the Audio Bubble: MARTA Commuters and Spotify's Playlists

The procrastination economy does not focus on commuters' social lives, but it does provide music services that many commuters use while they socialize. A full 83% of respondents in my MARTA survey reported listening to music during their commute. Reasons for listening included music as a good way to kill time, to make the commute seem shorter, and to block out the noise of others on the train. Respondents also listed the types of music they preferred and the reasons for these preferences, including keeping alert, focusing for the day, boosting energy, and helping with relaxation. It is clear from the results that people select their music intentionally, based on perceived suitability to the commute setting. Examples from chapter 2 show that music in the workplace was often selected for its ability to provide background noise and noise cancellation. On the commute, music selection is related to the time of the day and the energy associated with it. Many respondents reported listening to music in the morning that gave them energy to face the day and listening to soothing music at the end of the day. Entertainment companies that provide content for the procrastination economy understand that commuters want to set a mood for themselves. Paul Allen Anderson has observed streaming media services investing in music options to provide background noise and mood setting.[91] For example, Spotify purchased the playlist-design software company Tunigo in 2013 and began offering programmed playlists to fit the rhythms of people's lives.[92] Throughout the day, Spotify's "browse" function updates its programmed playlists with mood-based categories and contexts including "chill," "workout," "commute," "focus," and "party." In an interview with Rocio Guerrero, Spotify's head of product

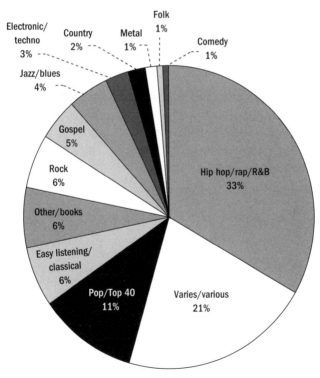

Figure 3.5. Music listened to by MARTA commuters, by genre

programming for the US Hispanic, Latin American, and southern European regions, she stated her belief that people often do not know what they want to listen to, so they use Spotify, which offers mood playlists when people are not looking for something specifically but want to relax and discover new music.[93] Guerrero's depiction of a passive audience is consistent across the "lean-back" subscription services that typify the procrastination economy. Spotify interprets context and mood, matches them with their licensed content, filters them through algorithms, and creates playlists that privilege a certain aesthetic associated with the commute.

Consider the Spotify playlist "Driving Commute," which features rock that is classified as "driving rock to help drive you forward."

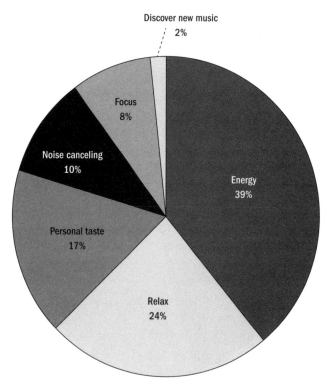

Figure 3.6. Reasons MARTA commuters listen to music

THE COMMUTE | 101

This playlist provides upbeat rock anthems from the most recent few years, omitting ballads and "oldies." Compare this offering to that of the "Morning Commute" playlist, which is chock-full of pop music and is advertised with the promise, "Make it to work the right way. Music on, volume up, smile on face. Day . . . started." Spotify's definition of the "right way" to arrive at work is informed by its access to contemporary pop music and a desire to appeal to its mostly young subscriber base. The "Evening Commute" playlist offers content similar to the morning-commute playlists, focusing primarily on recent pop music, despite claims that the playlist is supposed to relax instead of prepare.[94] Each of these playlists presents an idea of the commute couched in aesthetic assumptions and economic imperatives. In curating these playlists, Spotify imagines what commuters want; in the morning, the company's selections are organized around the idea of workers enthusiastically heading to the office. As Anderson notes, valorization of work is not unlike the reasons many offices in the 1950s pumped music into workplaces; the invention of Muzak (and others) was designed to be useful music to help employees concentrate and produce more efficiently.[95] The evening-commute playlists function similarly, suggesting that listening to a relaxing soundscape will send the commuter home in "style," a fitting reward for a job well done. These playlists reflect the taste of Spotify's subscribers and present their preferred aesthetic as the default desire for music on the commute.

Comparing Spotify's playlists to the listening tastes of MARTA commuters, it is clear that the company is off target for this demographic. Pop music was popular with the survey respondents, rock music to a lesser degree. The most obvious difference, however, is the complete omission of R&B music from Spotify's commuter playlists. This genre was the most popular among MARTA commuters. According to the respondents, R&B is a versatile genre, frequently used for relaxing on the commute but also providing energy and noise cancellation. R&B was particularly popular with African American MARTA commuters. On the basis of Spotify's

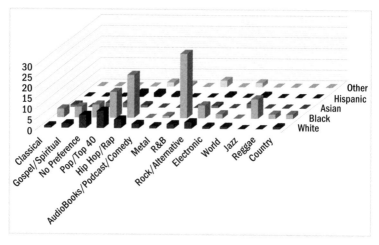

Figure 3.7. Music preferences of MARTA commuters

commuter playlists, it is clear that the company's definition of "relaxing" differs greatly from the survey respondents'.

The disconnection between MARTA riders and Spotify may lie in the streaming-music company's programming practices. Guerrero described Spotify's programming process as similar to traditional disc jockey curation. She explained that Spotify has four divisions that target different global markets: North America, Latin markets / southern Europe / US Latin, Europe, and Asia. For these markets, editors curate playlists on the basis of their musical tastes and their understanding of the target market. They publish the playlists to test their popularity and the popularity of each individual song. Songs that do not perform well are replaced by the editor, who is assisted by an algorithm they call Keanu (a reference to the movie *The Matrix*); the algorithm analyzes users' playlists for songs that are similarly grouped with those on the playlist. Thus, the creation of Spotify playlists begins with editors' music tastes and then becomes refined through Spotify's algorithm, which tabulates users' preferences. Surprisingly, Spotify does not analyze the 500-plus user playlists that are labeled "commute."

Spotify may see its listeners as passive subscribers, but Anderson notes that many listeners prefer to balance their playlists with their own collection of music:

> For many adults, deliberate musical listening is mostly nostalgic listening. Recent experimental work shows how often nostalgic listening reinforces positive and ego-fulfilling thoughts. Thinking and feeling nostalgically alongside musical triggers, the researchers speculate, helps some individuals conceive of their life as positively meaningful in terms of the self's continuity from past to present. Such nostalgia has a specific conceptual and emotional content and can be distinguished from the more generic and non-individualized content of archetypal mood music.[96]

Playlist creation can even be an opportunity for activism and community building. Meagan Perry of Toronto, Canada, created StationaryGroove.com, a site that operates as a community-based music chart where people can indicate what they listen to on their commute and learn what others are enjoying.[97] Similarly, the Human Connectedness Group at MIT embarks on projects to better design mobile applications to foster social connection, including through the sharing of music.[98] Both of these efforts demonstrate a desire to connect with fellow consumers and to create a community-generated playlist that could unite the individual listening habits of commuters. Listening to mobile devices can be as meaningful as community building or as passive as listening to a prefabricated Spotify playlist, but it is always an active space of engagement where purchasing decisions are made, moods are altered, and connections are made in between the hustle and bustle of everyday life.

Conclusion: From Passive Subscriber to Active Emojis

The procrastination economy of the commute offers a variety of subscription services because media companies see commuters as anxious, busy, and in need of entertainment. Those who can pay for the subscription services receive media content that helps them lean back and enjoy the ride and ignore the urge to continue working on the commute. The option to unwind on the commute by listening to some music or watching a show in between destinations is especially enticing given the demands of the modern workday. Not all commuters can afford the subscription prices or access streaming media on their commute. Additionally, media habits on the commute are much more context specific, as the choice of background music or audio is based on context, mood, and taste. Subscription services may be the preferred business model of the commute, but the passive idea of the audience is not reflected in studies of commuters' mobile habits. Commuters are much more likely to be text messaging and playing their preferred songs that personally alter their moods. While media-industry companies already provide streaming media for multitasking, digital divisions are beginning to invest in products and services to incorporate intellectual property in the conversations of the commute.

Some of the strongest offerings from these software companies are apps such as Giphy, Riffsy, Blippy, PopKey, and Kanvas.[99] These apps may sound like the tech world's version of the Seven Dwarves, but the apps are actually innovative products that provide mobile users with GIF databases and multimedia embellishments to enhance text message conversations.[100] Jason Eppink, of the Museum of the Moving Image, has described GIF use as an example of the "cinema of affiliation": people share GIFs with one another to express an emotional reaction or to punctuate a point.[101] The successful sharing of a GIF relies on the ability of the receiver to understand the reference and share the sender's familiarity and interpretation. Eppink describes a successful use of a GIF: "The result is a digital slang, a visual vocabulary unencumbered by authorship, where countless media artifacts are viewed, deployed and elaborated upon as language more than as art product. Even though individuals process the pixels, communities make the GIFs."[102] GIFs are like quotations of popular culture in that they appropriate popular-culture moments from film and television, making them relevant in everyday conversation.[103] These interactions foster social bonds among commuters and other populations alike.

In Barbara Klinger's study of film fans, she observed that quoting, or "karaoke cinema," was useful to community ties in a variety of ways.[104] According to Klinger, "The repeated text becomes a launching pad for experiences of mastery, solace, and observant engagement. In this sense, rereading is work without suffering."[105] Reflecting on the work of Roland Barthes, Klinger argues that as quoting "delivers the reader from commitment to narrative chronology and simple consumption of the story, rereading indulges in a kind of play that remakes the text into a plural text—'the same and new.' This play opens the text to a potentially intense refashioning, which, while perhaps frustrating for the aesthete invested in a concept of textual self-determination, nonetheless represents an active process of appropriation."[106] This process is similar to Henry Jenkins's concept of "textual poaching," in which fans gain power over the meaning of a text through the act of remixing or decontextualizing.[107] The legal scholar Lawrence Lessig takes these claims a step further, arguing that remixing is the way that culture evolves.[108] The GIFs populating the feeds of Tumblr users speak to the political importance of this practice. The moving image scholar Graig Uhlin describes the politics of the GIF as

> a type of cultural appropriation that acts as a counterweight to the restrictions on the use of moving images when treated as commodities. Though GIFs may not establish communities on their own, their sharing forges communal bonds that sustain existing relationships. The GIF walls that populate Tumblr, for instance, are often organized around personal identity (gays and lesbians, graduate

students, individuals who came of age in the 1990s, etc.)—groups that, in other words, already maintain shared experiences and lexicon. GIFs entail a spectatorial engagement with popular culture inflected around these identities.[109]

The integration of popular culture into new contexts inspires creativity that leads to the next generation of storytelling and thought. Using GIFs, emojis, and quotes puts the audience in a crucial position of adding, detracting, or augmenting the value of the brand through everyday interactions.

The unpredictability of audience remixing and the lack of a revenue model for GIFs have made some entertainment companies wary of this use of their intellectual property. The National Football League, Ultimate Fighting Championship, and the NCAA all requested that social media platforms remove GIFs and video clips of their sporting events.[110] The protectionist policies of these sports leagues contradict the ethos that made GIFs popular. The file type has persisted since the 1980s because it is an open-source file, compatible on any platform.[111] Uhlin explains, "GIFs were designed for the purpose of easy transmission, for uninhibited movement. The restriction on the circulation of cultural products through antipiracy efforts and copyright enforcement means that it is more difficult for the original to 'travel' and to some degree, the popularity of the decidedly mobile GIF is a response to the relative immobility of the source material."[112] Companies such as Betaworks (the creators of Giphy) have embraced this ethos and developed databases of popular user-generated GIFs, making them searchable and easy to insert into conversations.[113] Companies such as Disney and Facebook have rewarded Betaworks for this strategy; both companies embrace this use of their intellectual property and have hired Betaworks to provide software support for their own GIF databases.[114] The streaming-video service Hulu and the social media platforms Tumblr and Twitter have made decisions to facilitate the distribution of GIFs.[115]

This trend reflects industry-wide recognition that there are branding and marketing opportunities in the procrastination economy that provide value beyond the revenues of subscription services. Disney's decision to launch its own GIF app came after a marketing campaign with Twitter that resulted in over one billion views of the company's *Star Wars* emojis.[116] For major media brands such as *Star Wars*, there is promotional value in integrating stories, quotes, and characters into the procrastination economy. Marketing campaigns for *Star Wars* and *Fast and Furious* have used navigation apps such as Waze and GoogleMaps to reach commuters.[117] Whether it is C-3PO's voice navigating traffic or a Homer Simpson GIF expressing a desire for pie, marketing campaigns and GIF databases allow people to integrate popular culture into everyday life. These campaigns rarely provide direct revenue to the media companies, but they do inform consumers of new products and reinforce brand loyalty.

Investments in emoji keyboards, GIF databases, and meme generators are on the rise, but their influence on the procrastination economy is dwarfed by efforts to launch subscription streaming platforms that reinforce the image of the passive commuter audience. Over the course of 2015, two mobile phone companies made strategic plans to invest in the procrastination economy. AT&T acquired the satellite television service DirecTV, two companies from industries (wireless providers and satellite TV services) whose financial outlook had peaked or flattened in the wake of new consumer habits.[118] Meanwhile, AT&T characterized the acquisition as a chance to "accelerate innovation and growth" in the growing mobile video market.[119] The justification of innovation is one typically used by companies involved in mergers and acquisitions to reassure nervous regulators. The promise, however, turned out to be an actual consumer strategy, as AT&T rolled out the "All in One" mobile content plan. The plan offered customers a one-stop shop for mobile coverage and television content and included the ability to watch television on AT&T mobile devices for a reduced cost. Not to be outdone, the wireless carrier T-Mobile announced a plan to allow its mobile customers to stream unlimited video regardless of data limits, a practice known as "zero rating."[120] The plan, titled "Binge-On," envisions a mobile space that is dedicated to viewing television in public spaces. AT&T CEO Randall Stephenson makes this ambition clear in a postmerger statement: "With our national retail presence, coast-to-coast TV and mobile coverage, and pervasive broadband footprint, we're positioned like no other to lead the evolution of video and shape the future of the industry. We have the premier set of assets to redefine TV everywhere and deliver an entertainment experience that is truly unique."[121] Both plans characterize the procrastination economy, and the commute specifically, as a space in which people retreat to watch television, rather than a space for reaching out to the rest of the world. While GIFs and emojis reflect the desire to socialize on the commute, these indirect economic benefits are not as alluring to investors and content creators as are direct profits from subscription services.

In addition to the passive articulation of the consumer experience, the focus on mobile television viewing has implications for regulatory policy. The Obama administration announced plans to classify the Internet as a common carrier in 2014. This shift in classification would reverse a decades-old policy that fostered economic development and the privatization of the Internet. A Title II designation signifies the generative functions of the Internet, prioritizing the active use of culture over the passive consumption of culture. Klint Finley, writing for *Wired*, sees the efforts of telecommunications companies as attempts to shape mobile viewing practices that favor a privatized Internet and established content companies.[122] Finley explains, "The idea of zero-rating would seem to stand in stark contrast to the principle of net neutrality, where all services are treated equally, whether they're music streaming services, file sharing applications, or any other type of service—and whether they're operated by well-funded startups or by rag-tag community non-profits."[123] As these types of mobile service plans become widely available, regulatory policy may shift to favor consumption instead of conversation or creative remixing of content. The procrastination economy is big enough for subscription services and GIF databases, but the two services reflect different ideas of the commuter and foster different mobile habits. The economic incentive behind subscription services suggests that the passivity and isolation that critiques attribute to public mobile device usage is being encouraged by media companies despite commuters' interest in using their travel time to socialize.

4

The Waiting Room

Profiting from Boredom

The National Football League's annual championship game, the Super Bowl, is widely regarded as the most important advertising opportunity of the year. Super Bowl commercials are infamously expensive because they reach a large and attractive audience.[1] The 2015 Super Bowl broadcast included a commercial from mobile game company Supercell, featuring Liam Neeson. This brief advertisement became one of the most popular videos on YouTube and was selected as the best ad of the night by *Billboard*.[2] In the commercial, Neeson "kills time" at a coffee shop by playing the game *Clash of Clans* on his mobile phone. In the short time it takes for him to receive his scone, Neeson's virtual village is destroyed, causing him to vow revenge on his gamer foe—delivered in the dramatic style he perfected as the star of the *Taken* film franchise. The spot's success relies on the incongruous drama of Neeson's reaction to the loss of virtual lives and property on his mobile game. The humor succeeds because it derives from a recognizable scenario: namely, that people play mobile games while they wait.

This chapter turns a critical eye to the issues presented in the commercial for *Clash of Clans* by arguing that mobile games document the value of mobile users' downtime. Each time people complete a level or advance in a mobile game, they are reminded that the time they spend waiting has value. People can use their wait time for productive tasks, but the procrastination economy of mobile games reimagines the act of waiting as an opportunity for personal achievement and control. These positive attributes help people navigate the spatial politics of the waiting room. Through an analysis of the relationship between spatial politics, the entertainment industry, and the mobile audience in the waiting room, this chapter shows that "killing time" in the procrastination economy is about making a mark and asserting the value of a person's time. Killing time is an act not exclusive to waiting rooms; the bathroom, for example, is another popular location for using a mobile devices.[3] Additionally, playing mobile games is not exclusive to time spent in waiting rooms. Rather, like television programs, mobile games are designed for a particular context.[4] The chapter describes mobile games in a similar fashion; mobile games are part of the procrastination economy's culture, specifically designed for spaces like the waiting room. Specifically, this chapter argues that the mobile games industry is a part of the procrastination economy in that it categorizes the waiting room audience as a group looking to extract value from their downtime.

Critics of mobile phone culture and the ubiquitous Internet see mobile device use in waiting rooms as a crutch. The media ecologist Lance Strate revisits the work of Neil Postman when attributing individualism and arrested development to the constant connectedness of mobile devices.[5] Excessive mobile device use is linked with addiction and an inability "to be present" and maintain a work-life balance.[6] This chapter counters these critiques as they apply to the politics of the procrastination economy and the power dynamics of waiting. Following Anna McCarthy's work on site-specific analysis, I identify the media businesses that both target the waiting room audience and apply their practices to the procrastination economy of the mobile phone.[7] These business strategies determine content, including video games, which in turn makes up the culture of the waiting room. Following Ian Bogost's work on the procedural rhetoric of video games, I argue that mobile games, or casual games, amplify the politics of waiting and offer mobile users an opportunity to assert themselves and their value.[8] Documentation of the gamer community for the mobile game *The*

Simpsons: Tapped Out provides evidence that this content helps people "kill time" in creative ways. Examining the various elements of the procrastination economy of the waiting room reveals that mobile devices are far from simple, corrupting diversions and are central tools for documenting the value of people's time.

CNN Airport and the Business of Waiting

Waiting rooms often have televisions and magazines to help entertain, relax, or inform people as they struggle with boredom and frustration. Mobile devices have changed the dynamic of the waiting room from an ephemeral experience into a way for people to document the value of their time through virtual achievements on their mobile devices. The change is partly explained by the technological differences between mobile devices and waiting room televisions. Another explanation is the economic difference between the business models of waiting room media. The waiting room is an arena of the procrastination economy that, like the commute, has historically been targeted by advertisers. Mobile games, on the other hand, derive revenue through the freemium business model that thrives on micropayments. Advertising on waiting room televisions is dedicated to attracting desirable demographics through entertainment and information that they would enjoy and associate with the sponsoring products.

The dominance of advertising in waiting rooms has historically contextualized the waiting room experience, offering entertainment or information as a pacifier for the boredom, stress, and frustration of waiting. Anna McCarthy's analysis of "ambient television" identifies specialized companies that program for waiting rooms and attempt to monetize and discipline the behavior of those who are waiting. McCarthy explains that the programs on waiting room screens inherently present an ideological concept of identity and citizenship. Television has long been associated with assisting in the demarcation of public and private spaces and with encouraging passivity.[9] Turner Private Networks is one of the companies that creates content for waiting rooms. McCarthy identifies language in Turner Private Networks' industrial literature that explains how the company uses entertainment and news in airport waiting rooms as a "time-warping companion within the waiting area, an environmental distraction that somehow changes the overall affective experience of being there."[10] McCarthy goes on to describe how television screens in doctors' offices and government buildings are used for an additional purpose. Here, she says, the screen is less about distraction and is more focused on teaching those who are waiting about the institution and its services.[11] These latter two examples reframe waiting as supposedly empowering opportunities that will make waiting productive to society and enrich people's lives. Overall, McCarthy's message is that television screens in waiting rooms attempt to distract and discipline their audiences.

This chapter updates McCarthy's work by returning to one of the purveyors of the waiting room procrastination economy, Turner Private Networks, and analyzing its business practices in the age of mobile media. Following in the tradition of media industries scholars such as John Caldwell, Vicki Mayer, and Jennifer Holt, my analysis of CNN Airport shows how day-to-day operations and revenue expectations define the waiting room experience as a safe place to be informed.[12] This approach combines interviews, on-site observations, textual analysis, and trade discourse analysis to describe how the company defines success in its field. Revisiting CNN Airport 15 years after McCarthy, it is apparent that the network has changed its programming strategies to adapt to numerous and occasionally unanticipated pressures such as ever-evolving digital technologies, the "war on terror," and shifts in the Turner corporate structure. McCarthy's evaluation of Turner Private Networks was primarily based on promotional materials that she interpreted according to a discourse analysis framework. This interpretation formed her understanding of the waiting room's ideological structure. In researching this book, I met with members of Turner Private Networks in Atlanta and visited their work environment. My experiences there confirmed many of McCarthy's assertions and provided me with unique insight on how the network has evolved.

CNN Airport is a division of Turner Outdoor Networks that provides television programming to entertain and relax travelers in waiting rooms. Launching in 1991 in three airports, CNN Airport is now available in 47 airport waiting rooms around the world. The network estimates its audience at 20 million viewers but makes note that it is a different type of audience because they have no control over what they are watching. Programmers at the network are mindful of this fact but rely on audience surveys to see what programming people enjoy while they wait. These surveys show that people find the television comforting and that they look for different kinds of programming at different times of day. For example, CNN Airport programs the morning with news to help people stay informed as they begin a day of travel. In the afternoon and evening, the network programs variety programming such as clips from *Conan* and segments from *Real Sports with Bryant Gumbel.* According to Turner's internal audience research, the content selected by CNN Airport's programming team is accomplishing the desired goals.[13] Audience surveys provide evidence of the effectiveness of the network and encourage advertisers such as Starbucks, Absolut, Banana Republic, Kenneth Cole, and Verizon that look to the waiting room audience as a constituency with immediate contextual needs and affluence.[14] Often these companies will partner with CNN Airport to produce branded content that unites the company's products and Turner content around shared themes.

Turner Private Networks also distributes and produces content for Accent Health, a network shown in 13,000 medical waiting rooms that reaches 14 million viewers across the country. Additionally, the Gas Station TV network is available in 2,000 gas stations, reaching 37 million drivers per month. Each of these "waiting room" contexts fits neatly within the corporate logic of combatting boredom with the Turner content library. To monetize this service, CNN Airport collaborates with advertisers and matches each one with relevant content. Television scholars describe the marriage of audience and advertisement as one of the most fundamental realities of American television. Raymond Williams provided the term "flow" as the way to describe the weaving together of commercial solutions and narrative tension.[15] In the context of the waiting room, commercial messages promise relief from the worries of travel through the comforts of consumer goods.

Despite these earnings, CNN Airport's real value to Turner lies not in advertising revenue but in the promotion of other Turner properties. Like the procrastination economy of the workplace, the programming in the waiting room is connected to corporate branding efforts. Making consumers aware of content is crucially important in the era of media fragmentation and the explosion of content choices across media platforms. CNN Airport may not have the ratings success to compete with other television networks, but its ability to attract a desirable demographic and alert those people to shows across the Turner universe is essential to Turner's overall success: TBS, TNT, and Cartoon Network ranking in the top-ten most watched cable networks is one potential result of this strategy.[16] As has been discussed throughout the book, the procrastination economy is a key site where brand management occurs and where customers are primed to anticipate upcoming content. CNN Airport has spent nearly 25 years perfecting these practices, which are, in turn, informing mobile media engagement in the procrastination economy.

The concept of using CNN Airport for cross-promotion is not new, but it does take on new significance as CNN has struggled in recent years to maintain its value in a competitive environment. In the winter of 2012, CNN hired former NBC Universal CEO Jeff Zucker to oversee the network and to improve its declining ratings. CNN was facing an "identity crisis" as cable news was increasingly becoming the domain of partisan counterparts Fox News and MSNBC.[17] Zucker's solution was to invest in original content such as documentary series and reality shows while retaining the journalistic reputation of the network.[18] Zucker was the architect of NBC's *Today* show, which expertly packaged news and feature programming into short segments that people could enjoy while getting ready to go to work in the morning. Additionally, Zucker ran NBC, making him familiar with the ways one show relates to another and how a network develops a brand across platforms and channels. According to the *Hollywood Reporter* media critic Tim Goodman, Zucker's arrival at CNN was a major organizational shake-up that shifted the day-to-day operations away from a group of decision makers to a central vision coming from the new CEO.[19] That vision is clear in the green-lighting of projects and the cancellation of existing programming. For example, Zucker canceled the interview and debate shows that formed CNN's early identity.[20] Instead, he promoted original unscripted shows hosted by popular reality television stars such as Mike Rowe and Anthony Bourdain and documentaries produced by movie stars such as Tom Hanks.[21] CNN's news coverage often supports the unscripted content by featuring stories on similar topics.[22] The cross-promotion strategy demonstrates a dedication to exploring an issue from many angles and introduces audiences to programming on a variety of CNN platforms.

Alison Hashimoto, vice president of programming for Turner Private Networks, noted in an interview that CNN Airport has never received instructions about programming from the corporate leadership. However, Zucker's decision to invest in original content, such as documentaries and unscripted shows, conveniently builds the Turner library that CNN Airport uses to fill its programming schedule. John T. Caldwell provides the term "critical production practice" to describe the "proclivity by the industry for deconstruction and reflexivity assigned to their own programming or artistic decisions."[23] Caldwell contends that if we look at the decisions that media professionals make in the same way that we have traditionally looked at the decisions audiences have made in their meaning making, we can identify the logic and culture of a company or the entertainment industry.[24] CNN Airport's programming lineup is a good example of how media professionals make sense of their jobs and the meaning of their content. Hashimoto and her team must make decisions about what is appropriate for the waiting room context within the fixed parameters of the Turner content library. Much like the commercial content that audiences adapt to their own social and ideological needs, the CNN Airport team looks at the growing Turner content library as potential fodder for the waiting room audience and then makes decisions about the library's meaning and utility. Zucker may not have told the CNN Airport programmers what to put on the air, but they accept and use the Zucker-prescribed content as appropriately entertaining and informative for the waiting room audience. CNN Airport is promoting Turner content, but it is also contextualizing this content within the specific taste culture and psychology of its waiting room audience. CNN Airport is identifying certain Turner content as relaxing and informative for the beleaguered traveler. Turner's brand, as CNN Airport is curating it, is comfortable, easy to digest, and mass audience oriented, something that is appealing both in waiting rooms *and* when people are unwinding at home in front of their televisions.

In keeping with the network's goal of providing a relaxing environment for travelers, CNN Airport has had to become increasingly cross-promotional in the age of global terrorism. After 9/11, CNN Airport justifiably worried about displaying scenes of violence and other traumatic footage in airport waiting rooms. Hashimoto explained, "Graphic video is something we do not air on Airport Network. The airport is a charged environment, and people can't leave and walk away from their gate; we are sensitive to those realities."[25] Although the network often uses CNN's broadcast feed, it switches to pretaped segments or weather fore-casts to avoid live coverage of international incidents, especially events relating to airplane crashes or violence.

The network's approach to sensitive content became particularly difficult to manage in the spring of 2014, when CNN dedicated a majority of its programming time to the missing Malaysia Airlines jet.[26] CNN's coverage, despite the lack of new details about the disappearance, was a ratings success for the cable network but a tricky obstacle for CNN Airport.[27] The programming team at CNN Airport organizes the broadcast day into 15-minute segments. Since the team could not use CNN's content (most of which concerned the Malaysia Airlines jet's disappearance), they faced a serious dearth of programming. To fill the void, they used documentaries, lifestyle programming, and short features from across all the Turner networks. Hashimoto explained the CNN Airport programming flow as similar to the day parts assigned to traditional television. In the morning, it runs informative content for people with early flights who have not had an opportunity to see what is happening in the world. In the evening, the programming is more relaxed and light for people who are traveling home. Above all, the programming has to be family friendly, since there are frequently children in the audience at the gate. Hashimoto cited segments from *Real Sports with Bryant Gumbel* (HBO), Turner Classic Movie filmmaker or actor profiles, *Conan* (TBS) comedy segments, Anthony Bourdain's travelogue show *Parts Unknown* (CNN), and TruTV's magician show *The Carbonaro Effect* as content that was informative, family friendly, and suitable for the transitional environment of the airport waiting room. Like content discussed in chapter 2, these shows are "snackable" diversions meant to be pleasing but unsubstantial breaks in the middle of a busy day. Additionally, the programming strategy performs a promotional function for the media conglomerate, as all of the segments introduce the captive waiting room audience to the variety of shows available across the Turner networks.

THE WAITING ROOM | 119

Media companies such as CNN Airport have long targeted the waiting room audience and attempted to promote a sense of waiting that is predicated on the tastes and desires of the affluent travelers whom its advertisers are courting. In the case of Turner Private Networks, this content has mass appeal and leans toward masculine confidence and exploration of the world. Anthony Bourdain's *Parts Unknown*, for example, has been described as "macho but not overbearing" and "barbed humanism";[28] Mike Rowe's *Somebody's Gotta Do It* champions engineering and hard work; and Playtone's documentary about the 1960s valorizes the "greatest generation." These shows reflect a characterization of the waiting room audience that is decidedly older, masculine, and work oriented. This audience characterization makes sense for the network's advertisers and the constraints of the network, but it also limits the idea of what people want to watch while they are waiting.

The variety of games and experiences available on mobile devices expands the options for the person in the waiting room; it also provides interactivity, socialization, and a sense of control that improves on the narrow CNN Airport definition of "relaxing" in the waiting room. Mobile devices are a distinct threat to such networks as CNN Airport as they compete for the attention of people in the waiting room. Hashimoto says that television networks that target the home viewer face similar competition from these screens. In addition, the waiting rooms provide a variety of distractions. Providing content and graphics that are "eye popping" and attention getting, the programmers hope to get viewers engaged for a few segments and commercial breaks. Hashimoto's explanation makes sense given the specifics of her job and the restrictions of programming for a wide audience, constraints that do not hinder mobile screens. There are plenty of apps and services on mobile devices that use the advertising business model, but many mobile games use the freemium business model, which allows them to offer a different kind of value to the waiting room audience.

Casual Games in Stressful Places

"Casual games" is the name of the category for mobile games that are intuitive enough to be enjoyed in the first few moments of play.[29] These games are extremely popular on mobile devices, as their gentle learning curve makes them friendly to the in-between moments when a person is seeking entertainment in a waiting room. They are distinct from console games, which are associated with more intense and lengthy gaming sessions. Casual games are also much less expensive than console games and usually feature a freemium, or free-to-play, revenue model that allows people to play the game for free but entices players to spend money as they advance through the game. The premium enticements make casual games the highest grossing apps on mobile devices.[30] Casual games, particularly the subgenre of strategy games, challenge the player to manage resources and complete a series of tasks or puzzles. A player takes his or her turn playing the game in a free moment and then waits for the other player or for the game to allow him or her to take the next turn. Thus, the games themselves are often about waiting and the accomplishments gamers can accumulate in their downtime. Players who choose to spend extra money or time on the game can speed up the waiting process. Elizabeth Evans describes this process as the "impatience economy" and argues that the structure of the game allows people with money to bypass the structured waiting periods.[31] These games reflect the real-life politics of the waiting room, since players with the capital to pay for the shortcuts within the game do not have to wait their turn. Unlike traditional waiting rooms, these games offer an ability to document the value of wait time. Through achievements in the game and the fostering of community, casual games turn wait times into a moment of accomplishment and competition. A mobile device changes the act of waiting from "killing time" to earning recognition and documenting the cumulative value of one's time.

Casual games change the political dynamics of the waiting room, providing mobile device users with an opportunity to derive value from inconvenience. According to Barry Schwartz, the act of waiting is a crisis moment in modernity that alerts people to their position within the social hierarchy.[32] Anna McCarthy observes that the inclusion of diversions in the waiting room, such as television sets, is designed to distract and ease this sudden social discomfort.[33] Television recasts waiting as an opportunity for efficiency and self-improvement, as in learning about health from CNN's Dr. Sanjay Gupta. Turner Private Networks views this kind of programming as empowering people with information to live their lives in a healthier way.[34] McCarthy has shown that these efforts to distract backfire, often alerting people to how long they have been waiting.[35] Thus, the media content designed to disguise the social order and reassure people actually causes people to concentrate on their exclusion and alienation. Casual games function similarly: they heighten the audience's awareness of waiting through the gameplay mechanics and the revenue model. At the same time, casual games help people reclaim control of waiting by providing a way to document the value of their time.

McCarthy's methodology for analyzing the waiting room audience focused on site-specific ethnographic analysis. Though I have applied this method throughout the book, in this chapter I focus specifically on the video game culture on mobile devices played in waiting rooms. To this end, the chapter considers the gameplay of casual games and the community it attracts. The video game scholar Ian Bogost has proposed the idea of investigating the "procedural rhetoric" that video games teach through the structure of their gameplay. Bogost explains, "video games are not just stages that facilitate cultural, social, or political practices; they are also media where cultural values themselves can be represented—for critique, satire, education or commentary."[36] The ideology that a game espouses is apparent through the game's characters, situations, and dialog but is most evident in the rules that "construct the meaning of the game."[37] When mobile users play casual games in waiting rooms, they experiment with the rules of the game. From this experimentation, or play, they interpret the meaning of the game.

Casual games can be played over many years and store the efforts of the players on mobile devices. Each time players log into their game, they can observe the value of their waiting time as they see their progress through the game. In addition, the more avid gamers can build community around their gameplay and their shared pride of the value of their accomplishments during their downtime. The ability to document progress through the game enhances the political implications of the game, as it is a constant reminder of a person's achievements when waiting. Prior to mobile devices, handheld games such as the rolling-ball puzzles that first became popular in England in the 1840s offered similar abilities to gamify waiting. Mattel and Tiger Electronics created and sold electronic versions of these handheld amusements in the 1970s. As discussed in the chapter 1, Nintendo enhanced the variety of these electronic handhelds with the launch of the Game Boy in 1989. Modern mobile games, and indeed casual games, share similarities with these early handhelds, but the proliferation of mobile phones has brought the act of playing casual games into the mainstream. The first mobile phone games were similar to early computer games such as *Tetris* and *Snake*. The arrival of smartphones allowed for greater sophistication and interconnectedness, making casual games the fastest growing segment of the video game business.[38]

There are three major subgenres of casual games: puzzle, strategy, and side-scrolling/endless-running games. Puzzle games are favored by an older female demographic; strategy games are favored by males; and side-scrolling games are favored by younger players.[39] Puzzle games are electronic adaptions of board games and brainteasers; they are the digital amplification of the earlier mobile culture of the crossword puzzle. Strategy games are simplified versions of larger massive multiple player online games, in which the objective is to build up settlements and complete tasks for short narratives. Often in strategy games, the player is in competition with others in the online community. Players are encouraged to use their social media networks to reach out to potential challengers. Side-scrolling games are similar to early video game console games of the '80s and '90s, such as *Pitfall* (Atari) and *Super Mario Bros.* (Nintendo). The objective in these games is to navigate the perils of an environment while continuously moving forward and accumulating points.

Two principles unite these games, making them unlike previous waiting room pastimes. They each feature a freemium revenue model and a social networking option, making them ideal for quick bursts of play during in-between moments and for social

Table 4.1. Categories of Casual Games, with a List of the Most Popular Mobile Games

Genre	Examples	Producer
Puzzle	*Candy Crush Saga*	King (owned by Activision/Blizzard)
	Puzzle & Dragons	Gung-Ho
	Angry Birds	Rovio
	Words with Friends	Zynga
	Solitaire	MobilityWare
	Piano Tiles	Hu Wen Zeng
	Two Dots	Betaworks One
	2048	Ketchapp
	Trivia Crack	Etermax
Strategy	*Clash of Clans*	Supercell
	Game of War	Machine Zone
	The Simpsons: Tapped Out	Electronic Arts
	Farmville	Zynga
	Boom Beach	Epic War
	Mobile Strike	
Side-Scrolling	*Flappy Bird*	Gears Studios
	Hill Climb Racing	Fingersoft
	Subway Surfers	Kiloo
	Temple Run	

Source: Taylor Soper, "Here Are the 25 Most-Used Mobile Apps, Games on iOS and Android," *Geek Wire*, November 4, 2014, www.geekwire.com.

sharing of game progress. To illustrate, the game *Trivia Crack* pits two players against each other as they take turns answering questions in the style of the board game Trivial Pursuit. Once a player has completed a turn, he or she must wait for the opponent(s) to complete theirs. A player can start another game with a different opponent to continue playing the game, but the number of simultaneous games is capped unless a person chooses to pay to keep playing. Similarly, turns on strategy games are governed by waiting periods connected to the completion of tasks. Players must strategically assign characters to jobs using the resources they have accumulated. Players cannot do anything until a character has completed the task or the resources are replenished, unless they pay a premium to remove the waiting period. As Ian Bogost explains, these games are designed for downtime or waiting because they rely on "disruptions as wellsprings for game experiences. This means that good asynchronous multiplayer games design these fissures as centerpieces, rather than detours."[40]

The media industries scholar Elizabeth Evans notes that these disruptions are designed to support the economic model of the game. According to Evans, these games monetize gameplay in two ways: through reinforcing a media brand and "by exploiting player impatience."[41] On average, mobile players spend five dollars a month on the ability to advance in the game.[42] Some players, referred to as "whales" in the casual game development world, pay much more to avoid these delays. In general, players accept the delays, as they only engage the games for short bursts of downtime throughout the day. Using Bogost's concept of "procedural rhetoric," it is clear that casual games offer the player "claims about the world, which players can understand, evaluate, and deliberate."[43] These games designed for the waiting room are also a metaphor about the act of waiting. Players can choose, based on their economic situation, whether these games should be short digressions or experiences that are more substantial. Players are faced with the question of whether to enhance their waiting experience with premium content and functionality.

These questions are particularly intriguing in the subgenre of strategy games, which challenge the player to manage resources while personalizing his or her individual game space. Evans explains, "Rather than agency over narrative events, these games prioritize the personalization of a virtual story space. The process of acquiring assets to enable this personalization is at the core of these games' economic strategies."[44] Following Evans, these games require the player to decide how they want to document their achievements in the waiting room. They can "grind" away at a task, slowly progressing through the game until they meet a goal that reflects the cumulative value of their downtime, or they can pay for a shortcut. These options require gamers to think about the politics of waiting and offer an opportunity to document their decision. Members of the gamer community for *The Simpsons: Tapped Out* game take pride in the achievements they have accumulated and award badges to those who avoid paying the premium prices. In this way, they assert their agency in the act of waiting and make delayed gratification their choice.

The politics of waiting are not limited to the physical space of the waiting room but extend to the larger media industries' economic strategies. As Evans points out, the premium payments are just one monetization strategy in casual games. The other strategy is promotional, as casual games are transmedia touch points designed to build brand loyalty. Preselling, reselling, and nurturing audience interest in media franchises is an ongoing process, one that occurs on the various platforms of media conglomerates. Entertainment companies need media franchises to maintain value because these provide recognizable and preowned intellectual property for television networks, consumer products, film series, and licensing agreements. The procrastination economy of the waiting room is a key site for a transmedia touch point, and entertainment companies see casual games as an opportunity to bring their brands into people's everyday routines.

Casual games are particularly intriguing to entertainment companies because of their broad appeal. Activision-Blizzard, the most profitable video game company to date, purchased King, the producer of the mobile game Candy Crush, for $5.9 billion. This amount is more than Disney paid for Lucasfilm ($4 billion). The price tag reflects the market potential: King reaches half a billion active users per month.[45] Unlike the audience for console games, the casual games audience is diverse, with larger numbers of female and older players.[46] These games have mass appeal because they are easy to learn and fit a need for entertainment throughout the day. Indeed, game designers often remark that mobile games killed soap operas.[47] The similarities between these two entertainment genres are striking. Both are daytime genres for a predominantly female audience. Both of their forms reflect the producers' belief that they attract a distracted or intermittent audience, creating an object that is "glanced" while doing other things like waiting for one's turn in a waiting room.[48] Critics have debated the true attentiveness of the daytime audience, but the form of the games reflects this assumed partial attention.[49] Soap operas feature repetitive exposition, attention-focusing audio queues, and multiple story lines, all of which provide opportunities for jumping in or out of the narrative. The gameplay of casual games is once again similar: the actions the player is asked to do are repetitive (sometimes referred to as "grinding"), the sessions are short, and the narratives are thin. The lack of complexity and the clear commercial aims of this everyday culture stigmatize both genres.

Despite the stigma, casual games have become the subject of blockbuster films. The broad appeal of these mobile games makes them presold intellectual property. Additionally, their position in the procrastination economy means that people integrate these characters and stories into their daily lives.[50] Unsurprisingly, video game companies are bullish on their emerging position in the media industries. Former game producers and movie studio executives see video games as a model for reverse engineering the entertainment industry by building audiences around games and then creating film franchises, instead of the more traditional cinema "mothership" and video game "satellite" arrangement.[51] The 2016 film adaptation of *Angry Birds* is one example of this new upside-down relationship. Producers' confidence arises from their belief that mobile games establish a "much more connected relationship with fans and players" because of the daily interactions.[52] Historically, video game movies have struggled at the box office, but typically they have been based on console titles popular among "hardcore" gamers.[53] The logic for adapting video games (and board games, for that matter) into movies is based on the belief that people establish a relationship with the characters and story world over time and repetition. As a daily activity, casual games do both.

The "Tappers" of *The Simpsons: Tapped Out*

Casual games are designed to induce and monetize impatience, and yet they offer people an opportunity to take control of their wait times. Casual gamers take pride in the creative ways they use their downtime. This pride can translate into social interactions and admiration within the gamer community. Not all casual games inspire online social communities, but those that do provide evidence of mobile device use while waiting. Henry Jenkins has argued that online forums "allow us to observe a self-defined and ongoing interpretive community as it conducts its normal practices of forming, evaluating, and debating interpretations."[54] To understand how mobile game players think about branding, spatial politics, and the social possibilities of the procrastination economy, consider the Electronic Arts' online forum for *The Simpsons: Tapped Out*. Members of the community, known as Tappers, are united by their *Simpsons* fandom and their dedication to building impressively detailed virtual cities. Interactions between Tappers reveal the pride and sense of control they derive from playing a mobile game.

As an example of the empowering possibilities of the procrastination economy, *Tapped Out* is an intriguing case because its gameplay and stories are shaped by the *Simpsons* brand of satire and self-awareness. *Tapped Out* promotes the brand by maintaining the self-reflexive satirical style of the television show. The television scholar Jonathan Gray describes this self-reflexive commercialism as a complex exchange with the audience's own awareness of the machinations of capitalism.[55] *The Simpsons* has a long history of being an irreverent show that appealed to its audience through satirical critique of contemporary culture and crass commercialism. It uses intertextual references and satire to identify the ways in which the culture industries, political institutions, and ideological institutions work to maintain the status quo. Gray explains, "the show deftly exploits televisual form so as to mock, ridicule, and take parodic swipes at advertising, but in doing so, it is aware of the complexity of advertising's infusion into contemporary culture, and calls on audiences to acknowledge their own complicity."[56] Gray claims that there is great power in a show such as *The Simpsons* that offers "critical intertextuality," or references to politics, media, and culture within the show that help the audience use the characters and stories to understand the incongruities of daily life.[57] Building on the work of Mikhail Bakhtin, Gray argues that parody and intertextuality allow the audience to "contextualize and re-contextualize other media offerings, and thus to teach and engender a media literacy of sorts."[58] *Tapped Out* maintains the sensibility of the *Simpsons* brand by bringing this same critical intertextuality to mobile devices. The parodic powers of *The Simpsons* are thus available to players in a variety of locations. The audience is invited to create associations between the game's humor and critiques of modern life within the waiting rooms of the institutions being critiqued. *Tapped Out* includes the same kind of satirical humor that made the television show so successful. In the use of characters, situations, dialog, and quests, the game successfully maintains the brand of *The Simpsons* and has been rewarded with a loyal following.

Tapped Out has consistently been a popular mobile game since its release in 2012. The game is among the top-ten highest grossing apps in the iTunes app store. It is also one of the highest grossing mobile games in the Electronic Arts catalog, averaging more than 16 million monthly players and earning over $130 million in its first three years.[59] To contrast, *The Simpsons* television show averages 11 million monthly viewers.[60] The discrepancy between these two data points highlights the fact that more people are experiencing *The Simpsons* via the mobile game than through television, the franchise's medium of origin. Nick Earl, senior vice president of Electronic Arts Global Social and Mobile Studio, announced in the press release for the game that *The Simpsons* was an "ideal brand" for mobile devices.[61] Earl's meaning of "ideal" is made clear through accompanying statements about the game—namely, that it had a built-in fan base that would incorporate the game into their "everyday" routines.[62] Electronic Arts enticed *Simpsons* fans by hiring the show's writers and producers to help design the game. This step helped to preserve the brand's "irreverent humor" and ensured the continuity of fans' "favorite characters."[63] The press release's language is not simply a promotional announcement; it is also a promise to fans that the game will be worth their attention and respect their values. The convergence culture scholars Henry Jenkins and Joshua Green have argued that in a digital environment, entertainment companies must see their audiences as partners.[64] This partnership is particularly vital for media franchises with large and vociferous fan constituencies that have strong opinions about the essential qualities of the series. Due to online platforms and collective action, fans can make their opinions heard, potentially to the brand's detriment if the community deems a product lackluster.[65]

Designing a mobile game based on a media franchise carries less risk of fan revolt than designing a console game based on one. Once a console game is released, it is difficult to improve the game to meet the demands of fans. Gray notes that television producers have long struggled to translate their properties into video games largely due to short production cycles, small budgets, and a production culture that writes off these efforts as a quick way to cash in on a gullible fan base.[66] Mobile games circumvent many of these issues, since they are frequently updated and therefore more nimble at responding to audience behavior and feedback. Evans has referred to these games as "never ending," as the developers are constantly creating new levels and tasks for the gamers.[67] Unlike games with a clearly defined narrative, casual games such as *Tapped Out* are a part of a promotional strategy that situates gaming as an ongoing brand relationship designed to promote the airing of new episodes and the launch of new endeavors. A good game experience could entice the audience to stay loyal to the brand.

The game makes good on the promise of "critical intertextuality" by opening with a joke about the "life-ruining" potential of mobile games. In the introductory mission, the player learns that Springfield, the hometown of *The Simpsons*, has been accidentally destroyed by the show's main character, Homer, because he was too distracted playing a casual game to attend to his job as a nuclear safety technician. The player takes on the role of a deity tasked with rebuilding the town. The game routinely remarks on its own commercialism, the procrastination economy of casual games, and the strategic cross-promotion pushed on it by its corporate owners. For example, in the second task of the game, "Springfield Cleaners Part 1," Homer remarks, "Cleaning, really!? I can't believe that's what passes for fun in games these days." This joke reveals the writers' skepticism of the form of casual games, particularly the practice of "grinding" that typifies much of the gameplay. The critique of casual games' form and mobile device habits is consistent throughout the game. During the 2016 election cycle, a new challenge was added to the game, called "Burns' Casino Event." The narrative setup for the challenge featured the miserly billionaire Mr. Burns creating a casino for the town. Marge Simpson dismisses skepticism about Mr. Burns's intentions by explaining, "Wealthy businessmen never have a hidden agenda. Otherwise I wouldn't be voting for Donald Trump." Homer concurs: "Agreed, Marge. Let's all be distracted by fun games while rich people control our future." This dialog reminds the audience that their gameplay is being monetized in the procrastination economy; it also makes a broader satirical point about casual games in relation to real political changes. The satire of the mobile game forces players to interpret their own gameplay in relation to the current political climate.

Tapped Out's critical intertextuality does not stop at a critique of the casual games form but extends to the freemium payment model as well. In the task "The Box, the Box!," Homer and Lisa Simpson introduce the player to the freemium model by explaining that a player can purchase donuts, the currency of the game, by completing tasks or through actual monetary transactions. These donuts can be exchanged for such things as the "mystery box," which could contain useful items. The player is asked to use six donuts to purchase the mystery box and is rewarded with 30 donuts. Homer exclaims, "Woo-hoo! Spend six donuts to get 30? What a deal!" Lisa responds, "It might just be beginner's luck," to which Homer says "The only way to find out is to buy 100 more of those boxes!" Homer's outrageous suggestion is meant to highlight the inequities of the freemium model. Even the name of the game itself, *Tapped Out*, references the game's efforts to entice players to use all their money on the construction of a virtual town. The brand of *The Simpsons*, the dialog, and the gamer community reinforce an ethos of critical consumerism. Players are aware of mobile gaming's role in their everyday lives and the efforts to make a profit off the game players. They align their community values against the commercial system that is attempting to manipulate them, and they look down on players who are not smart enough to avoid vanity and mindless consumption.

Reflecting on the gaming community for mobile strategy games, Evans notes that there is a general respect for players who avoid shortcuts and earn rewards through perseverance and skill.[68] The community's dedication to avoiding premium payments is evident in a number of ways. The ability to manage the imposed waiting times of *Tapped Out* while also achieving goals and acquiring desired buildings and characters is a point of pride for the gamers, who would otherwise have very few strategies for avoiding life's waiting periods. The conversation on the "Oddest Place / Time to Play TSTO" thread of the Electronic Arts *Tapped Out* forum reveals the ways Tappers have mastered waiting. Players report playing in the bathroom, in traffic, at work, in the shower (putting their tablet in a plastic bag), while receiving chemotherapy treatments, in church, while cooking, in class, in a coffee shop, in meetings, while breastfeeding, and in a hospital waiting room while waiting for the birth of a granddaughter.[69] Members of the forum are experts at documenting their in-between moments by integrating gameplay throughout their downtime.

Not only do Tappers take pride in how and when they wait, but they derive value from their control of the games characters. Tappers choose how their characters spend their time, which tasks the characters are assigned, and how the characters complete selected goals. The games offer control over virtual space that is unavailable in most waiting rooms. But casual games are not strictly for escapism and a false sense of control: the freemium model reinforces the player's personal economic realities. Strategy games are not the only games that engage with the politics of their surroundings. The games scholar Shira Chess argues that the *Dash* franchise of casual games features workplaces that reflect the work-leisure balance that mobile game players manage in their real lives.[70] These games offer control over space. The player decides what goes where, what gets prioritized, and how resources are allocated, all while sitting in a location such as a waiting room, when the player is most keenly questioning the allocation of resources in an environment that is outside his or her control.

Indeed, discussions about the placement and arrangement of Springfield's town landmarks feature prominently on the Tappers' discussion forum. The subforum "Springfield Showcase" features over 23,000 messages on over 1,300 topics, with new contributions appearing each day.[71] In this subforum, Tappers engage in debate and discussion over the best way to organize Springfield. It is one of only two subforums out of six not dedicated to game strategy or technical issues. Explanations for placement decisions range from personal taste to the show's canon, revealing the collective engagement and meaning making the fans produce as they navigate spatial politics both inside the game and outside. Henry Jenkins cites fan discussions as important meaning-making practices that occur online and influence communities' understanding of a media property.[72] Some members of the forum take great pride in their ability to re-create the exact topography of Springfield by following a fan-made "Guide to Springfield" map that lays out the location of each building on the basis of analysis of episodes and ancillary materials.[73] The forum participant Bravewall meticulously planned a city based on this map.[74] Fellow Tapper Emmcee1 points out that the source is imperfect because the writers of *The Simpsons* manipulate the geography to suit their storytelling, "so the layout consistently changes."[75] Issues of canon are typically important to fans, but they do not stifle creativity. There is significant support for Tappers who creatively appropriate the buildings and remix them to represent other things. Tapper member MrClutch111 used the Rancho Relaxo spa to create a mansion setting, while DaoudX used a variety of details to create a tableau of a car accident.[76] Decisions on how to decorate depend on an individual Tapper's own taste, but the community universally values planning, effort, and detail. These attributes attest to Tappers' ability to control space and resources and to express themselves within the game.

It is not unusual for a player to report a hasty start to the game in which he or she haphazardly designs a city in an attempt to accumulate resources and buildings and in order to progress quickly through the opening levels. Often players will reach a point where they want to bring more organization to their town. This urge seemed to be particularly popular in August and September 2015, when a monorail became a feature of the game.[77] The advent of the monorail required Tappers to squeeze a disruptive mass-transit system into their already-crowded cities. Players frequently debated whether they should start over in their design, given the spatial difficulties presented by the monorail. When contemplating a redesign, community members urged each other to plan the locations of their buildings first, with some members suggesting that the buildings should be organized into zones or districts such as the town square, the wharf, rural areas, and upscale neighborhoods.[78] Once these buildings were placed, some Tappers encouraged arranging decorations around the buildings to provide detail, distinction, and bonus points. Certain buildings were singled out as ideal transitional buildings from one zone to the next.[79]

Tappers upload screenshots of their towns to the forum for the approval and praise of their peers. The level of care and effort that goes into these designs is astonishing. Tappers who master the game tools are lauded for their creativity and planning. In creating a highly detailed version of Springfield, they express personal statements about either mastery over space or extensive knowledge of *The Simpsons* or both. The care, community, and collaboration that occur on the forum indicate the level of thought put into the management of resources and the city planning. Fans of this game also use the forum as an opportunity to have everyday conversations. The "Off-Topic Discussion" subforum is the second most popular discussion board on the *Tapped Out* forum, demonstrating that when Tappers are not thinking about the arrangement of their towns, they are connecting with each other.

Just as television episodes are understood through real-world associations, casual games bring the world of the story to the politics of everyday life and its downtime. When players encounter characters in the context of waiting, they initiate a relationship with the story in a different place than the storyteller imagined. The politics of waiting can influence the audience's interpretation of the text. The Tapper forum just described illustrates that many *Simpsons* fans experience the show's story lines within an ongoing conversation about city planning, spatial politics, and the public sphere. For example, in the *Simpsons* episode "The Day the Earth Stood Cool," the politics of gentrification and public breastfeeding are the episode's featured topics. The player first meets these issues and characters when playing *Tapped Out* in public space (often a waiting room). The freemium model of the game means that players have the opportunity to draw associations between the politics of breastfeeding, gentrification, and their actual surroundings. The player might think about how he or she would react in a similar situation if it occurred in the current location. The player's experience of that story line while out in public can affect his or her perceptions of the narrative when it is aired later that week on television. Additionally, mobile devices offer a network of interaction via social media, messaging services, and telephone calls that allows players to discuss the issues presented in the game. As discussed previously, waiting in public spaces presents an opportunity for reflection about the power dynamics of daily life. Introducing a media franchise into this environment encourages reflection on the text, particularly as these games emphasize the inequities of waiting through their freemium revenue model.

There is no doubt that *The Simpsons: Tapped Out*, because of its history of satire and its focus on city planning, is a particularly loaded example for considering the politics of the procrastination economy. Not all casual games are as explicit in their intertextual references and use of satire to comment on efforts to monetize the mobile audience. Yet Jonathan Gray sees television and television series as the "crown domains of intertextuality" because of the variety of genres, mediums, and audiences it addresses.[80] Hyperintertextuality provides many opportunities for critical intertextuality, in which the audience is invited to draw associations outside the text. The media theorists J. David Bolter and Richard Grusin point out that digital media are defined by their intertextuality, since their texts are able to take the form of any other medium via the arrangement of their malleable binary code.[81] A casual game such as *Tapped Out* contains elements of a television text, branded entertainment, advertising messaging, board games, and video games. Following Gray, this intertextuality offers opportunities for reading the text critically in relation to the environment or users' experience with the referenced texts.[82] Gray points out that the openings in the textual form offered by intertextuality offer a new ordering paradigm around parody or other critical avenues.[83] For *Tapped Out*, the parody within the game operates in much the same way as it does in the television show: as a way to comment on the commercial system in which the audience is engaged. Few casual games include this level of parody, but their inherent intertextuality offers other organizing logics that are similarly self-reflexive. Thus, most casual games, because of where they are played, the generic forms they marshal, and the freemium business model that organizes their procedural rhetoric, invite reflection and association.

In the hope of maintaining brand value, entertainment companies are increasingly looking to the procrastination economy as a place to engage consumers. For the waiting room, this means the world of casual games and the freemium business model. Even when games are not connected to a television show, casual games still maintain their relationship to waiting and offer their audience an opportunity to take control. When media companies hitch their story worlds to these games, the audience uses those characters as tools for engaging with the issues present in everyday life. In the case of *Tapped Out*, the game DNA insists on this kind of active use and reflective thinking about power and capitalism. It advocates for critical reading and reminds the mobile device audience of its relationship to business strategies. *Tapped Out* is an extreme example, as is *The Simpsons* on television, because of the game's inherent embrace of parody and satire, which contrasts sharply with the structure of delay and waiting that is consistent across casual games. This structure brings along an invitation to people who cannot afford to avoid waiting to make associations between the economics of their gameplay and the world around them.

Conclusion: The Value of Waiting

In a *New York Times Magazine* feature from April 2012, the author Sam Anderson refers to mobile games as "stupid games" and warns against their addictive and exploitive potentials.[84] Anderson's evidence is anecdotal, as he cites his and his wife's attraction to the games as well as industry reporting on their popularity. Casual games are compared to more "hard-core" console or desktop games, which he elevates to the level of legitimate art form. The popularity of and quotidian and feminine qualities associated with casual games reconstitute debates once had between television and film. Television, with its advertising sponsorship, was seen as a crass medium that encouraged such nicknames as the "idiot box" and the "boob tube." Television scholars have argued that these critiques were due to suspicion of popular culture and fear of mass media.[85] The feminist media scholars Charlotte Brunsdon's and Dorothy Hobson's research on soap operas reveals that much of the prejudice toward television emanates from gendered assumptions and the politics of taste.[86] Casual game developers see their work as the "new soap operas," culturally popular and critically maligned contributions to everyday life.[87] Applying a television studies approach to these games reveals that they are much more than simple diversions.

The similarities between casual games and soap operas extends beyond cultural value to their shared relationship with domestic labor. Historically, women's leisure time was squeezed between first-shift labor outside the home and second-shift domestic labor.[88] Melissa Gregg's work on the changing demands on employees in the Internet age argues that the affective labor and interpersonal capabilities of workers, once the purview of largely female careers, have become the currency of most white-collar careers.[89] The leisure gap between the sexes is becoming more of a leisure shortage in a society in which we seem to have less and less time. Despite more equality in terms of housework and collaborative marriages, women still feel guilty about taking time for themselves.[90] As men begin to take more of an active role in the second-shift work, they too see their leisure time shrink. In this economic situation, people are increasingly looking to moments in the waiting room as an opportunity to assert their agency and value.

Casual games on mobile devices offer agency and value by giving people an opportunity to play and achieve something in their downtime. Video game history demonstrates that games have been crucial to the introduction and adoption of new technologies.[91] Thus, the habits associated with casual games and their relationship with waiting are key attributes of mobile culture. The argument and evidence presented in this chapter explain that casual games are self-reflectively engaged with the politics of waiting. Playing these games is not the mindless escape from reality that it may seem. Just as television has come to be studied as a sophisticated medium used for a myriad of cultural practices, so too should casual games. People use popular culture in their everyday lives to navigate the politics of space and social networks. Casual games provide people with tools for taking control of their wait times. For people who find pleasure in casual games, wait times transform from a moment of boredom and stress into an opportunity for socializing, competition, and creativity.

Those entertainment companies looking at mobile devices as an exhibition platform would benefit from considering the politics of waiting. If waiting is a moment in which people reflect on their power in relationship to larger institutional structures, then it would follow that games that empower players to take control of space would be ideal. Games such as *Tapped Out* that cleverly engage with the realities of playing in public space and address the desires of audiences to connect with others or to adapt existing popular culture will be as successful as the television shows that identified the family sitcom as an appropriate genre for the living room audience. At the same time, these games are specifically designed so that the average player cannot entirely disappear into his or her fictional world. People will still have to face the realities of waiting because the games themselves are built on delays. In this way, casual games are an amplification of the politics of space, and they provide users with more options for managing the frustration of waiting.

5

The "Connected" Living Room

The Idiot Box Gets a Diploma

My daughter, like many other two-year-olds, is an enormous fan of Disney's *Frozen*. A couple of months after receiving a voice-activated television remote control from our cable provider, she decided to take a break from her coloring. She toddled over to the remote, held it up to her face, and whispered "*Frozen*." The television was off at the time, so her request went unheeded; however, it is interesting to note that she had figured out the basic mechanics of putting her movie on the screen without any parental intervention or instruction. This moment was similar to the promises Samsung made when the company rolled out its 7500 and 8000 series "smart" TVs in 2012. In a commercial for those televisions, titled "Hi, TV," a toddler observes each family member control the television through voice and gesture commands. Just like my daughter, the toddler in the commercial figures out how to operate the television—no button pushing, menu navigating, or fine motor skills required. The commercial ends with the toddler uttering possibly her first words, "Hi, TV!"[1]

The next year, Samsung's smart TV technology advanced, allowing people to control their TVs by using their mobile devices. In another Samsung commercial ("It's Not TV"), a teenage boy controls the television with his tablet, synchronizing the mobile screen with the living room television.[2] The boy's mother asks that he not watch TV right now. In response, the son pulls up a YouTube video with his tablet, claiming that he is no longer watching TV but watching YouTube. After being rebuked again, the son brings up a number of options, with his tablet displaying the variety of online content now available on the living room television. Finally, his mother uses her phone to deactivate the television.

Each of these examples demonstrates that mobile devices and "smart" television technology have altered the social dynamics of the family living room. Audience studies scholars including David Morley, Roger Silverstone, and Ian Ang have documented how the living room television relates to family dynamics and social power.[3] These authors also recognize that family leisure time in the living room is the foundational currency of the television industry.[4] The arrival of mobile devices in the living room has resulted in the amplification of both family dynamics *and* the monetization of domestic leisure time. Samsung's commercials focus on how the company's technology affects the social dynamic and obscure the ways in which these televisions monetize the living room.

Shrewd observers, however, did not miss the economic and privacy implications of this new technology. Not long after Samsung's smart television models became available, concerns arose over the televisions' ability to record private conversations and spy on the activities of the living room.[5] In February 2015, Shane Harris of *The Daily Beast* scrutinized Samsung's privacy policy and discovered a passage that stated, "Please be aware that if your spoken words include personal or other sensitive information, that information will be among the data captured and transmitted to a third party."[6] While many people reacted with concern, David Meyer, a writer for the technology blog *Gigaom* pointed out that this loss of privacy could be the price of living with smart technology.[7] "Smart" technology, especially as applied in televisions, is "intelligent" because the software "learns" about its users with each interaction. Over time, smart software can predict users' preferences on the basis of usage patterns. Additionally, consumer data can be collected by hardware and software manufacturers and then packaged and sold to media companies. The consumer electronics industry is not the only sector of the media industries working to connect the living room. Television networks hire social media consultants and staff digital marketing departments, digital entrepreneurs develop mobile apps for the living room, and social media platforms have marketing departments dedicated to monetizing the time we spend in the living room. In this way, mobile devices and smart technologies intensify the economic stakes and social functions of the family living room, by quantifying and wrangling audience attention as it shifts from away from the television screen.

The procrastination economy of the "connected" living room, like its siblings in the workplace, the commute, and the waiting room, is dedicated to monetizing the in-between moments that traditional media industries struggle to reach. In this case, the procrastination economy's target is the wandering eye of the living room television audience. The television networks and advertisers want mobile devices to help focus attention and conversation on programs and advertisements that draw the family to the living room television in the first place. This chapter presents the strategies and assumptions inherent to the living room procrastination economy with a particular focus on Twitter, the social media platform that is most invested in this work. The desire to corral wandering attention motivates the development of products and services for the "connected" living room and privileges viewers who want to sync their interactive technologies with the programming flow. However, many viewers do not meet this profile and instead use their mobile devices to navigate family power dynamics and change the politics of how families watch television together. Evidence of this shift is gathered from the discussion boards of cable and satellite providers, bolstered by existing audience research on the integration of mobile devices into family dynamics, and rests on the foundational research of scholars who first observed the ways television viewing functions as a social experience.

Digitizing Attention: The Procrastination Economy of the "Connected" Living Room

The procrastination economy of the living room is designed to integrate mobile devices and other interactive technologies with television programs. While the pairing of mobile devices and television screens can enrich some viewers' television experience, there is a distinct economic advantage to organizing the entertainment in this way. The television industry's dominant revenue model relies on the assumption that the home audience pays attention to the advertising that accompanies their evening's entertainment. Television-ratings and audience-measurement companies assure advertisers that people are watching and receiving the sponsored messages. In the early 2000s, the popularity of mobile devices and the development of "quality TV" reinvigorated conversations about audience attention.[8] On the one hand, mobile devices provided a second screen that could encourage multitasking or even replace television. On the other hand, prestige programming that started on cable channels but eventually spread across the television landscape enticed filmmakers and auteurs to create content for television. These technological and aesthetic shifts raised television's cultural status while simultaneously calling into question the industry's viability.[9] The solution, as many people in the entertainment industry see it, is to bring digital devices in line with the prevailing logics of television.[10] Instead of regarding mobile devices as competition for audience attention, the entertainment industry, advertisers, and social media platforms have collaborated to create a procrastination economy meant to redirect the living room audience's wandering attention back onto television programming. The living room procrastination economy attempts to colonize the daydreaming and multitasking that often takes place while we watch television. This procrastination economy seeks to eliminate the distractions of the living room and redefine television viewing as a focused, interactive cultural experience.

Examples throughout this book demonstrate how the procrastination economy monetizes the in-between moments of daily life by bringing mobile devices into the "flow" of television programs—a foundational principle of television programming. Techniques of programming flow, such as the manipulation of narrative arcs, the minimization of credits, the altering of volume, and the shortening of intro music, are all tried-and-true methods for channeling audience attention from one program, commercial, or interstitial to the next. Television flow strategies do more than prevent viewers from changing the channel; they also keep viewers' attention on the television. This can be an especially challenging task in the complicated context of the living room. The audience studies scholar Dan Hassoun points to a long history of industry anxiety about the attention of the home audience. Hassoun refers to "a widely cited study by Charles Allen that found substantial percentages of the audience would 'eat, drink, sleep, play, argue, fight, and occasionally make love' in front of the TV set rather than giving undivided attention to the programming or ad onscreen."[11] Hassoun sees mobile devices as merely the latest technology employed by the entertainment industry to combat inattentiveness.

The procrastination economy of the connected living room is composed of a variety of technologies designed to make mobile devices support television programming. Regardless of whether these products are labeled "second screens," "social TV," "connected viewing," or "co-viewing," they are all designed to redirect attention back to the television screen. In previous work, I have argued that second-screen mobile apps reinforce traditional revenue models by promoting synchronous viewing or mobile access to content.[12] Apps designed for these purposes are essentially mobile versions of what the television scholar Will Brooker has called "textual overflow," additional content for those viewers who want to extend the show experience to a digital platform.[13] Adam Cahan, the CEO of IntoNow, a Yahoo-branded second-screen app, describes a common rationale for this technology: "If you're watching a Green Bay game, the app will automatically pull in any breaking news about players like Aaron Rodgers. You can see what's going on around the league or dive deep into what's going on with one player."[14] As Cahan sees it, these apps anticipate the questions that could potentially lead viewers' attention away from the primary screen. The new media scholar Karin van Es argues that second-screen apps "envelop" television content by providing context and depth that makes television viewing a richer and more curated experience.[15] Hye Jin Lee and Mark Andrejevic provide a more critical view with their "second-screen theory," which states that second-screen apps "build on and complete" the traditional marketing goals of the past.[16] Consistent among these arguments about the uses of mobile devices for programming flow is the acknowledgment that our mobile devices are designed to support television programming by anticipating viewers' curiosity.

The focus on serving viewers' curiosity and anticipating questions plays into the functionality of second-screen apps. These functions are very attractive to advertisers, as sponsors want to be associated with satisfying the audience's urges. Research on second-screen mobile apps shows that the functionality has evolved over time to privilege the reactive engagement experiences preferred by advertisers.[17] Additional research on second-screen apps by Elizabeth Evans explains how these apps "gamify" television viewing by inviting audiences to predict the outcome of the show during lulls in the narrative.[18] Evans encourages researchers to think of the second-screen experience as a "layering" of attention across multiple screens. When an audience member's attention declines on the primary screen, he or she turns to the secondary screen to fill the attention gap. Consequently, media companies can redirect attention back to the primary screen through interactive content. Cahan of IntoNow cites user data confirming that audiences layer attention across multiple screens: "User activity [on mobile devices] rises during big games and award shows, events that do not require constant attention. But there are large dips during well-written dramas, followed by a burst of activity once the show ends. It seems device owners can contain themselves for quality content."[19] Cahan's findings are supported by research that shows genre as a major factor in how people layer their attention between the living room screen and the mobile screen.[20] The research and common wisdom on second-screen use reveal a relationship between genre, advertising, and functionality that makes mobile devices ideal companions for anticipating curiosity and encouraging anticipation during live-event programming.

Live events have many commercial breaks, creating multiple opportunities to shift attention from the programming. Second-screen apps combat waning attention by offering questions, answers, and trivia during these breaks in programming. Audience research by Lora Oehlberg et al. shows that the visual cues of "fade outs," "fade ins," and other scene transition devices are invitations to disengage with the television screen.[21] This evidence shows that commercial breaks are not the only moments when viewers' attention strays from the television screen. The functionality of second-screen apps attempts to monetize other moments when people's eyes wander to mobile devices. Television programming conventions such as roundtable discussions and interviews have been shown to cause inattention.[22] In addition to these aesthetic triggers, the tone or rising suspense of a television narrative can cause viewers to turn to their mobile devices as a place to "relax" during moments in programs that were stressful.[23] These examples show many reasons that people shift attention from the television screen. Second-screen apps offer trivia and enticements to these viewers to keep them interested in the program even when television flow fails.

Television has always suffered from disruptions in programming that allow viewers to become distracted. The procrastination economy of the living room offers products and services to mitigate a decades-old problem that has become even more concerning in an era of media fragmentation. The television theorist John

Ellis has argued that television is best understood through the notion of "glance theory" because the home audience often watches television in a state of distraction, with family life, multitasking, and interruption constituting the natural state of television viewing.[24] Following this theory, people watch television in intermittent glances, in which they attempt to follow the plot and then refocus during key moments. The nature of the medium itself contributes to the opportunities for distraction and shifting attention. Ellis argues that television programs consist of "small sequential unities of images and sounds whose maximum duration seems to be about five minutes. These segments are organized into groups, which are either simply cumulative, like news broadcast items and advertisements, or have some kind of repetitive or sequential connection, like the groups of segments that make up the serial or series."[25] Lee and Andrejevic see mobile apps as an attempt to organize this segmentation around industry logic, to colonize the interpretive breaks by reinforcing a dominant reading of the text.[26]

Mobile devices allow television networks and advertisers to reach viewers on an additional screen and influence their understanding of a show. People already use their mobile devices to comment and discuss television programs with others while they are watching.[27] The functionality of second-screen apps encourages this activity and frames the discussion with content meant to anticipate audience questions and confusion. Not only do second-screen apps frame the terms of conversation, but they monetize this conversation through the sponsorship of discussion platforms. Some media executives are advocating to take this monetization strategy further by offering audiences incentives for discussing programs on industry-preferred apps. Dennis Adamovic, senior vice president of brand and digital activation for Turner Broadcasting, told *Broadcasting and Cable*, "Down the road, [second-screen apps] will allow users to download a coupon or even buy a ticket for a movie."[28] In this scenario, viewers who allow mobile devices to shuttle their attention between the television screen and the second-screen app will be compensated for their time. Deborah Brett, vice president of mobile sales at Viacom, sees second-screen advertising as an extension of the television business model, saying, "the ad that is running on-air to create awareness of a brand [can now be tied] to a second screen that in effect makes the TV ad clickable."[29] This would make ads more relevant to consumers than the current ratings system does, by targeting particular users instead of broad demographics. In September 2015, the veteran mobile-industry analyst Benedict Evans promoted a chart from Flurry Analytics and the US Department of Labor Statistics showing that people made in-app purchases at an astounding rate, generating what is believed to be more revenue than mobile advertisements do.[30] Of course, these targeted advertisements and two-screen experiences create a powerful and potentially manipulative commercial system, what Lee and Andrejevic call a "digital enclosure," in which the interpretive process is shaped by the advertisers and programmers designing the mobile apps.[31] Despite these concerns, it is important to remember that the television industry already monetizes our leisure time; the system proposed by these executives creates a more direct relationship between advertiser and audience and provides some form of compensation.

Despite these strategies, second-screen apps have largely failed to attract a wide audience, causing many ventures to fold, consolidate, or shift strategies.[32] Part of the problem is that the market was immediately oversaturated, with over 200 second-screen apps available in 2012.[33] Ian Aaron, cofounder of the second-screen company ConnecTV, provides an additional theory: "Our research found that about two-thirds didn't want all that ancillary content."[34] Media companies may have been too eager to expand advertising opportunities through narrative and textual overflow and turned off viewers who did not want such a tightly programmed interactive experience. Another reason for the failure comes from interviews with Andrew Seroff, junior software developer for Miso and later Viggle, who explained that his group's goal was to create a mobile app that would help the company be acquired by Hollywood. The economic motivation to be bought out by an entertainment company led them to create a second-screen experience that fit more with the strategies of media companies, such as channeling attention back to the primary screen, and less with the way people actually use their mobile devices.[35] The strategy of creating apps for television's business model worked out for some companies, such as the social TV company Beamly. Beamly was hired to create the software for the apps of television networks, while other second-screen companies transitioned into big-data companies or more expansive lifestyle and culture apps.[36] Many second-screen apps failed to offer advertisers the numbers of viewers available on the more dominant social media platforms, Twitter and Facebook, but as it turns out, that may not have been as important to these start-ups as the goal of being purchased by larger media companies.

"The World's Biggest Living Room"

Many second-screen apps failed despite creating functionality designed to channel attention to the living room screen.[37] Twitter, however, had enough users to implement the logics of the procrastination economy on a much grander scale. It is fair to say that Twitter has staked its financial future on its relationship with the television industry. The company is proud of its role in facilitating a social television experience, but it is the variety of conversations on the platform that distinguishes Twitter from television-network- or show-specific second-screen apps. Research from Donghee Yvette Wohn and E. K. Na shows that users preferred Twitter because it helped them selectively seek out the conversations they were interested in, rather than constraining them to the conversations happening within curated second-screen experiences.[38] This preference makes sense, given that viewers who shift their attention from the television screen are often interested in a different program or in a completely different subject matter.[39] Twitter is a portal to a variety of conversations happening all over the world and thus provides a wide array of diversions from which to choose. The desire to organize multiple screens of entertainment is similar to Evans's description of screen "layers" or Markus Stauff's term "screen stacking," both of which describe how a viewer alternates between devices to fill attention gaps.[40]

While Twitter offers a variety of conversations on every topic, the site has developed a reputation as the destination for conversations specifically about television. Twitter refers to itself as "the world's biggest living room" because of the volume of tweets generated by television programs.[41] Twitter organizes conversations through the use of hashtags, which allow users to find communities of like-minded individuals wanting to discuss a particular television show.[42] Because Twitter does not foster much back-and-forth conversation, tweeting about a show becomes a second arena of entertainment that provides a snapshot of viewer reaction. Users visit the site to voice their thoughts and read other viewers' tweets, but rarely is there substantive interaction. In addition, people are much more likely to read others' tweets than to tweet themselves.[43] Agence France-Presse described Twitter as a "must-have tool for journalists, activists and celebrities" but noted that the platform "has struggled to show it can expand beyond its devoted 'twitterati' to become a mainstream hit."[44] This description demonstrates how Twitter is composed mainly of people cultivating a brand and performing the act of watching television. Considering that the mobile screen is "stacked" or "layered" with the living room screen, it is not surprising that there is a dearth of in-depth conversation on Twitter or other social media platforms. If people were conversing during the show, they could miss an important scene or plot point. People turn to Twitter when attention wanes: they look for some diversion and then return to the television after a commercial break or during a climactic moment.

The procrastination economy of Twitter shapes the audience's perception of television viewers' reaction.[45] The belief that Twitter reflects the audience's reaction is concerning given that some estimates claim that Twitter readers outnumber Twitter authors 50 to 1.[46] Despite the relatively small percentage of people actively tweeting, conversation on the social media platform is often accepted as evidence of public sentiment. Consider ABC's *The Bachelor*, one of the most tweeted-about television shows, with 156,000 people routinely commenting on the reality show. This number is dwarfed by the number of people (an estimated 3.5 million) who read tweets while watching but do not tweet themselves.[47] Despite the discrepancy, the researcher Philip Pond found that viewers see themselves as an imagined community of people watching together.[48] Advertisers and television producers assume that Twitter reflects a similar reality and see Twitter as a direct line to feedback from the audience. This somewhat-faulty assumption means that a handful of people have enormous capability to shape the conversation about a television show and its reception. José Van Dijck has noted the outsized influence held by a minority of the Twitter community in her critiques of the social media platform.[49] She explains, "Twitter-the-ambient-utility promoting user connectedness finds itself at odds with Twitter-the-information-network exploiting connectivity to help businesses promote their brands among users."[50] The implication of Van Dijck's claim is that in the pursuit of a stable business model, Twitter must monetize its users even though the opinions expressed by that group represent only a small portion of the actual, full audience. Twitter largely defines the procrastination economy of the connected living room, but it does so by capitalizing on a rather incomplete view of how people spend their in-between moments on the couch.

Twitter Amplify

Twitter Amplify, the backbone of the living room procrastination economy, epitomizes the ways the economic desire to monetize viewers' in-between moments is based on the activities of a minority of mobile phone users.[51] Introduced in 2013, Twitter Amplify is the social media platform's second-screen advertising product. Twitter Amplify operates through the following process: a customer such as Fox Broadcasting Company, for example, purchases time on Twitter Amplify to promote its prime-time shows and to earn advertising revenue on its exclusive video clips. During a show's broadcast on the Fox network, Twitter Amplify sends out promotional tweets featuring video clips, audience polls, and other interactive content, all designed to drive viewers to the broadcast program. In addition to promoting shows currently on the air, the clips also include sponsor messages in the form of "preroll" advertisements. An advertiser could purchase ad time during the broadcast of a show and during the Twitter Amplify campaign, ensuring that no matter where the audience looks, they will see the marketer's message. Twitter Amplify capitalizes on the social media platform's status as television viewers' favorite alternative to the living room television by ensuring that television advertisers and programs can reach audiences on both screens.

Twitter Amplify was the outcome of a systematic pursuit of profits, meant to appease nervous investors. Van Dijck notes that Twitter's redesigns in 2010 and 2011 were clear indicators of how "the company's ambitions transformed from wanting to be a global, neutral communication channel for citizens that might be used in defiance of governments, to wanting to be a profitable venture that must obey the laws of those countries where it seeks to attract customers."[52] This shift was also evident in partnerships forged with advertisers and in Twitter's acquisition of BlueFin, an audience-measurement company. Twitter's path to success would be through its relationship with television, capitalizing on the television chatter already occurring on the social media platform.[53] Adam Bain, Twitter's president of global revenue, described Twitter Amplify as a way to "connect people across screens, and tap into the social conversation on Twitter with complementary TV video clips."[54] These monetization strategies reveal how the living room procrastination economy is designed to function. It privileges mobile users who enjoy multitasking and sharing content while watching television. Van Dijck refers to this form of socializing as "connectivity," which she contrasts to "connectedness": "connectivity" involves companies encouraging and profiting from social behavior that was previously difficult for them to penetrate.[55]

The desire to attract partners to Twitter Amplify led the company to focus the procrastination economy on live-event programming. Twitter Amplify's first advertising deal was with ESPN and Ford to deliver instant-replay video clips and ads during college football games.[56] Viewers who used their digital devices to follow ESPN on Twitter could find highlights and instant replays of game action following a "preroll" advertising message from Ford.[57] The sponsored tweets, which Twitter calls "two-screen sponsorships," operate in two ways: First, the commercial content reaches consumers looking at their mobile devices during commercial breaks or gaps in attention. Second, these clips entice people who might not be watching the broadcast to turn on ESPN to see the game where the clip originated. This strategy is supported by the research of Judit Nagy and Anjali Midha, who found that when people discovered a conversation about a television show on Twitter, they changed the channel to the corresponding show 45% of the time.[58] Turner networks and Coca-Cola signed a similar partnership to support the broadcast of the NCAA March Madness tournament, another sporting event that draws a large live crowd.[59] Twitter also signed a "six-figure ad deal" with Heineken to use Amplify on highlights from the UEFA Champions League soccer tournament.[60] Broadcasters around the world flocked to the service to provide a mobile media presence for regional sporting events. Coverage of a deal between Twitter and an Indian cricket network touts the partnership's ability to "enhance viewer experience" and deliver "high-quality clips of sporting action."[61] This rhetoric reveals aesthetic and viewing assumptions about the procrastination economy. The partnership assumes that viewers will accept advertising messages on their mobile devices in exchange for highlights that "enhance" the viewing experience. Each of these assumptions speaks volumes about the way Twitter understands audience members' preferences for satisfying their waning attention.

The image of the procrastination economy of the living room is one of rabid media consumers looking to use their mobile device to monitor multiple programs at once. This is clear in the reporting on Twitter Amplify's relationship with ESPN by Christopher Heine, who describes the advertising platform as a boon for viewers, who can now avail themselves of "the ability to focus on single games via the living room flat-screen TV while getting snippets galore of other contests on [their] laptop, tablet or smartphone."[62] This promise to enhance the viewer experience is one of the platform's key selling points. Not only do these enhancements entice superfans, who attempt to be aware of everything happening in the sports world, but they also help more casual sports fans multitask and discover all the "extras" offered by the broadcast. The "amplify" in Twitter Amplify's meaning is clear: working with sports leagues, Twitter Amplify aims to create fans who do not just watch a single game but consume an entire league or sports landscape. Twitter Amplify promotes the idea that fans should never miss breaking sports news or live events. The invitation to amplify one's fandom recalls the audience labor issues described by John T. Caldwell, as he depicted Internet extensions of television programs as "second-shift" labor for fans.[63] If viewers actually used Twitter in the ways that marketers believe, watching sports would be a lot of work.

Twitter Amplify has over 200 partnerships in 20 countries, including relationships with individual sports leagues and each of the major broadcasting companies.[64] The advertising platform is especially popular with sports broadcasts because these typically draw big audiences and attractive audience demographics. As I have written before, sports programming is ideal for the procrastination economy because highlight clips fit neatly within the in-between moments of the day.[65] Highlight clips are also a boon for advertisers. For example, Heineken and the United States Tennis Association posted a clip of a 54-shot rally in the US Open tennis tournament via Twitter Amplify that was retweeted 1,500 times; this promotion translated into 12 million impressions and 2,300 new followers to Heineken.[66] Impressive as these numbers may be, the real Twitter Amplify powerhouse is the NFL. Advertisements embedded with NFL highlight clips were clicked on four and a half times more than were advertisements attached to the average Amplify message.[67] In the past, legacy licensing deals limited the online efforts of sports leagues. New rights deals account for social media integration, opening up new ways to generate revenue for sports leagues and advertisers alike.[68] As I have argued elsewhere, the procrastination economy is lucrative not only for sports leagues but also for ancillary revenue sources such as fantasy sports leagues.[69] People use their mobile devices to check the status of their virtual "teams" while watching a live game on the television. This activity demonstrates how the procrastination economy amplifies the act of watching sports.

The procrastination economy applies this same amplification of audience labor to watching other live events as well. In 2013, Viacom used Twitter Amplify to deliver ad-supported highlights and behind-the-scenes videos of the live 2013 MTV Video Music Awards broadcast.[70] Pepsi was another promotional partner in this venture and garnered 9,000 new Twitter followers through advertisements it placed at the start of awards-show clips. This example illustrates Andrejevic's assertions that corporations use data to gauge an audience's affinity for content and then use that affinity to forge an emotional connection with a brand or person.[71] Twitter provides advertisers with data about how a live event is being received, and then an advertiser customizes its message to match the prevailing sentiment. This form of "affective economics" requires the advertiser to ingest the data and quickly churn out a relevant, pithy reaction that connects with the audience. Similar strategies were used in Twitter Amplify deals that supported live coverage of the 2012 election, comedy roasts, the Kids' Choice Awards, concerts, and the Academy Awards.[72]

In addition to awards shows and sporting events, Twitter Amplify has contracted with shows that have enthusiastic fan support and active Twitter communities, such as *Duck Dynasty* (A&E), *The Mindy Project* (Fox), *Glee* (Fox), *New Girl* (Fox), *Brooklyn Nine-Nine* (Fox), and *Pretty Little Liars* (ABC Family).[73] Viewers of these shows tend to watch the episodes when they premier on television so that the stories are unspoiled and they can weigh in with their thoughts and read the reactions of others. By placing ads before *Pretty Little Liars* clips, Johnson & Johnson netted 4.7 million impressions from the show's Twitter followers.[74] Despite the impressive analytics earned by a few shows, television producers see Twitter Amplify as more relevant for live events.[75] Searching for an alternative to entice partnerships with prerecorded television content, Twitter purchased SnappyTV, a company that created software that enables users to quickly edit and share clips from TV.[76] Like Twitter Amplify, this new feature asks viewers to contribute more effort to watching television; however, instead of monitoring two screens for a complete viewing experience (as with Twitter Amplify), SnappyTV uses viewers to promote the show through the sharing of clips with friends and family.

Twitter Amplify provided Twitter with a revenue model for monetizing its users' interest in television, but Twitter sealed its relationship with television through a partnership with the Nielsen audience research company. Nielsen created the currency of the television industry in the 1950s. Eileen Meehan has expertly dissected the meaning behind the Nielsen rating system, explaining how it turns the audience into a "commodity" for transactions between advertisers and networks.[77] The emergence of Twitter and its audience metrics represented a challenge to Nielsen's sovereignty in this arena. The media industries scholars Allie Kosterich and Philip M. Napoli have documented how Nielsen pacified the challenge of social media metrics by assimilating Twitter and the creation of the Nielsen Twitter TV Ratings.[78] The partnership with Twitter not only extended Nielsen's brand to social media but also organized the metric around linear viewing.[79] The emphasis on linear television validates Nielsen's existing television rating system while adding the metric of social conversation, or what advertisers categorize as "earned media," to the menu of products that the company can sell to advertisers and networks.[80]

To illustrate Nielsen's new range of offerings, consider these rankings, based on data gathered during the 2014–2015 television season. NBC's *Sunday Night Football* was the highest rated show (an average of 20.8 million viewers), while CBS's *The Big Bang Theory* was the highest rated scripted show (an average of 19 million viewers).[81] The show with the highest social media score, the number of tweets associated with the show, belonged to NBC's Super Bowl XLIX broadcast, with 16.1 million tweets; the most tweeted scripted series was Fox's *Empire*, with 5.9 million tweets.[82] Of the top ten for the year, the shows with the highest social media scores were *The Walking Dead* (480,000 average tweets per episode), *The Bachelor* (156,000 average tweets per episode), *Game of Thrones* (107,000 average tweets per episode), *American Horror Story: Freak Show* (239,000 average tweets per episode), and *Empire* (627,000 average tweets per episode).[83] The highest rated television shows were traditional "lean-back" television series, such as the three-camera sitcom *The Big Bang Theory* (19 million viewers) and the police procedurals *NCIS* (18.2 million viewers) and *NCIS: New Orleans* (17.4 million viewers).[84]

In general, the difference between the traditional audience-size metric and the social media score is the willingness of viewers to display their fandom on Twitter. The Nielsen Twitter TV Ratings take into account a group of viewers who have been historically ignored: enthusiastic viewers who want to share their thoughts with others. Twitter's director of global brand and agency strategy, Jean-Philippe Maheu, declared that people who tweet about what they are watching are different kinds of viewers: "People who are tweeting don't go to the kitchen or bathroom—they stay in the room."[85] While the inclusion of these types of viewers expands the types of viewing counted by ratings companies, privilege is still given to people watching in real time. Binge watchers and time shifters, who watch more than a week after a show originally airs, are still not accounted for under this new system. Researchers have shown that there is also a robust conversation occurring on Twitter about shows that are viewed on demand and/or after a significant amount of time has passed since the original airing.[86] Even more striking is the way that both the traditional Nielsen ratings and the social media metrics reinforce gender conventions: men are much more likely to glance at Twitter while watching sporting events, and women are more likely to check Twitter during dramatic series or reality programs.[87] It is unclear how these metrics would change if data collection went beyond the initial broadcast and considered long-term conversation and engagement. Twitter acknowledges that there are nearly 8,000 tweets sent about television programs in the days between airings, but the company does not harvest these tweets because there is no established revenue model for monetizing data that track this activity.[88] Nielsen recognizes that these conversations "can open new doors for networks, agencies, and advertisers" to think about television viewing differently, but to date, the company has not figured out how to turn a profit from these tweets.[89]

Twitter doubled down on its relationship with linear television by pursuing a streaming-media deal to broadcast live events. Twitter beat out Amazon and Verizon for the digital rights to stream live NFL games.[90] It is the first time Twitter will stream live sports, but the deal follows a number of initiatives to monetize the living room procrastination economy. Twitter's first streaming-video deal was with the BBC. In October 2013, the company made a deal with the BBC to create streaming-video news reports focused on trending social media stories.[91] A month later, Twitter struck a partnership with SeeIt that would allow Comcast subscribers to access certain television shows by following links in promoted tweets.[92] Next, Twitter tested live streaming through the integration of video services from the celebrity-focused Twitter Mirror and the global video app Periscope.[93] While testing its video capabilities, the company also fostered relationships with sports leagues through its Twitter Amplify contracts. With the relationships and technology established, Twitter decided to take the next step by offering live games and reaping profits from the increased advertising opportunities. The deal was met with skepticism: Todd Spangler of *Variety* explained, "Twitter is a place for sharing short snippets of text, photos or video. It has never been a destination for viewing long-form video, and live NFL games go against the grain of its entire user experience."[94] Unlike the deal with SeeIt, the NFL deal does not require cable subscriber authentication and is available worldwide free of charge. For Twitter and the NFL, the deal made sense as a way to grow the global audience and attract more advertising dollars. Twitter CEO Jack Dorsey explained, "People watch NFL games with Twitter today. Now they'll be able to watch right on Twitter Thursday nights."[95] The move to embrace streaming content comes at a moment when investors are concerned about Twitter's stagnation. Lou Kerner of Flight Venture Capital believes Twitter needs a profound change in design and functionality in order to "reignite engagement."[96] According to Dorsey, streaming video is one possible solution to the problem of stagnation, one more step down the path Twitter has followed since first identifying television as a revenue source.

Twitter's search for viable revenue streams has shaped the living room procrastination economy. Upon discovering that user activity spiked around television broadcasts and live events, Twitter invested in technology that fosters behavior complementary to the business model of television. Twitter created its Amplify product for the purpose of exposing viewers to advertisements, even though viewers commonly use Twitter to escape commercials on the living room television screen. In an effort to become a market leader in television-industry insight, Twitter partnered with Nielsen to create the Nielsen Twitter TV Ratings, which reassert the importance of linear programming by collating Twitter-based discussions occurring during live broadcasts. Twitter's streaming deal with the NFL essentially transforms mobile devices into a television, neutralizing the difference between the virtual living room and the actual living room. Every move Twitter has made contributes to monetizing the time that people spend disengaged with the living room television. To take a more cynical view, Twitter's decisions have created the conditions of the digital enclosure feared by Lee and Andrejevic.[97] Fortunately, for people with similar fears about the procrastination economy, strategies for monetizing audience behavior rarely work as smoothly as presented in corporate boardrooms.

Of Apps and Cable Boxes: Technologies of Living Room Control

Marketing strategies, product design, and the content of the procrastination economy do not determine how people behave with mobile devices in the living room. The products and services of the procrastination economy do not account for all the established practices, audience research, and contextual evidence. The remainder of this chapter situates mobile device use in the living room by revisiting audience studies research that describes the spatial and familial politics of television viewing. This foundational audience research provides context for understanding how mobile apps fit within established spatial dynamics. In particular, mobile apps that offer audiences "platform mobility," or the ability to access television on a mobile device in any location, are promoted as a tool for navigating family viewing dynamics.[98] Evidence of using these mobile apps can be found on the discussion forums of the companies that provide them. Combining audience studies with this documentation of users' habits provides a picture of how mobile devices increase flexibility within the spatial and family dynamics of the living room. These uses of mobile devices offer empowerment in ways that the preferred products of the procrastination economy, Twitter Amplify and other second-screen apps, often suppress.

In the book *On-Demand Culture*, the television and media industries scholar Chuck Tryon expertly analyzes the marketing materials of cable, satellite, and new-media companies that promise platform mobility. In the mold of Lynn Spigel, Tryon looks at the advertisements for these platform mobility technologies in order to chart how the new technologies fit within the connected home and "resolve family conflict."[99] Tryon cites the example of a Verizon ad called "Shining Star," in which family members are attending to their own mobile screens while putting up the Christmas tree, "without any conflicts over a central television set."[100] Tryon outlines a number of critiques of this viewership, noting Charles Acland's argument about rising informality, Mark Andrejevic's appraisal of monitored mobility, and Dan Schiller's assertion that users are just exchanging one screen for "a self-service vending machine of cultural commodities."[101] In the end, Tryon rightly points out that the advertisements for these mobile platforms foregrounds individuality and personalization.[102] Tryon does an excellent job of describing the marketing claims that these products are the key to maintaining family unity by putting an end to squabbles over the remote control. Tryon's use of an advertisement for UltraViolet software is a particularly direct example, as the ad carries the promise of "no more fighting over the main TV when Dad wants to watch football at the same time the kids want to watch cartoons."[103]

Tryon's ideological critique is sound, but the marketing materials' depictions of conflicts between family members accurately reflect the family dynamics of many living rooms. David Morley's seminal research on television viewing found that the choice of what to watch is a "complicated interpersonal" activity that is determined by "inter-familial status relations, temporal context, the number of sets available, and rule-based communications conventions."[104] Morley concludes, based on his extensive ethnographic research of television audiences, that the act of watching television can only be understood in its social and spatial context because "'watching television' cannot be assumed to be a one-dimensional activity of equivalent meaning or significant at all times for all who perform it."[105] Studies of the television audience often acknowledge that much television viewing is actually an excuse to share the same physical space as loved ones.[106] In these cases, what is on the screen is of secondary importance to the feeling of togetherness and the spontaneous conversation that can occur.

Considering years of television audience research, platform mobility apps would seem to expand the ways in which people manage familial dynamics and share the living room. These apps provide family members who are lower in social standing with a wider array of choices in how they share space with loved ones, and the app companies promote their products with this goal in mind. Before platform mobility apps, family members used a variety of diversions while "watching" whatever the person with the remote control chose as the evening's entertainment. Mobile devices deliver access to television that may have been previously denied by the person claiming the remote control. Mobile devices provide family members without power with a path to watching what they want while still sharing the space with loved ones.

In the Dish Network advertisement called "Who Wears the Pants?," a family fights over control for the television by struggling to fit into a pair of men's khaki trousers.[107] A voice-over explains that with the Dish Network DVR, everyone in the family can have control over the television by recording their favorite shows and watching on any device or television in the house. The depiction of equality offered by digital technology is something that the audiences in Morley's study would have eagerly embraced. Indeed, even people who are annoyed by the perceived social disconnect that mobile devices bring into the living room recognize that this phenomenon is an amplification of spatial politics that already exist. For example, a study by Sherryl Wilson on the use of mobile devices in the living room reveals this compelling exchange between mother and daughter: "Sue [mother] 'feels she is watching alone especially when Ruby [daughter] is using Facebook; she wants Ruby to do one thing or the other, which she then acknowledges as 'hypocritical' because she (Sue) will read the newspaper while the TV is on."[108] This example updates Morley's point that family television viewing includes many different types of engagement. Wilson found that "the majority of respondents report turning to social media as an adjunct to television viewing when not fully immersed in a TV show and are used to 'chat' with friends or absent family members."[109] Overall, Wilson's research suggests that mobile devices "allow for a companionship, a sharing of the same space while (dis)engaged with the primary screen."[110] The living room has seldom been a time of harmonious, in-depth engagement. The procrastination economy was alive and well in the living room; mobile devices are simply the newest way of navigating the socio-spatial dynamics of the living room.

Reviewing user comments on customer support forums of major cable and satellite providers reveals the roles that mobile devices play in family dynamics. To examine the amplification of these family dynamics, I searched the discussion forums for Comcast, Time Warner Cable, DirecTV, AT&T U-Verse, Verizon Fios, and Apple TV looking for discussions of family life. These discussions revealed that living room gender politics still exist but that mobile apps are providing a work-around for dealing with these issues while also preserving the spirit of the communal living room.

Dealing with Patriarchy

One of Morley's most important findings about television audiences is how gender and power influence the choice of what appears on the living room television. Indeed, the television scholar William Uricchio recognizes the introduction of the remote control as a key moment when the communal act of watching television as a family became more about the interests of the person with the remote control (often the oldest male in the room).[111] Morley cites examples related to economic status, such as a viewer who explained that the breadwinner of the house is perceived to have earned his or her leisure time and therefore is granted control over the television.[112] This power structure affects the types of programs that are selected, as the men in Morley's study preferred content that commanded full attention, while women reported preferring programs that allowed them to multitask. One respondent explained that she liked to knit while watching so that she did not feel like she was wasting time simply watching television.[113] Morley notes that women are typically excluded from programming decisions because of cultural expectations around domestic labor and the attending guilt of indulging in leisure time.[114] Despite the numerous shifts in household power structures in recent years, responsibility for domestic labor remains imbalanced between the sexes, with women continuing to do more of the work around the house.[115] This imbalance results in situations such as those chronicled by Morley, in which the head of the household selects a show for everyone else to watch.

Mobile apps from cable and satellite providers, while not erasing the power dynamic, do offer alternatives for family members who are excluded from control of the television. For example, commenters in customer service forums described their use of the mobile app as a way of accessing preferred television shows when the living room television was being controlled by another member of the family. As Belfast5348 describes the situation, "I am a football wife and watch online while husband watches TV."[116] DoConnor6408 recounted using her mobile device to watch the local news while his or her spouse was watching something else on television.[117] Multiple people, including Carols46 and TheJessle, reported using mobile devices to watch television while their husbands played video games.[118] Some people use the apps to watch television in entirely different rooms from their partners, as in the case of RH2514.[119] While comments generally suggest that women use the apps as a way to access preferred television programming, there were also examples of men ceding control of the living room TV to the rest of the family and relying on mobile devices to keep tabs on sporting events. For example, TheDaveMitchell wrote, "My wife and kid have the TV held hostage. I need to watch the Giants."[120] For some users, the decision to rely on the second screen is rooted in financial realities, as in the case of RayGoQuestions, who stated, "There are times my wife is watching one thing and I would like to be able to watch something else. . . . Getting a second TV is not an option in our present home."[121]

While critics of these apps might interpret these comments as evidence of the desire for individualism leading to social isolation, an alternative interpretation is to see mobile viewing apps as empowering for people who traditionally have not had control over the television. Remarks from QuessP and Majesty1919 reflect a sense of feeling empowered by taking ownership of their leisure time. QuessP states, "I have a suggestion for the TV mobile app. It would be nice if I could categorize my recordings by user, kind of like how Netflix does it. When I log into Netflix, I choose my user and then am shown shows I've recently watched, suggestions for me based on my viewing history, etc. I would love to NOT have to scroll through my daughter's Disney Jr. shows and my husband's comedy shows."[122] In addition to these comments, Majesty1919 requests an ability to protect her shows from her daughter's attempts to delete them, while bob wants the ability for him and his wife to "own" separate DVRs for their content.[123] The quest for greater personalization and customization concerns many critics of new media; however, increased individual control over viewing preferences also gives family members a sense of agency with regard to their leisure time, which is an improvement over the living room dynamics of the past.

Children's Screen Time

Mobile devices also give parents a sense of control over their children's viewing habits, mood, and behavior. Debates over the effects of "screen time" on children are hotly contested. Regardless of what pediatricians and child psychologists recommend, mobile devices are frequently used as parenting tools, since they are a platform for age-appropriate interactive apps and children's television shows that often invite participation and learning.[124] Parents sometimes rely on mobile apps to help manage their children's behavior, whether the device is used as a reward, as pacification, or simply as a tool to stave off complaints of boredom. Parents are eager to find child-appropriate content on these mobile devices, as cnunes6636 explains: "Hi, i use my phone and tablet alot to let my daughter watch tv and i noticed you do not have nicktoons on your xfinity go app, i would love to see it on there as shes asks for it alot! Im not to sure as to why you do not have it on there as you have nick on there."[125] Parents want access to preferred content to manage their children's behavior. These devices are particularly useful during times of stress. Tiffany_Ivanov describes the importance of her mobile viewing app during military redeployment: "I will not have household goods until Army only knows when, and I highly doubt with inprocessing, and keeping a cranky 2 year old from flipping out and screaming for the next few weeks because she can't find her favorite toy, blanket, cup, etc, that I will find even a spare moment to sit at yet another computer, for another 6 (50) minutes waiting to 'chat' with an expert. Could you please square me away or tell me to buy the Blu-Ray of whatever movies I just can't live without?"[126] Mobile devices provide access to platform mobility that can be useful to parents, especially during transitional moments (such as moving or vacation) and in the daily activity of raising children. Alexandra Samuel has argued that screen time is a feminist issue, stating that mobile devices are crucial tools for parenting that are vital to mothers who want to give themselves a break.[127] As with the case of competition over the living room screen, mobile device use in the house is connected to issues of gender and the ability to carve out some time to reenergize.

Remote Control

In addition to carving out personal time and screen time in the busy workday, the procrastination economy of the "connected" living room can create a vicarious living room for families that are not occupying the same space or even the same zip code. Some families engage in password sharing for streaming services as a way to provide similar television options for all members of the family, even ones who do not live under the same roof. This practice is well documented and is even acceptable to some media companies.[128] While the decision to share passwords is partially financial in nature, it also presents an opportunity to foster conversation between family members around a virtually shared television experience. Morley's investigations of family viewing dynamics support this idea; he describes television "as a common experiential ground for conversation. In this kind of instance, television is being used for something, which is more than entertainment. It is being used as a focus, as a method for engaging in social interaction with others."[129] Parents providing children with access to mobile apps may help maintain familial lines of communication. This motivation is clear from Bella1213's comments on the Xfinity forum when she writes, "My son and daughter are away at college and I want them to be able to access Showtime and HBO on their computers. We subscribe to both. How do I set that up for them?"[130] Tryon's analysis of the authentication software for UltraViolet rightly points out that the rhetoric of familial closeness is employed to foster digital rights management (DRM) restrictions, but these restrictions do not negate families' desires to share account access for reasons of unity and conversation.[131]

Across each of these examples, mobile devices and apps are consistently used as tools for negotiating family dynamics in particular spatial situations. Within many households, platform mobility enables access to and control over television content that was previously unavailable. The examples from the user comment forums show that these apps are particularly useful in navigating gendered power issues, managing children's behavior, and fostering conversation across long distances. Markus Stauff, building on the work of Matthias Thielle, claims, "The couch figures as a joint between community and society, between intimate contact with friends and family, as well as the possible encounter and conversation with a stranger."[132] Mobile devices and streaming-media apps extend the political implications of the living room couch. The utility of mobile devices is borne out in the very body postures that mobile devices have fostered. According to Stauff, using a mobile device in the living room "combin[es] watching and communication, seeing and touching, leaning back and leaning forward."[133] Each tap on a mobile device communicates a relationship to the rest of the family. The ways mobile apps are integrated into the living room amplifies tactics and habits that family members have used since television first arrived in the 1950s. Only by considering the reports from mobile device users can we see how this technology relates to spatial politics and the procrastination economy. From the findings available on the comment boards of cable and satellite companies, it is clear that mobile devices have provided new abilities for socializing and multitasking with family.

Conclusion: Mobile Devices versus Smart TVs

The procrastination economy of the living room is different for those who experience it through mobile devices as opposed to other interactive technologies. For example, smart televisions promise to enhance the living room and capture the audience's wandering attention through the capabilities of digital technology, but the appeal to the audience is entirely different. Unlike mobile device apps, these smart technologies tend to replicate the gendered, patriarchal dynamics of traditional television viewing observed by Morley. James Bennett has examined the interactive satellite channels SkyActive, SkyGamestar, and SkyVegas and discovered a striking carryover of the pre-digital-television era's gendered assumptions.[134] Similarly, Daniel Chamberlain believes that the interfaces for smart televisions obscure differences in technology and unify the experience of interactive television as a "bland corporate space" organized by the programming, viewing rhythms, and data-collection exchanges of large media conglomerates.[135] Smart television interfaces offer personalization in the form of "wishlists, queues, playlists, top rated" in exchange for data that help content companies see into the living room in ways that previous audience research has lacked.[136] Smart technologies are dedicated to giving the person with the remote control increased dominion over living room viewing while simultaneously determining the household's value to the marketplace.

Consider, for example, the Comcast X1 box, which offers smart capabilities that enable a user to look up an actor's biography while watching a show. The box also enables the person controlling the television to split the screen in order to simultaneously watch a program and view sports scores. These enhanced functions are designed to replace the viewer's reliance on a mobile device and to keep the viewer's attention focused on the living room television. Comcast advertises these services as being "smarter, richer and more personalized."[137] This personalization may be useful to whoever uses the remote control but at the expense of the other family members in the room, who are subjected to the screen manipulations and multitasking of the person pressing the buttons. Whoever controls the remote shapes the viewing experience: that person's whims determine the textual information displayed. Karen Orr Vered argues that the increased integration of interactive components on television screens means that the viewer becomes a part of the "supertext" of meaning making along with the programming lineup, the advertisements, the interstitials, and other textual content.[138] In effect, smart television interfaces suture the meaning-making process of the person using the remote into the viewing experience. Watching television on a smart TV is like watching through the mind of the person with the remote.

While mobile devices are seen to be technologies that individualize and personalize the viewing experience, it is clear from the evidence just presented that they offer opportunities for sharing communal space and providing agency in viewing decisions. Smart televisions, on the other hand, reinforce the tastes of the person with the remote control by taking the attention-harnessing techniques of second-screen apps and installing them on the living room television. Both mobile devices and smart television technology disrupt the flow that characterized the communal experience of watching television, but smart television technology reinforces the interpretive experience of the person with the remote control. Smart television interfaces change television viewing into a mixed-media experience that complicates the communal nature of watching television.

As much as smart televisions focus on the experience of a single viewer, mobile apps provide tools for undermining the programming decisions of the person with the remote control. Often the same passwords that provide distant family members with access to television on their mobile devices also grant users the ability to control the living room television. Some users capitalize on this capability to assist less technologically savvy friends and family members. Cable and satellite company comment forums include comments such as those from Wildrisc, who wrote about his desire to remotely "setup recordings" of baseball and PBS programming for his in-laws.[139] Mobile devices also enable more mischievous family members to play pranks on their loved ones, as in the case of Ckpeck, who enjoyed the "snide power of changing [her] husband's TV to Teletubbies."[140] JPL also got in on the fun, explaining, "you can mess with your kids' heads with [the mobile app]. I started changing the channels on them when they were watching TV in another room. It took a lot of restraint to wait for the 'Dad! There's something wrong with the TV!'"[141] These pranks, while not the mobile app's primary use, demonstrate how the living room is now accessible by the networked technologies of the outside world. People can set up their DVR, change the channel, discuss a favorite show with an online community, or access recordings through their mobile device. They can effectively access their living room, and the living rooms of others, from anywhere in the world. While this can foster a sense of individualism, as Tryon has argued, it also offers tactics for navigating spatial politics, as has been demonstrated throughout this book.

The living room procrastination economy is dedicated to monetizing the in-between moments that our televisions fail to capture. Twitter has built its business by capitalizing on these moments through the promotion of live television events and enthusiastic television conversation. While mobile devices in the living room invite this second-screen experience, the technology also offers new tools for navigating family dynamics. Mobile devices and streaming-video apps enable previously marginalized members of the family to take more control of their leisure time, while allowing them to coexist in the shared space of the living room. Although mobile devices are factored into strategies that support traditional viewing, they still offer forms of engagement that amplify existing practices and bring into the mainstream audience practices that were previously ignored by television producers and consumer product designers.

Conclusion

The Procrastination Economy in the Era of Ubiquitous Computing and the Internet of Things

Across the procrastination economy, media companies create content and services for a mobile day part made up of people's in-between moments. Assumptions about mobile device use provide a template for companies attempting to monetize the habits of valuable audience demographics. Attempts to woo these demographics affect the products and services produced for all mobile devices. The examples throughout this book demonstrate the habits that the procrastination economy attempts to foster and monetize. In the workplace, the procrastination economy offers media snacks for hardworking cubicle dwellers who want to check in on their favorite media franchises in anticipation of upcoming games, episodes, or film premieres. On the commute, subscription services help mobile users create a media bubble for relaxing on the way to and from work. In waiting rooms, casual games attempt to capitalize on impatience as people look to their devices to extract value and document achievements during their downtime. In the living room, second-screen apps and Twitter Amplify attempt to anticipate the needs of television viewers by making mobile devices companions for television viewing. In each of these examples, economic models including promotional flow, subscription services, micropayments, and advertising define the mobile day part. While the procrastination economy does not account for all mobile device habits, services, or functionality, its logics are pervasive, as they provide media companies with strategies for understanding and monetizing context-specific mobile device usage.

The lessons of the procrastination economy, particularly the habits and audiences that are privileged, are relevant not only to the development of mobile media but to future efforts to integrate digital technology into everyday life. To conclude this book, I argue that the lessons of the procrastination economy are applicable to the era of ubiquitous computing and the Internet of Things. As these technologies promise to bring digital efficiency and increase the productivity of daily life, it is crucial to remember the procrastination economy as a defining logic that will most likely inform the design of future site-specific media technology. The application of the procrastination economy to the technology of the Internet of Things is different from the way it is experienced on mobile devices. The Internet of Things boasts an automated and interconnected digital ecosystem in which technology will anticipate human needs. The procrastination economy that has developed around mobile devices shows how user data and business practices shape understandings of human needs. As the procrastination economy is deployed across the Internet of Things, particular contexts will be shaped by algorithms that foster certain behaviors and media usage. Looking at early examples of the Internet of Things, it is clear that the logics of the procrastination economy have made their way into appliances, locative media, and augmented reality technology. Each of these technologies makes assumptions about how people use their in-between moments in particular contexts. Examples throughout this book demonstrate that the assumptions contained within the procrastination economy often ignore particular consumers or activities that do not align with the entertainment experiences offered on mobile devices. The designers of the next age of public computing would benefit from a broader consideration of the cultural and social dimensions of public space.

The Internet of Things

The Internet of Things promises to expand the logic of the procrastination economy by bringing digital technology to every public space. The logic that defines digital media use in the workplace, commute, waiting room, and living room will soon apply to other contexts as the Internet of Things promises (or threatens) a future in which our every move and every object is cataloged and used to predict desires and actions. This technology will be continuously location and context aware and seamlessly integrated with human action to create "ambient intelligence."[1] Much as the procrastination economy for mobile devices champions leisure activities for users' in-between moments, the rhetoric for the Internet of Things promises to empower people, increase safety, and maximize productivity. While these promises are lofty, Rob Kitchin and Martin Dodge note that this future is stalled because "in its contemporary deployment is highly partial in nature, uneven, and unequal in distribution, density, penetration, sophistication, and form."[2] The process of integrating all digital technology is a daunting task that is more likely to be achieved by individual companies, such as a digital ecosystem that aligns all Samsung or Google products. While the rhetoric suggests a future in which all digital technology is seamlessly integrated and informing our experience of public space, it is more likely that there will be as vastly different experience of the Internet of Things as there is of the Internet.[3]

Integrating a variety of Internet-connected technology will provide these companies with larger sets of data than is currently accessible. More data, however, may mean more complication, as the statistician Nate Silver warns that Big Data suffers from a problem of "overfitting," in which data is used to justify interpretations that are not reflected in the raw numbers.[4] Big Data is alluring because it offers a statistical glimpse into everyday habits that were previously too numerous to quantify. While the wealth of data generated by the connected world is staggering and potentially useful, considering context and history is essential to gaining a more nuanced understanding of human behavior.

This book is partially an attempt to address the problem of overfitting by focusing on specific contexts of mobile device use and understanding them through the lens of cultural studies. This approach involves investigating audiences' uses of popular culture as reactions to their surroundings. The algorithms and designs of the technologies of the future must account for established behaviors and social habits. It is likely that only some behaviors will be included, as companies cater to the habits of those that best fit their products. Just as in the procrastination economy, the coding of human actions has a tremendous impact on our understanding of human behavior. As Kitchin and Dodge put it, "In designing and writing software, developers make, on the one hand, critical, ontological decisions about what to capture, categorize, and represent in the world."[5] The strategies of the procrastination economy are likely to be present in the design of technology for the Internet of Things because the products and services for mobile devices are already connecting algorithms with specific locations. The logic that fostered media snacking, subscriptions, micropayments, and companion apps came from the same considerations that programmers face as they design the next generation of digital technology. Considering three examples of proto–Internet of Things technologies, Samsung's Family Hub refrigerator (part of its Smart Hub line), Snapchat's "lenses" and "filters" functionality, and the augmented reality game Pokémon Go, shows how these efforts to employ ubiquitous computing relate to assumptions about the ways people want to use digital technology to change their surroundings.

Smart Appliances and the Internet of Things

In 2016, Samsung made an early effort to define the Internet of Things by launching a line of Internet-connected appliances targeted at affluent customers with busy lives. For those who cannot afford the smart appliances, the commercials act as an endorsement of Samsung as an aspirational brand capable of presenting a vision of the future in which technology makes life easier. Crucial to this appeal is the suggestion that smart appliances are the key to domestic harmony. These technologies make it possible for people to use their in-between moments to complete small tasks that free up leisure time and help complete everything on the to-do list. The Smart Hub advertises itself as a technology of efficiency, but it is also connected to the same politics of the domestic sphere that typifies the procrastination economy of the living room.

Like advertisements for the technology of the connected living room, the commercial for Samsung's smart refrigerator, the Family Hub, connects domestic tranquility with particular spaces in the home, in this instance the kitchen.[6] Starring the real-life celebrity couple Kristen Bell and Dax Shepard, the advertisement depicts the ways the Family Hub assists in the preparation for their daughter's birthday party. In marketing materials, Samsung refers to Shepard and Bell as "the ultimate multi-tasking couple," and the commercial features examples of the refrigerator assisting them as they juggle responsibilities.[7] Shepard uses his phone to access the refrigerator's internal camera to peer inside to see if he needs to pick up eggs while he is at the store. Next, the couple uses the refrigerator's touchscreen to order more "squeezy yogurts" and have them delivered. Shepard uses his phone to leave a romantic message, like a sticky note, on the refrigerator's tablet screen for Bell. With his message delivered, Shepard uses the refrigerator to access a streaming-music service so they can share a dessert and listen to music at the conclusion of a busy party. The commercial ends with the tagline, "the home has a new hub."

The scenario described in this commercial situates the Samsung refrigerator as an essential component of completing daily tasks. The refrigerator's functionality means that it can be functional as an impromptu grocery list and entertainment console. The appliance makes grocery shopping easier by creating a way to purchase things the moment you think of them and to check the refrigerator to make sure not to buy something you already have. Much like the procrastination economy on mobile devices, the functionality is designed to assist people in their in-between moments. In this instance, it puts into action thoughts that a person has throughout the day. Now when someone thinks, "I need to pick up milk," he or she can use the Internet of Things to complete that task instantly. Whereas the mobile screen is used as a source of leisure and control over surroundings, the procrastination economy of the Internet of Things is dedicated to efficiency and productivity.

The presence of the procrastination economy on smart devices has implications for the functionality of the Internet of Things. It shows that disruptions and creativity need to be figured into the era of the Internet of Things. The overriding belief in efficiency and productivity makes sense if one assumes that people are always looking to streamline their activities. This philosophy is shared by many smart appliances designed to anticipate human needs and make home life more efficient. Lynn Spigel notes that there is a long history of technologies designed for domestic efficiency paving the way for these smart technologies.[8] Television screens are a part of this history, and the Smart Hub combines the promise of mobile privatization and efficient housework. One of the concerns about these technologies is that they can be too efficient to the point of constraining and surveillance. The automation of the Internet of Things could make people overly reliant on companies that make this interconnected technology possible.[9] Certainly, Samsung's suite of smart technologies is designed to integrate with its mobile devices, thus making a closed system in which consumers are reliant on Samsung to organize their everyday routines. If something was to go wrong, such as when Samsung did a product recall on its phones, this could disrupt the operation of the household.[10]

The amplification of automation, prediction, and recommendations that the Internet of Things promises would further solidify the logic of the procrastination economy. In the case of Samsung, this would mean making all in-between moments opportunities for planning and being productive. Evidence throughout the preceding chapters shows that people often reject the suggestions of the procrastination economy. People use their mobile devices in unique ways that go beyond the commercial opportunities provided to them. The technology of the Internet of Things promises automation that would further emphasize assumed activities for killing time. Yet central to this "smart" appliance is the integration of the mobile phone as the controller of the Internet of Things experience. In public-relations materials that accompanied the launch of the Smart Hub, Samsung explains how the use of the smartphone will control what is posted on the refrigerator screen.[11] While it is easy to predict that the smartphone will be the recipient of notifications reminding users to be productive with their downtime, the evidence throughout this book shows that people use their mobile devices in unexpected ways. If Samsung is any indication, mobile devices will be the key entry point to interacting with the Internet of Things.

Snapchat and Locative Media

Mobile devices are also central to locative media technologies that will inform the Internet of Things of a person's changing spatial context. Mobile applications such as Snapchat use locative services to enable particular features such as "filters" and "lenses" that are associated with physical spaces. As discussed previously in the book, mobile users turn to social media platforms, such as Snapchat, in the in-between moments of the day. As the Internet of Things promises to surround people in a constantly updating digital relationship with "smart" objects in their environment, locative media technology will be central to this operation.

Locative media technology is not typically considered a part of the procrastination economy, as it has a strong association with navigation. People rely on location services when they are consulting a mobile map or traffic apps. Consulting these services can change people's understanding of their surroundings and their interactions with particular people. Mobile apps such as Four-square and Yelp rely on geographic and demographic information to provide recommendations for how a person should navigate a location and find a favorable destination such as a coffee shop or a restaurant. A study of the algorithm logic that organizes this navigation shows that geographical and demographic information are mapped together to create a depiction of a place through an understanding of the user's taste.[12] These recommendations may save time, but they also present a map of the city that changes depending on the person using the app. In the name of efficiency, locative media services construct an idea of space on the basis of the demographic profile of the user. The algorithm has a "diversity-accuracy dilemma," in which the more accurate the system predicts a person's taste, the less diverse options he or she is given next time.[13] These services can cause recommendation homogeneity, effectively reducing the options within a location to the most likely to satisfy but also least likely to surprise.

Many navigation apps operate under the assumption that people are in a hurry and trying to make a quick decision that will get them directly to their destination. This is a fair assumption when people use navigation software, but as location services expand to incorporate other activities in public space, networked information could benefit from data that recognize that different social situations, moods, temperaments, and spatial circumstances relate to different preferences. Snapchat, like other social media services, uses geotagging when people post to the platform. Accounting for mood and social activity in a post, particularly posts done spontaneously in the in-between moments of the procrastination economy, could provide location services with a better understanding of the nuances of the ways we travel through the world. Indeed, many navigation apps encourage social media integration to provide demographic information in their algorithms.

Of course, sharing social media data between corporations raises questions about privacy and the ability to interpret the data. Even the design of the social media applications influences how people's activities are contextualized. For example, the social media app Snapchat offers popular features called "lenses" and "filters" that utilize location services. Lenses augment pictures according to various themes. The Dog Lens is a popular version of the feature, as it superimposes animated dog ears, nose, and tongue over the image of a person's face. Special lenses and filters are only accessible in particular locations. People and companies can pay to create and host a filter at a certain location for a certain amount of time. Populated locations, such as football stadiums, are more expensive ($12,000 for three hours) than are less populated locations, such as a residence ($20 for three hours). People and companies that can afford the prices can literally frame how people present themselves in public space. Following the logic of the Internet of Things, these photographs could be used to make determinations about mood and social situation that would influence the way other technologies would react to the person.

For example, consider how media companies are currently using Snapchat as a model for the Internet of Things. Media companies purchase time on Snapchat and brand particular spaces or events with filters and lenses that people use to document their downtime. This relationship brings branding and advertising into the social media experience in ways similar to Twitter Amplify's efforts in the living room. Snapchat and Viacom agreed to a multiyear partnership after a Snapchat filter became a success during the 2015 MTV Video Music Awards.[14] The filter framed photos of the audience and home viewers to create branded selfies that captured people's reactions to the show. The lens feature is even more intriguing, as it changes the image of the person's face through either a caricature or brand integration. According to Snapchat, the lens feature is used over 30 million times a day. 20th Century Fox was the first company to completely take over the lens feature in promotions for the film *X-Men Apocalypse*, replacing the usual lenses with nine different characters.[15] The branding attempt followed the success of Taco Bell and Gatorade, which received hundreds of millions of photos and hours of brand engagement.[16] These experiences are the kind of affective economics that Mark Andrejevic warns about, as they essentially place a person and his or her social network within the message of an advertisement.[17] In the future of the Internet of Things, these apps would not only integrate brands into identity but then also shape the way other connected technologies would react.

The procrastination economy thrives at the intersection of branding, public space, and digital technology. As our digital lives become entwined with our real lives, there will be material consequences in the ways we move through locations. The actions we take in our in-between moments will contribute to our personal presentation. J. Sage Elwell calls the blending of the digital with the real life the "transmediated self," in which our online activity will have everyday consequences as networked technologies read our posts and adjust themselves to their perception of our moods and desires.[18] Once again, the mobile device is a key component of this proto-version of the Internet of Things. The smartphone that hosts Snapchat provides the hardware that reveals the locative technology that is operating in relation to the individual user. Mobile devices are also the places where people will make decisions about how to interact with their digital surroundings. Lessons from the procrastination economy suggest that their reactions may not reflect the desired brand integration that the Internet of Things encourages. While the Internet of Things will predict how people will want to spend their in-between moments in different locations, people will still have control through their individual smartphones.

Pokémon Go and Augmented Reality

Locative media services such as Snapchat are not the only technologies that offer digital enhancements for physical spaces. Augmented reality products create virtual worlds atop real space. Sometimes this technology is restricted to particular theaters, as with virtual reality goggles and controls, but increasingly augmented reality displays are becoming portable via mobile devices and wearable technology. People often use augmented reality technology to enhance a tour or play a game. As this technology becomes a feature of the Internet of Things, the procrastination economy will inform the design of augmented reality. People can turn to augmented reality in the in-between moments to imagine their surroundings in a different way.

The best example of the procrastination economy's relevance to emerging augmented reality technology is the most popular mobile app of 2016, Pokémon Go. Created by the Nintendo subsidiary Ninantic, Pokémon Go transforms real-world space into an environment crawling with fantastic creatures known as Pokémon. These creatures are products of a popular media franchise that began in the 1990s. The game allowed fans of the franchise to virtually inhabit the storyworld by collecting and battling Pokémon. In order to find these creatures, the game player had to walk in the real world until one came upon their path. The requirement that players go out in the world set this game apart from other popular mobile games. Coverage of the game discussed the ways it helped people incorporate exercise into their gameplay.[19] Indeed, Nintendo advertisements and promotions for the game emphasized the activity required to play the game, with the slogan "Get Up, Get Out, and Explore."[20] Initial reports of these explorations focused on the sensational, with stories of gamers finding dead bodies, getting robbed, invading private residences and sacred sites, and getting in turf wars over political differences.[21] The game became a phenomenon but began to lose players as the novelty wore off.[22] The players who remained were those who incorporated gameplay into their daily routines.

The advertisements for the game make Nintendo's focus on the procrastination economy clear. The commercial called "Get

Up and Go" depicts a player using the app while exercising and commuting.[23] Interviews with players who continued to use the game months after the others quit discuss the ways they integrate gameplay into their routines.[24] Kris Siddiqi is one of those still playing months after the launch. He explained that he opens the app "on bike rides to and from work."[25] While many set aside time for playing the game and build their day around it, the longevity of games such as this one will be how they fit within our in-between times such as the commute. The procrastination economy of augmented reality technology suggests that people should use their in-between moments to change their perspective, particularly as they go through their daily routines. People choose to reach for their phones to enhance these in-between moments, and augmented reality technology provides a way of reimagining the space where one is killing time. Unlike other examples of the Internet of Things that work on prediction and recommendations, augmented reality is the closest to the forms of user-controlled procrastination that allow digital device users to change their spatial circumstances.

Final Thoughts: The Future of Entertainment

Smart appliances, locative media, and augmented reality technologies provide glimpses of the future of the Internet of Things. From these examples, it is clear that the procrastination economy will be a part of the future of Internet-connected technology. Indeed, the business models and the way they frame the mobile audience are attractive schemas for media and technology companies designing products and services for our everyday lives. Most of this technology assumes that people want to increase their efficiency and productivity. The examples throughout this book point out that people want much more from their in-between moments than an additional opportunity to do some work.

No matter what users are looking to do with their in-between moments, it is clear from these early examples of the Internet of

Things that mobile devices will become even more crucial to how people interact with their surroundings. Mobile devices will be the personal remote control for the Internet of Things. People's ability to manage notifications, recommendations, and automation through their mobile devices will be integral to their experience of the procrastination economy. Nintendo, Snapchat, and Samsung recognize that the Internet of Things will shape the future of consumer behavior. Each of these companies is applying the logics of the procrastination economy to their products. They are also looking to advertisers, brand managers, subscription services, and micropayments to capitalize on the ways they integrate digital technology with people's routines. The ability that people have to manage their in-between moments depends on the level of control they have through their mobile devices. Henry Jenkins cites the mobile device as "central" to "the process of media convergence."[26] This argument is doubly true, as the Internet of Things promises to bring media companies into all aspects of our daily lives.

The rise of these technologies mirrors a shift in the entertainment industries away from singular products to the maintenance of ongoing media brands. Part of this brand maintenance will be done in the procrastination economy, as transmedia storytelling, character licensing, and interactive play will appear on smart devices. Entertainment companies have been moving toward media brand strategies since the 1980s.[27] In the book *Empires of Entertainment*, the media historian Jennifer Holt provides context for this strategy, chronicling the ways in which media industry deregulation paved the way for consolidation and created the need for popular franchises.[28] Following this consolidation phase, growing media companies embraced marketing-driven media content to minimize risk and maximize audience appeal.[29] These strategies became increasingly popular as media companies developed a global footprint.[30] Targeting a global audience meant adopting a strategy that Paul Grainge calls "total entertainment," in which media franchises are constantly circulated across media platforms.[31]

The procrastination economy is a key site for the circulation of brands. Media companies fill our in-between moments with leisure options in the hopes of establishing an affective relationship with the audience. Scholars such as Axel Bruns and Henry Jenkins have demonstrated that the feedback loop between producers and consumers provides more opportunities for participation and intervention.[32] In addition, Joe Turow, Amanda Lotz, and Chuck Tryon have shown that digital technologies have changed the way media companies measure their audience and distribute content.[33] These changes have led to more personalized and nichified cultural production and distribution, a trend that is sure to continue as the Internet of Things adopts the logic of the procrastination economy and personalizes our downtime with the "appropriate" brand for a corresponding spatial context.

The procrastination economy is clearly apart of convergence culture, as it establishes a relationship between the daily lives of the audience and the development of media brands. While mobile devices have become essential to the entertainment industries as vehicles of promotion, branding, distribution, and engagement, audiences use smartphones, tablets, laptops, and wearable technology to wield the culture and conversation of the procrastination economy as a tool for navigating public space. As new immersive technologies embrace the procrastination economy, it is highly likely that media brands will become a part of smart appliances, locative media, and augmented reality offerings. Media brands have appeared on clothing, lunch boxes, posters, and toys for decades. Mobile devices have changed the way we use these media brands in our everyday routines in two significant ways. They provide versatility in how we incorporate media brands, and they act as a conduit to media producers that can shape the future of the brand on the basis of the habits and routines of our everyday lives.

The centrality of mobile devices as the conduit to media producers and the Internet of Things requires functionality and regulation that will empower users. Smartphones include functionality that enables users to control the notifications and surveillance that goes on without their active engagement. People have different levels of familiarity and ability to use these functionalities, but mobile device literacy will be essential to those who want to manage the procrastination economy. Privacy legislation such as the FCC's 2016 decision to stop broadband companies from collecting and selling data on the habits of mobile users will also be crucial to people's abilities to use their phone to control their surroundings.[34] Efforts to connect the procrastination economy and transmedia branding strategies will only increase as computer technology is woven into all aspects of daily life. The mobile phone is the place where people will encounter this digital marketing strategy. People are going to need all the tools and protections they can get.

ACKNOWLEDGMENTS

I have been preoccupied with the subject of this book ever since my wife insisted that I get an iPhone in the spring of 2011. Neither of us anticipated how many conversations we would have about mobile devices or how many of our friends and colleagues I would rely on to broaden my understanding of this technology. I am particularly grateful to the mentors Jennifer Holt, Constance Penley, Anna Everett, and Henry Jenkins who helped me develop the initial arguments for this book. I would also like to acknowledge the staff and faculty of the Carsey-Wolf Center: Media Industries Project, including Michael Curtin, Joshua Green, Kevin Sanson, Ron Rice, LeeAnne French, and Elissa Nelson, who helped me get access to the media industry professionals and their workplaces. I owe the research team of the Connected Viewing Project, including Sharon Strover, Matthew Thomas Payne, Paul McDonald, Patrick Vonderau, Amanda Lotz, Aynne Kokas, Chuck Tryon, and Max Dawson, thanks for the many discussions about digital distribution and mobile devices that we had during that research project. During those initial months of research, I relied on the suggestions and creativity of my fellow graduate students, including my dear friends Meredith Bak, Ryan Bowles, Dan Reynolds, Nicole Starosielski, Jeff Schieble, Joshua Neves, Jade DaVon, Maria Corrigan, Regina Longo, Rahul Mukherjee, John Vanderhoef, Lindsay Palmer, and David Gray.

I would also like to thank the many media professionals who patiently and graciously granted interviews and visits to their workplaces, particularly Keith Allen and Alison Hashimoto of CNN, Judy Hoang and David Hill of Fox Sports, Gary Newman of

20th Century Fox, Josh Koppel of Scrollmotion, Rocio Guerrero of Spotify, and Andrew Seroff of Viggle. I also had tremendous help recruiting participants for my surveys thanks to the help of Abbie Hamilton at Outfront Media. I also thank the staff and leadership of Ameravant, Latitude 34, and the other workplaces that permitted me to observe their workplace culture and the mobile media habits of the employees. Thank you to all of the employees who agreed to conversations following their long workday.

The ideas in this book were profoundly influenced by the enjoyable conversations at conferences with Elizabeth Evans, Jennifer Gillan, Derek Kompare, Jason Mittell, Ethan Thompson, Derek Johnson, Myles McNutt, John T. Caldwell, Denise Mann, Jonathan Cohn, Alex Kupfer, Dawn Fratini, Drew Morton, Jen Moorman, Harrison Gish, Jaimie Baron, Jason Gendler, Jennifer Porst, Vicky Johnson, Beretta Smith-Shomade, Erin Copple Smith, Alfred Martin, Kristen Warner, Julia Leyda, and Chris Becker. A special thank-you to Aymar Jean Christian, Courtney Brannon Donoghue, and Elizabeth Ellcessor for the encouragement and advice on this book and beyond. Thank you to my colleagues at Georgia State University for the support both intellectually and administratively, including Greg Smith, Alessandra Raengo, Ted Friedman, David Cheshier, Jennifer Barker, Sharon Shahaf, Amelia Arsenault, Shawn Powers, Philip Lewis, Greg Lisby, Mary Stucky, Angelo Restivo, Sheldon Schiffer, and Holley Wilkin. Alisa Perren and Kathy Fuller-Seely were also tremendously helpful in the early stages of this book and continued to be supportive and helpful even when they were no longer down the hall from me.

A special thank-you to Nedda Ahmed, Derek Kompare, Amanda Lotz, Eric Zinner, and Lisha Nadkarni for their help transforming this book from a rough draft to completion. Also essential to the completion of this book are the many excellent graduate students I have worked with, including Hemrani Vyas, Caren Pagel, Andy Kemp, Christopher Cox, Erik Clabaugh, Kyle Wrather, Lauren Cramer, Liza Cabral, Brooke Sonenreich, Matt

Boyd-Smith, Neal Hinnant, Tanya Zuk, Sara Stafford, Jayson Quearry, John Roberts, and Alec Latimer.

Thank you to Jeremy Nguyen, Glenn Musa, Phil Befus, Mihai Samartinean, Kyle Marquez, Chris Valenzuela, Nick Valenzuela, Aaron Lassner, Phil Izdebski, Brian Gernak, Justin Kaufman, and Jeff Kissinger for the many text message conversations that informed my thinking on this topic. Thank you to my family, Tod Tussey, Christina Tussey, Elyse Tussey, Tyler Tussey, Emily Tussey, Christine Tussey, Christianna Jarvis, and Sam Jarvis, for the support and encouragement. Finally, thank you to Becky for initiating this research and for being beside me every step of the way.

NOTES

INTRODUCTION

1 Jones, "Music in Factories," 727.

2 Ibid., quoting S. Wyatt, and J. N. Langdon, *Fatigue and Boredom in Repetitive Work*, Medical Research Council, Industrial Health Research Board, Report 77 (London: Medical Research Council, 1937).

3 Jones, "Music in Factories," 731.

4 Harold C. Schonberg, "The Sound of Sounds That Is New York," *New York Times*, May 23, 1965.

5 Cotton Delo, "U.S. Adults Now Spending More Time on Digital Devices than Watching TV," *Advertising Age*, August 1, 2013.

6 Maeve Duggan, "Cell Phone Activities 2013," Pew Research Center: Internet & Technology, September 19, 2013.

7 For examples of moral panics over mobile devices, see Kevin McSpadden, "You Now Have a Shorter Attention Span than a Goldfish," *Time*, May 14, 2015; Stephen Marche, "Is Facebook Making Us Lonely?," *Atlantic*, May 2012; Joanna Walters, "Tablets and Smartphones May Affect Social and Emotional Development, Scientists Speculate," *Guardian*, February 2, 2015; Graeme Paton, "Internet and Mobile Phones Are 'Damaging Education,'" *Telegraph*, September 9, 2009; Carolyn Gregoire, "How Technology Is Warping Your Memory," *Huffington Post*, December 11, 2013; Helen Lee, "How Your Cell Phone Hurts Your Relationships," *Scientific American*, September 4, 2012.

8 Couldry and McCarthy, introduction to *MediaSpace*, 2.

9 Aaron Smith, "A 'Week in the Life' Analysis of Smartphone Users," chap. 3 in *U.S. Smartphone Use in 2015*, Pew Research Center: Internet & Technology, April 1, 2015.

10 Michele Himmelberg, "Everybody in the Pool: The NCAA Basketball Pool: Morale Booster or Death of Productivity?," *Orange County Register*, March 25, 1997.

11 Grant Robertson, "A New Temptation for Office Workers, Online TV: March Madness Sets Audience Records," *Globe and Mail*, March 20, 2006.

12 Diego Vasquez, "The Dreadful Price of March Madness: Figure $3.8 Billion in Lost Productivity at Work," *Media Life*, March 16, 2006.

13 Jack Shafer of *Slate* does a good job making this point in his March 2006 article "Productivity Madness: The Press Swallows $3.8 Billion Worth of Junk Economics," *Slate*, March 20, 2006.

14 Ibid.

15 Bull, *Sound Moves*, 22.

16 Jeff Buttle, "Street Shows Turning into a Big Business," *Vancouver Sun*, July 22, 1989.

17 Eileen McNamara, "Waiting Room Awaits Us All," *Denver Post*, May 23, 1996.

18 Patricia Davis, "Master Bathrooms Triple in Size and Function," *Wall Street Journal*, February 15, 1999.

19 Radway, *Reading the Romance*; Jenkins, *Textual Poachers*; Klinger, *Beyond the Multiplex*.

20 Anna McCarthy, "Geekospheres: Visual Culture and Material Culture at Work," *Journal of Visual Culture* 3, no. 2 (2004): 213–221.

21 Marvin, *When Old Technologies Were New*.

22 Ibid., 68.

23 Robert Sklar, *Movie-Made America: A Cultural History of American Movies* (New York: Vintage Books, 1994), 14.

24 Spigel, *Make Room for TV*.

25 Boddy, *New Media and Popular Imagination*.

26 As an example of mobile technologies' current status in the stage of "economic distribution," consider that while advertising revenue online, including on mobile platforms, has increased consistently since 1996, with a spike in the first decade of the 21st century, digital advertising revenue only replicated television advertising revenue in 2016, demonstrating that it has reached a pivotal moment of economic stability. "U.S. Internet Ad Revenues Reach Historic $13.3 Billion in Q1 2015, Representing 16% Increase over Q1 2014 Landmark Numbers, According to IAB Internet Advertising Revenue Report," press release, Internet Advertising Board, June 11, 2015; Ingrid Lunden, "2015 Ad Spend Rises to $187 Billion, Digital Inches Closer to One Third of It," *TechCrunch*, January 20, 2015. George Slefo, "Desktop and Mobile Ad Revenue Surpasses TV for the First Time: Digital Advertising Saw $72.5 Billion Revenue in 2016, a 22% Upswing from the Previous Year," *Advertising Age*, April 26, 2017.

27 Tom Lowry, "As the World Wide Web Turns," *Business Week*, April 2, 2007.

28 Brian Stelter, "Noontime Web Video Revitalizes Lunch at Desk," *New York Times*, January 5, 2008.

29 Nicholas Carlson and Kamelia Angelova, "Chart of the Day: Lunchtime Is the New Primetime," *Business Insider*, October 1, 2009.

30 Carole Angelo, in discussion with author, December 21, 2009.

31 Monica Anderson, "Technology Device Ownership: 2015," Pew Research Center: Internet & Technology, October 29, 2015.

32 Rishika Sadam, "NBC Signs Deal to Create Original Content for Snapchat," Reuters, August 8, 2016.

33 Spigel, *Make Room for TV*; McCarthy, *Ambient Television*.

34 For examples of scholars who examine software studies from its technological perspective, see Manovich, *Language of New Media*; David Trend, ed., *Reading Digital Culture* (Malden, MA: Blackwell, 2001); Marshall McLuhan. "The Medium Is the Message," in *Media and Cultural Studies: Keyworks*, ed. Meenakshi Gigi Durham and Douglas M. Kellner (Malden, MA: Blackwell, 2006), 107–116; David Porter, ed., *Internet Culture* (London: Routledge, 1997); Donna Haraway, "A Cyborg Manifesto: Science, Technology, and Socialist-Feminism in the Late Twentieth Century," in *Simians, Cyborgs and Women: The Reinvention of Nature* (New York: Routledge, 1991), 149–181.

35 Galloway, *Interface Effect*; Manovich, *Language of New Media*.

36 Benkler, *Wealth of Networks*; Pierre Levy, *Collective Intelligence* (New York: HarperCollins, 1997).

37 Bogost, "Procedural Rhetoric," in *Persuasive Games*; Van Dijck, *Culture of Connectivity*.

38 Alisa Perren and Jennifer Holt's anthology *Media Industries Studies* and John T. Caldwell's *Production Culture* present an agenda for combining political economic and cultural studies approaches in understanding the media industries.

39 For examples of descriptions of scholars who describe digital technology as empowering to citizens, consider Nicholas Negroponte, *Being Digital* (New York: Vintage, 1995); Pierre Levy, *Collective Intelligence: Mankind's Emerging World in Cyberspace* (New York: Plenum, 1997); Sherry Turkle, *Life on the Screen: Identity in the Age of the Internet* (New York: Simon and Schuster, 1997); and Benkler, *Wealth of Networks*. For examples of scholars who describe the exploitation of digital consumers, see Castells, *Rise of the Network Society*; Mark Andrejevic, *iSpy: Surveillance and Power in the Interactive Era* (Lawrence: University Press of Kansas, 2007); James Carey, "Historical Pragmatism and the Internet," *New Media and Society* 17, no. 4 (2005): 444.

40 Benkler makes the connection between folk culture and Internet culture by arguing that people have always wanted to collaborate and communicate

but were restrained by cost and access to the distribution infrastructure and the production standards of the entertainment industry. He believes that digital technology has lifted those barriers, providing consumers with increased autonomy and the ability to establish new distribution networks that transcend financial relationships and concentrate on social network relationships. See Benkler, *Wealth of Networks*, 23.

41 Castells, *Rise of the Network Society*, 15–17.

42 For an example of research that applies structuralist economic approaches to new media technology, see Andrew Currah, "Hollywood versus the Internet: The Media and Entertainment Industries in a Digital and Networked Economy," *Journal of Economic Geography* 6 (2006): 439–468; Lessig, *Free Culture*.

43 Two of the best examples of work that combines political economic analysis and cultural studies approaches in the examination of digital media are Henry Jenkins, *Convergence Culture: Where Old Media and New Media Collide* (New York: NYU Press, 2006); and Klinger, *Beyond the Multiplex*.

44 Augé, *Non-places*, 105.

45 Souza e Silva, "From Cyber to Hybrid Mobile Technologies."

46 McKenzie Wark, *Virtual Geography: Living with Global Media Events* (Bloomington: Indiana University Press, 1994), xiv.

47 Bull, *Sound Moves*, 22.

48 McCarthy's sixth chapter in *Ambient Television* is titled "Television While You Wait"; it includes an analysis of the programming for the waiting room created by the CNN Airport network and her site-specific ethnographic observations of the space.

49 Jenkins, *Convergence Culture*, 258.

CHAPTER 1. THE PROCRASTINATION ECONOMY AND THE
MOBILE DAY PART

1 Neetzan Zimmerman, "Louis C.K.'s Explanation of Why He Hates Smartphones Is Sad, Brilliant," *Gawker*, September 20, 2013.

2 Williams, *Television*.

3 Spigel, "Portable TV."

4 Kobayashi and Boase, "Tele-cocooning."

5 Sterne, *Audible Past*.

6 Michael Bull, "No Dead Air! The iPod and the Culture of Mobile Listening," *Leisure Studies* 24, no. 4 (2005): 343–355.

7 Campbell, "Mobile Communication and Network Privatism," 3.

8 Papacharissi, *Private Sphere*.

9   Ibid., 24

10 Campbell, "Mobile Communication and Network Privatism," 7.

11 Ibid., 3.

12 Sydney Shep, "Books in Global Perspective," in *The Cambridge Companion to the History of the Book*, ed. Leslie Howsam (New York: Cambridge University Press, 2015), 55.

13 Ibid.

14 There are multiple accounts of this kind of literary regulation, including Jacqueline Pearson, *Women's Reading in Britain, 1750–1834: A Dangerous Recreation* (New York: Cambridge University Press, 1999); and Belinda Jack, *The Woman Reader* (New Haven, CT: Yale University Press, 2012).

15 Mary Hammond, "Book History in the Reading Experience," in *The Cambridge Companion to the History of the Book*, ed. Leslie Howsam (New York: Cambridge University Press, 2015), 242.

16 Michael Brian Schiffer, *The Portable Radio in American Life* (Tucson: University of Arizona Press, 1991).

17 Ibid., 41.

18 Ibid., 42.

19 Ibid., 66.

20 Ibid., 181.

21 Ibid.

22 Ibid.

23 Ibid.

24 Ibid., 214.

25 Ibid., 223.

26 Murray Schafer, *The Tuning of the World* (New York: Knopf, 1977).

27 Hosokawa, "Walkman Effect."

28 Ibid., 176.

29 Spigel, "Portable TV," 60.

30 Ibid., 80.

31 Ibid.

32 Ibid., 88.

33 Ibid., 71.

34 Goggin, *Cell Phone Culture*, 24.

35 Ibid., 28.

36 H. Lacohée, N. Wakeford, and I. Pearson, "A Social History of the Mobile Telephone with a View of Its Future," *BT Technology Journal* 21, no. 3 (2003): 205.

37 Goggin, *Cell Phone Culture*, 35.

38 Ibid.

39 Du Gay et al., *Doing Cultural Studies*.

40 Ibid., 48.

41 Ibid., 60.

42 Ibid., 62.

43 Tobin, *Portable Play in Everyday Life*. 20. Tobin argues that portable games such as Nintendo's Game & Watch, Game Boy, and later DS should be seen as evolving from earlier toys and novelties such as the Robot Hand and other periscoping technologies that extended the body and reworked perception in humorous ways.

44 Ralph Blumenthal, "Electronic-Games Race," *New York Times*, December 14, 1980.

45 Jason Wilson, "Distractedly Engaged: Mobile Gaming and Convergent Mobile Media," *Convergence* 17, no. 4 (2011): 351–355.

46 Tobin, *Portable Play in Everyday Life*, 21.

47 Ibid.

48 Ibid., 23.

49 Goggin, *Cell Phone Culture*, 32.

50 Ibid., 37.

51 Larissa Hjorth and Ingrid Richardson, "The Waiting Game: Complicating Notions of (Tele)presence and Gendered Distraction in Casual Mobile Gaming," *Australian Journal of Communication* 36, no. 1 (2009): 26.

52 Certeau, *Practice of Everyday Life*, 29.

53 Browne, "Political Economy of the Television (Super) Text."

54 Tania Modleski, "The Search for Tomorrow in Today's Soap Operas: Notes on a Feminine Narrative Form," *Film Quarterly* 33, no. 1 (1979): 12–21.

55 Browne, "The Political Economy of the Television (Super) Text," 71.

56 Other scholars who have described the relationship between television and the structuring of everyday existence include Torunn Selberg, "Use of Television in Everyday Life: Ritualisation of Everyday Culture," *Lore and Language* 16, nos. 1–2 (1998): 104–114; Fiske, *Television Culture*; Modleski, "Rhythms of Reception."

57 See Dawson, "Little Players, Big Shows"; Will Brooker, "Living on Dawson's Creek: Teen Viewers, Cultural Convergence, and Textual Overflow," *International Journal of Cultural Studies* 4 (2001): 456–472; Chuck Tryon, *Reinventing Cinema: Movies in the Era of Convergence* (New Brunswick, NJ: Rutgers University Press, 2009); Evans, *Transmedia Television*; Jennifer Gillan, *Television and New Media: Must-Click TV* (New York: Routledge, 2011); Ross, *Beyond the Box*; Jostein Gripsrud, *Relocating Television: Television in* *the Digital Context* (New York: Routledge, 2010); John T. Caldwell, "Convergence Television: Aggregating Form and Repurposing Content in the Culture of Conglomeration," in *Television after TV: Essays on a Medium in Transition*, ed. Lynn Spigel and Jan Olsson (Durham, NC: Duke University Press, 2004), 41–74; Graeme Turner and Jinna Tay, eds., *Television Studies after TV: Understanding Television in the Post-Broadcast Era* (New York: Routledge, 2009); Paul Grainge, ed., *Ephemeral Media: Transitory Screen Culture from Television to YouTube* (London: BFI, 2011); Caldwell, "Second-Shift Media Aesthetics"; Thompson, *Frodo Franchise*; Michael Curtin, "Matrix Media," in Turner and Tay, *Television Studies after TV*, 9–20; Gray, *Show Sold Separately*.

58 Henry Jenkins, "YouTube, Multichannel Networks and the Accelerated Evolution of the New Screen Ecology," *Confessions of an ACA-Fan*, April 26, 2016, http://henryjenkins.org.

59 Meehan, "Why We Don't Count."

60 Ibid., 127.

61 Ibid.

62 Evans, "Economics of Free Freemium Games."

63 Zittrain, *Future of the Internet*.

64 Chris Anderson and Michal Wolff, "The Web Is Dead. Long Live the Internet," *Wired* 18.09 (August 17, 2010).

65 Apple, "iPhone Premieres This Friday Night at Apple Retail Stores," press release, June 28, 2007.

66 Alice Z. Cuneo, "iPhone: Steve Jobs," *Advertising Age*, November 12, 2007; Beth Snyder Bulik, "iPhone 3G: Phil Schiller," *Advertising Age*, November 17, 2008.

67 Apple, "Elliot," iPhone commercial, 2007.

68 Facebook, "Facebook Launches Additional Privacy Controls for News Feed and Mini-Feed," Facebook Newsroom, September 8, 2006.

69 Jessi Hempel, "Facebook's News Feed Turns 10," *Backchannel*, September 6, 2016.

70 A *Tech Crunch* review prior to the release of the feature described News Feed as "an attention metastream, where page views aren't the currency that matters but rather how effectively the service allows users to communicate." Michael Arrington, "New Facebook Redesign More than Aesthetic," *Tech Crunch*, September 5, 2006.

71 Warren St. John, "When Information Becomes T.M.I.," *New York Times*, September 10, 2006; Nielsen, "Tops of 2015: Digital," Nielsen Newswire: Media and Entertainment, December 17, 2015.

72 Alex Woodson, "Gewecke Goes Digital at WB," *Hollywood Reporter*, December 13, 2007.

73 Georg Szalai, "Time Warner: Flixster Is Key to Cloud-Based Content Plans," *Hollywood Reporter*, May 25, 2011.

74 Tryon, *On-Demand Culture*, 43.

75 Kimberly Nordyke and Carolyn Giardina, "Warner Bros. Adds 'Inception,' 'Harry Potter' Movies to Facebook Rentals," *Hollywood Reporter*, March 28, 2011.

76 Georg Szalai, "Warner Bros. Offers 'Dark Knight,' 'Inception' Downloads via Apple Apps," *Hollywood Reporter*, February 16, 2011.

77 Chris Marlowe, "Warner Rolling with BitTorrent First to Use Open P2P for Output," *Hollywood Reporter*, May 9, 2006.

78 Ben Fritz, "Digital Distribution: All Together Now," *Variety*, April 25, 2006.

79 Tryon, *On-Demand Culture*; Spigel and Dawson, "Television and Digital Media," 281.

80 Spigel and Dawson, "Television and Digital Media," 281.

CHAPTER 2. THE WORKPLACE

1 Laurie Flynn, "Finding On-Line Distractions, Employers Strive to Keep Workers in Line," *New York Times*, November 6, 1995.

2 Examples of books on productivity and strategies for managing your technology include Timothy Ferriss, *The 4-Hour Workweek: Escape 9–5, Live Anywhere, and Join the New Rich* (New York: Crown, 2007); Kory Kogon, Adam Merrill, and Leena Rinne, *The 5 Choices: The Path to Extraordinary Productivity* (New York: Simon and Schuster, 2014); Brian Tracy, *Eat That Frog! 21 Great Ways to Stop Procrastinating and Get More Done in Less Time*, 2nd ed. (Oakland, CA: Berrett-Koehler, 2007).

3 Studies that support his claim include Cecilie Schou Andreassen, Torbjørn Torsheim, and Ståle Pallesen, "Predictors of Use of Social Network Sites at Work: A Specific Type of Cyberloafing," *Journal of Computer-Mediated Communication* 19, no. 4 (2014): 906–921; J. Adams and R. J. Kirkby, "Excessive Exercise as an Addiction: A Review," *Addiction Research & Theory* 10 (2002): 415–437; M. S. Eastin, C. J. Glynn, and R. P. Griths, "Psychology of Communication Technology Use in the Workplace," *Cyberpsychology & Behavior* 10 (2007): 436–443; Don J. Q. Chen and Vivien K. G. Lim, "Impact of Cyberloafing on Psychological Engagement," paper presented at the annual meeting of Academy of Management, San Antonio, TX, August 2011; Vivien K. G. Lim, "The IT Way of Loafing on the Job: Cyberloafing, Neutralizing and Organizational Justice," *Journal of Organizational Behav-*

ior 23 (2002): 675–694; J. A. Oravec, "Constructive Approaches to Internet Recreation in the Workplace," *Communications of the ACM* 45 (2002): 60–63; L. Reinecke, "Games at Work: The Recreational Use of Computer Games during Working Hours," *Cyberpsychology & Behavior* 12 (2009): 461–465; J. M. Stanton, "Company Profile of the Frequent Internet User," *Communications of the ACM* 45 (2002): 55–59.

4 Andreassen, Torsheim, and Pallesen, "Predictors of Use of Social Network Sites at Work," 917.

5 Ibid

6 For further discussion of importance of the workplace in the meaning making process, see Hobson, "Soap Operas at Work"; and Dorothy Hobson, "Women Audiences and the Workplace," in *Television and Women's Culture: The Politics of the Popular*, ed. Mary Ellen Brown (London: Sage, 1990), 61–71.

7 V. K. G. Lim and D. J. O. Chen, "Cyberloafing at the Workplace: Gain or Drain on Work?," *Behaviour & Information Technology*, 2009, 1–11.

8 Andreassen, Torsheim, and Pallesen, "Predictors of Use of Social Network Sites at Work"; J. Vitak, J. Crouse, and R. LaRose, "Personal Internet Use at Work: Understanding Cyberslacking," *Computers in Human Behavior* 27 (2011): 1751–1759; R. K. Garrett and J. N. Danziger, "On Cyberslacking: Workplace Status and Personal Internet Use at Work," *Cyberpsychology & Behavior* 11 (2008): 287–292.

9 Marshall McLuhan, *Understanding Media: Extensions of Man* (Cambridge, MA: MIT Press, 1994), 8.

10 Ibid.

11 L. G. Pee, I. M. Y. Woon, and A. Kankanhalli, "Explaining Non-Work-Related Computing in the Workplace: A Comparison of Alternative Models," *Information & Management* 45 (2008): 120–130; R. K. Garrett and J. N. Danziger, "Disaffection or Expected Outcomes: Understanding Personal Internet Use during Work," *Journal of Computer-Mediated Communication* 13 (2008): 937–958; B. Verplanken and S. Orbell, "Reflections on Past Behavior: A Self-Report Index of Habit Strength," *Journal of Applied Social Psychology* 33 (2003): 1313–1330.

12 B. Liberman, G. Seidman, K. Y. A. McKenna, and L. E. Buffardi, "Employee Job Attitudes and Organizational Characteristics as Predictors of Cyberloafing," *Computers in Human Behavior* 27 (2011): 2192–2199.

13 The company chose to remain anonymous.

14 Marek Kaczynski, "Music at Work: Towards a Historical Overview," *Folk Music Journal* 8 (2003): 314–334.

15 Jones, "Music in Factories."

16 Celine Roque, "Can Listening to Music Boost Your Productivity?," *Gigaom*, July 12, 2010.

17 The referenced Spotify playlists can be located at the following URLs: Sarah-Louise Thexton, "Safe for Work (Pop)," http://open.spotify.com /user/115223202/playlist/4dWou8uj4IYfaaj9wCUnVR; ihascube, "Work Music (Clean)," http://open.spotify.com/user/ihascube/playlist/2JRocnWt cH6gwShnYZZyT4; Lisa Roach, "Work Playlist," http://open.spotify.com /user/1248940056/playlist/5RcBBrwJXrTpnglEB1BMfF.

18 Michael Bull, "'To Each Their Own Bubble': Mobile Spaces of Sound in the City," in *MediaSpace: Place, Scale and Culture in a Media Age*, ed. Nick Couldry and Anna McCarthy (London: Routledge, 2004), 283.

19 Klinger, *Beyond the Multiplex*.

20 Ibid., 139.

21 For more on the importance of identity exploration at work in the "new economy," see Lisa Adkins, "The New Economy, Property, and Person-hood," *Theory, Culture, Society* 22, no. 111 (2005): 111–130.

22 See debates about the relationship between eating lunch at one's desk and national identity from Nathalie Rothschild, "Swedish Lunch Disco," *Slate*, May 1, 2012; Rachael Larimore, "I'd Rather Eat at My Desk," *Slate*, April 24, 2012; and Rachael Levy, "Let's Do Lunch," *Slate*, April 20, 2012.

23 McCarthy, *Ambient Television*, 41.

24 Ibid.

25 Anna-Lisa Linden and Maria Nyberg, "The Workplace Lunch Room: An Arena for Multicultural Eating," *International Journal of Consumer Studies* 33, no. 1 (2009): 42–48.

26 Hobson, "Soap Operas at Work."

27 Morley, *Family Television*.

28 Bryan Long, "'Daily Show' Viewers Ace Political Quiz," *CNN.com*, September 29, 2004.

29 Kenneth Olmstead, Cliff Lampe, and Nicole B. Ellison, "Social Media and the Workplace," Pew Research Center, June 22, 2015.

30 Nielsen, "Web Traffic to U.S. Sports Sites Grew in August," Nielsen News-wire, October 3, 2008.

31 ComScore, "Official FIFA Cup Web Site Attracts Millions of Viewers and Billions of Page Views from Around the World in June," press release, July 13, 2006.

32 Kyle Stock, "Why NBC Doubled Down on the English Premier League's Small Audience," Bloomberg, August 11, 2015.

2009.

PalandPalandd

33 I. Nayeem, A. Rangachari, J. Trent, and R. R. Josyula, "A Flexible Security System for Using Internet Content," *IEEE Software* 14, no. 15 (1997): 52–59.

34 A. Urbaczewski and L. Jessup, "Does Electronic Monitoring of Employee Internet Usage Work? At What Cost?," *Communications of the ACM* 45, no. 1 (2002): 80–83.

35 Yvonne Jewkes, "The Use of Media in Constructing Identities in the Masculine Environment of Men's Prisons," *European Journal of Communication* 17 (2002): 222.

36 Evan M. Berman and Jonathan P. West, "The Effective Manager . . . Takes a Break," *Review of Public Personnel Administration* 27 (2007): 383.

37 Brent Coker, "Freedom to Surf: Workers More Productive If Allowed to Use the Internet for Leisure," *University of Melbourne News*, April 2, 2009.

38 Ibid.

39 Chen and Lim, "Impact of Cyberloafing."

40 Ameravant employee, interview with author, November 8, 2010.

41 Andreassen, Torsheim, and Pallesen, "Predictors of Use of Social Network Sites at Work."

42 For a description of the campaign and the creative process behind it, see "Wonderland Productions Finishes HBO 'Watercooler,'" *Mix*, April 16, 2004, http://mixonline.com. See the video for the campaign here: http://creativity-online.com/work/hbo-watercooler/10764. This campaign is also discussed in Jane Feuer, "HBO and the Concept of Quality TV," in *Quality TV: Contemporary American Television and Beyond*, ed. Janet McCabe and Kim Akass (New York: Palgrave Macmillan, 2007), 154.

43 Ellen Seiter, *Television and New Media Audiences* (Oxford, UK: Clarendon, 1999), 116.

44 Fiske, *Television Culture*.

45 Castells, *Internet Galaxy*, 127.

46 Christian, "Web as Television Reimagined?"

47 Fox Sports Digital, "Fox Sports Creates Digital Programming Unit," press release, September 9, 2009, www.foxsports.com.

48 Mayer, Banks, and Caldwell, *Production Studies*.

49 Paul Willis, *Learning to Labor: How Working Class Kids Become Working Class* (New York: Columbia University Press, 1981).

50 Austin Siegemund-Broka and Paul Bond, "Budget Breakdowns: What a Typical Movie and TV Pilot Really Cost to Make Now (and Why)," *Hollywood Reporter*, October 1, 2015.

51 The sitcom *The Big Bang Theory* was sold in syndication for $1.5 million an episode. For more on the syndication market, see Nikki Finke and Nellie

Andreeva, "Big Syndie Deals: 'Glee' to Oxygen; Modern Family to USA," *Deadline Hollywood Daily*, June 29, 2010.

52 Bruce Owen and Steve Wildman, *Video Economics* (Cambridge, MA: Harvard University Press, 1992), 48.

53 There are some exceptions to the lack of secondary markets for webisodes: *The Office*'s webisodes were compiled into a DVD, and *Dr. Horrible's Sing-Along Blog,* a web series produced by Joss Whedon, became one of the best-selling DVDs of 2008. For more, read Cynthia Littleton and Josef Adalian, "TV Shows Getting Ambitious," *Variety*, September 21, 2007; and Ryan Nakashima, "Hollywood Adds Money, Talent to Made-for-Web Shows," *Boston Globe*, December 21, 2007.

54 John Consoli, "FoxSports.com Tackles TV-Web Integration with Streaming," *Wrap*, May 9, 2010.

55 This strategy is often called "360 marketing" and has been a selling point at the television up-fronts since the middle of the first decade of the 21st century. See Lotz, *Television Will Be Revolutionized*.

56 Jennifer Gillan, *Television Brandcasting: The Return of the Content-Promotion Hybrid* (New York: Routledge, 2014).

57 Interview with author, December 16, 2009.

58 "Center placement" is the coveted location for web publication; it is equivalent to front-page news in the newspaper industry.

59 These statistics were provided to me by the *Lunch with Benefits* producers on the basis of data they received from Omniture and ComScore.

60 Victoria E. Johnson, "Everything New Is Old Again: Sport Television, Innovation, and Tradition for a Multi-platform Era," in *Beyond Prime Time: Television Programming in the Post-network Era*, ed. Amanda D. Lotz (New York: Routledge, 2009), 114–138.

61 Max Dawson and Jennifer Gillan describe the practice of unbundling content for digital platforms in genres other than sports. See Max Dawson, "Little Players, Big Shows: Format, Narration, and Style on Television's New Smaller Screens," *Convergence: The International Journal of Research into New Media Technologies* 13, no. 3 (2007): 231–250; Jennifer Gillan, *Television and New Media: Must-Click TV* (New York: Routledge, 2011).

62 Steven Melnick, in discussion with author, December 7, 2009.

63 The Twitter account is @Broslife.

64 Melnick, in discussion with author.

65 Marisa Guthrie. "'SNL,' Jimmy Fallon, Kimmel Turning Late Night Laughs into Digital Dollars," *Hollywood Reporter*, January 12, 2012.

66 Bill Carter. "How Jimmy Fallon Crushed Stephen Colbert (and Everyone Else in Late Night)," *Hollywood Reporter*. (December 16, 2015).

67 Jeanine Poggi, "Late Night Is Much More than TV," *Advertising Age*, February 17, 2014.

68 Guthrie, "'SNL,' Jimmy Fallon, Kimmel."

69 Michael O'Connell, "Trevor Noah's 'Daily Show' Mandate: Lure Millennials, Digital Heat," *Hollywood Reporter*, August 5, 2015.

70 Caldwell, "Second-Shift Media Aesthetics."

71 Ibid.

72 Elana Levine, "The Changing Fortunes of Daytime Television Soap Opera," in *Beyond Prime Time: Television Programming in the Post-network Era*, ed. Amanda D. Lotz (New York: Routledge, 2009), 36–55.

73 Raymond Williams, "Programming: Distribution and Flow," in *Television*.

74 John Ellis, *Visible Fictions: Cinema, Television, Video* (London: Routledge and Kegan Paul, 1982); Jane Feuer, "The Concept of Live Television: Ontology as Ideology," in *Regarding Television*, ed. E. Ann Kaplan (Los Angeles: American Film Institute, 1983), 12–22.

75 John Caldwell, in *Televisuality: Style, Crisis, and Authority in American Television* (New Brunswick, NJ: Rutgers University Press, 1995), makes the argument that an excess of style became a popular technique for differentiating programs as new technology brought increased competition for viewers.

76 Other scholars who have described the relationship between television and the structuring of everyday existence include Torunn Selberg, "Use of Television in Everyday Life: Ritualisation of Everyday Culture," *Lore and Language* 16, nos. 1–2 (1998): 104–114; Fiske, *Television Culture*; Modleski, "Rhythms of Reception."

77 Judy Boyd, interview with author, December 1, 2009.

78 While I was on set, I interviewed many of the crew members that produced *The College Experiment*. They repeatedly described the show as being the most provocative of the *Lunch with Benefits* lineup and cited problems that their material created for cross promotions and sponsorship.

79 Boyd, interview with author.

80 Producers and writers of *Lunch with Benefits*, interviews with author, December 2, 2009.

81 John Ourand, "Fox Feasting on Early Numbers for 'Lunch,'" *Sports Business Daily*, October 5, 2009.

82 Ibid.
83 Associated Press, "Fox Sports Cancels Show after Video Mocks Asians," Yahoo Sports, September 7, 2011.
84 Mikey O'Connell, "'The College Experiment' Ends at Fox Sports after Mocking Asian Students," *Zap 2 News and Buzz*, September 8, 2011.
85 Ibid.
86 For examples of content that was developed during the strike and received television deals, see Virginia Heffernan, "Serial Killers," *New York Times Magazine*, August 22, 2008; Chris Volgner, "Web Videos Helped Samberg Snag 'Hot Rod,'" *Dallas Morning News*, August 3, 2007.
87 Elizabeth Wagmeister, "HBO Brings Web Series 'High Maintenance' to TV with New Episode," *Variety*, April 20, 2015.
88 Ariana Bacle, "'Broad City' and Other Web Series That Made Surprising Jumps to TV," *Entertainment Weekly*, January 28, 2015.
89 Marx, "Missing Link Moment."
90 For an example of how media conglomerates use one industry to support another, see Christopher Anderson, *Hollywood TV: The Studio System in the 1950s* (Austin: University of Texas Press, 1994).
91 Hill is not the only one to use this metaphor. Throughout my research, industry executives such as Gail Berman, Lloyd Braun, and Steve Lafferty each applied this same metaphor to the emergence of digital media. Hill spoke these words in the PR launch for the series. Fox Sports Digital, "Fox Sports Creates Digital Programming Unit," press release, September 9, 2009, www.foxsports.com.
92 Boyd, interview with author.
93 Richard Sandomir, "Fox's Glazer Straddles Jobs as N.F.L. Reporter and Trainer," *New York Times*, May 27, 2010.
94 News Corporation, "Bill Richards Elevated to Coordinating Producer of 'Fox NFL Sunday' and 'The OT,'" *Business Unit News*, August 11, 2011.
95 Roy Cureton, "Robert Ryang '02's Stanley Cup," *Columbia College Today*, January 2006.
96 Gail Berman, interview by the Media Industries Project staff, Carsey-Wolf Center, University of Santa Barbara, May 21, 2010.
97 Peter Levinsohn, interview by the Media Industries Project staff, Carsey-Wolf Center, University of Santa Barbara, May 21, 2010.
98 Pierre Bourdieu, *Distinction: A Social Critique of the Judgment of Taste* (Cambridge, MA: Harvard University Press, 1984), 5–6.
99 Ibid., 111.

100 Joe Turow, *Niche Envy: Marketing Discrimination in the Digital Age* (Cambridge, MA: MIT Press, 2006).

101 Ibid., 18.

102 For examples of fan studies research, see Will Brooker, *Using the Force* (London: Continuum, 2002); Jenkins, *Textual Poachers*; Constance Penley, *NASA/TREK* (London: Verso, 1997); and Matt Hills, *Fan Cultures* (London: Routledge, 2002).

103 Certeau, *Practice of Everyday Life*, 25.

104 Ibid., 26.

CHAPTER 3. THE COMMUTE

1 M. Sheller, "Automotive Emotions: Feeling the Car," *Theory, Culture and Society* 21, nos. 4–5 (2004): 231.

2 Campbell, "Mobile Communication and Network Privatism," 3.

3 Mimi Sherry and John Urry, "The City and the Cybercar," in *The Cybercities Reader*, ed. Stephen Graham (New York: Routledge, 2004), 170.

4 Peter Walker, "Union Wins Travelling Time Case in European Court," *Guardian*, September 10, 2015.

5 Kenzie Burchell calls this management of communication via networked mobile device "networked time." Kenzie Burchell, "Tasking the Everyday: Where Mobile and Online Communication Take Time," *Mobile Media and Communication* 3, no. 1 (2015): 36–52.

6 Campbell, "Mobile Communication and Network Privatism," 3.

7 Studies of commuter advertising exposure go back at least as far as 1963, as evidenced by the work of ARF director of technical services Ingrid C. Kildegaard, "How We Commute," *Journal of Advertising Research* 5 (1965).

8 Examples of these commercials include the ad "Camp Out" by Google Nexus TV and "Band" by T-Mobile Monthly 4G TV.

9 Chuck Tryon, "Make Any Room Your TV Room: Digital Delivery and Media Mobility," *Screen* 53, no. 3 (2012): 287–300.

10 McCarthy, *Ambient Television*, 11.

11 John T. Caldwell has identified this tactic from the media industries' first efforts to create digital programming. Caldwell, "Second-Shift Media Aesthetics."

12 Bull, *Sound Moves*.

13 Ibid., 9.

14 Tryon, *On-Demand Culture*.

15 Caldwell, *Production Culture*.

16 Patrick Kevin Day, "Netflix Gets into the Awards Game with the Flixies," *Los Angeles Times*, February 28, 2013.

17 The nominees included *Louis C.K. Chewed Up, Dreamworks Shrek's Swamp Stories, Something from Nothing: The Art of Rap, Man vs. Wild, Portlandia, Weird, True & Freaky, Mythbusters, Shark Week, Punkin Chunkin', Best Food Ever, Oddities,* and *Wreckreation Nation.*

18 Josh Constine, "Twitter Becomes Its Own Second Screen with Dockable Videos that Play While You Browse," *TechCrunch*, October 27, 2014.

19 Paula Bernstein, "Netflix Expands Originals to Include Documentaries and Stand-Up Comedy," *IndieWire*, July 22, 2013.

20 Adam Epstein, "Netflix Is Cornering the Stand-Up Comedy Market," *Quartz*, January 18, 2017.

21 Todd Spangler, "YouTube Red Unveiled: Ad-Free Service Priced Same as Netflix," *Variety*, October 21, 2015.

22 McClung and Johnson, "Examining the Motives of Podcast Users."

23 Carly Mallenbaum, "Podcast Fans: Get a Ticket to the 'Party,'" *USA Today*, June 12, 2015.

24 Vincent Meserko has described how podcasts have empowered comedians to speak frankly and connect with their audience outside of their comedic performances. Vincent M. Meserko, "Going Mental: Podcasting, Authenticity, and Artist-Fan Identification on Paul Gilmartin's *Mental Illness Happy Hour*," *Journal of Broadcasting & Electronic Media* 58, no. 3 (2014): 456–4469.

25 Sarah Florini, "The Podcast 'Chitlin' Circuit': Black Podcasters, Alternative Media, and Audio Enclaves," *Journal of Radio & Audio Media* 22, no. 2 (2015): 209–219.

26 Julie Miller, "Marc Maron's President Obama Podcast: The WTF Host Takes Us Behind the Scenes," *Vanity Fair*, June 22, 2015.

27 Archie Thomas, "Brit Comic Joins the Pod People," *Variety*, December 19, 2005.

28 Andrew Bottomley's research makes the connection between radio genres and podcasting forms explicit. Andrew Bottomley, "Podcasting, *Welcome to Night Vale*, and the Revival of Radio Drama," *Journal of Radio & Audio Media* 22, no. 2 (2015): 179–189.

29 Shirley Halperin, "Why Podcasts Are Comedy's Second Coming: Adam Carolla, Marc Maron and Greg Proops Weigh In," *Hollywood Reporter*, September 29, 2011.

30 Carly Mallenbaum, "The 'Serial Effect' Hasn't Worn Off," *USA Today*, April 16, 2015.

31 Carly Mallenbaum, "'Serial' News: Incarcerated Adnan Syed Granted Appeal," *USA Today*, February 8, 2015.

32 Berry, "Golden Age of Podcasting?"

33 Natalie Jarvey, "Howl Launches Podcast Subscriptions with 'WTF with Marc Maron' Archives," *Hollywood Reporter*, August 17, 2015; Natalie Jarvey, "E. W. Scripps Acquires Podcast Network Midroll Media," *Hollywood Reporter*, July 22, 2015; Jenelle Riley, "*Comedy Bang-Bang*'s Scott Aukerman: From Screwing Around to a Podcast Empire," *Variety*, May 5, 2015.

34 Natalie Jarvey, "Pandora Gets 'Serial' Podcast in Exclusive Streaming Deal," *Hollywood Reporter*, November 2, 2015.

35 Spigel, *Make Room for TV*, 75.

36 Ibid.

37 Alex Heath, "This Is the Next Big Thing for Spotify—and It Has Nothing to Do with Music," *Tech Insider*, February 8, 2016.

38 Outfront Media, "Audience Targeting: African American-Black: Out-of-Home Advertising Solutions," www.outfrontmedia.com; Outfront Media, "Your Brand Story, Outfront: Media across the U.S.A.," accessed September 14, 2015, www.outfrontmedia.com.

39 Outfront Media, "Frank Beck Chevrolet Case Study," accessed September 14, 2015, www.outfrontmedia.com.

40 Outfront Media, "Designing for Out of Home," accessed September 14, 2015, www.outfrontmedia.com.

41 Ibid.

42 Outfront Media, "Mobile Advertising," accessed September 14, 2015, www.outfrontmedia.com.

43 Outfront Media, "JCDecaux and Outfront Media Launch the First Smart Bus Shelter in Los Angeles," press release, July 22, 2015, http://investor.outfrontmedia.com.

44 Ibid.

45 Steve Scauzillo, "Metro Works to Hook Up Subway Riders to Internet," *Inland Valley Daily Bulletin*, January 18, 2015.

46 AFA, "iFlirtero," Google Play Store, Vers. 6.0 (February 23, 2015), accessed September 25, 2015, https://play.google.com/store/apps/details?id=com.appplication.flirteroapp&hl=en.

47 Place-based mobile apps that allow context-specific collaboration include LifeKraze, ShareMyPlaylists, Yik Yak, Geocaching, Parallel Kingdom, SpecTrek, Parallel Mafia, Turf Wars, Landlord Real Estate Tycoon, Whisper, Jack'd, Spaceteam, nearpod, Ingress, Pacmanhattan, and iFlirtero.

48 Micah Wright, "5 Inexpensive Connected Cars with Available WiFi," *Gear and Style: Cheat Sheet*, March 28, 2015.

49 Goggin, *Cell Phone Culture*, 24.

50 For example, Chevy offers plans from $10 to $50 a month, Chrysler for $35 a week.

51 These software integrations are advertised as safer alternatives to distracting smartphones that allow drivers to accomplish common tasks without the danger of searching a mobile screen.

52 According to industry analysis from Pavel Marceux, one area that has seen an increase in growth in 2014 is Internet-enabled cars, perhaps a signal that entertainment will increasingly be integrated into this formerly business-focused commute audience. Pavel Marceux, "Why Digital Majors Are Moving into the Car Market," Euromonitor International, March 25, 2015, www.portal.euromonitor.com.

53 This functionality is limited only to the Apple apps iMessage, Calendar, and Maps.

54 Matthew Spadaro, "An Apple a Day," *U-Wire*, September 24, 2015.

55 Bill Vlasic, "U.S. Proposes Spending $4 Billion on Self-Driving Cars," *New York Times*, January 14, 2016.

56 Campbell, "Mobile Communication and Network Privatism."

57 Papacharissi, *Private Sphere*.

58 G. Simmel, "The Metropolis and Mental Life," in *The City Cultures Reader*, ed. M. Miles, T. Hall, and I. Borden (New York: Routledge, 2003), 12–19.

59 Simun, "My Music, My World," 925.

60 Morse, "Ontology of Everyday Distraction," 195. Because places only take on meaning as spaces, they can be disrupted by the enunciating capabilities of the people walking in them. Morse believes, however, that the spaces of modern life are already being enunciated as spaces through the economics of distraction and leisure.

61 Ibid., 199. Morse poetically describes this effect of displacement: "This interior duality has symbolic dimensions as well: oppositions between country and city, nature and culture, sovereign individual and social subject are neutralized only to be reconstituted within non-space in a multilayered compromise formation, a Utopian realm of both/and, in the midst of neither/nor."

62 For examples of this work, see Michael Bull, "'To Each Their Own Bubble': Mobile Spaces of Sound in the City," in *MediaSpace: Place, Scale, and Culture in a Media Age*, edited by Nick Couldry and Anna McCarthy (London: Routledge, 2004), 275; Stephen Groening, "From 'a Box in the Theater of the World' to 'the World as Your Living Room': Cellular Phones, Television and Mobile Privatization," *New Media and Society* 12, no. 8 (2010): 1331–1347; Michael Bull, "Automobility and the Power of Sound," *Theory, Culture and Society* 21, nos. 4–5 (2004): 243–259.

63 Nielsen, "Millennials Prefer Cities to Suburbs, Subways to Driveways," Nielsen Newswire, March 4, 2014.

64 Thulin, "Mobile Audio Apps"; Hosokawa, "Walkman Effect."

65 Groening, "From 'a Box in the Theater of the World,'" 1342.

66 Morse, "Ontology of Everyday Distraction," 200.

67 Williams, *Television*, 188.

68 Project for Public Spaces, "Technology Brings People Together in Public Spaces after All," *Project for Public Spaces Blog*, July 17, 2014, www.pps.org.

69 Ibid.

70 Ibid.

71 Chase Wright, "Metro North to Expand Quiet Car Program," *Hour*, March 21, 2012.

72 Randy Kennedy, "A Code to Crack Down on Subway Impoliteness: City," *New York Times*, July 22, 2003.

73 Ibid.

74 Ira Henry Freeman, "Subway Riders to Hear TV Voices with Advice on Safety and Etiquette," *New York Times*, August 21, 1953.

75 Ibid.

76 Robert Trumbell, "Campaign to Improve Etiquette on Trains Is Started in Japan," *New York Times*, August 2, 1959.

77 Ibid.

78 Daniel S. Hamermesh, "Not Enough Time?," *American Economist* 59, no. 2 (2014): 119; Kim Parker and Wendy Wang, "Modern Parenthood," Pew Research Center's Social & Demographic Trends Project, March 14, 2013.

79 Liz Bowie, "Teens under Stress in Top College Competition," *Baltimore Sun*, April 12, 2009.

80 Laura Dwyer-Lindgren, Greg Freedman, Rebecca E. Engell, Thomas D. Fleming, Stephen S. Lim, Christopher J. L. Murray, and Ali H. Mokdad, "Prevalence of Physical Activity and Obesity in US Counties, 2001–2011: A Road Map for Action," *Population Health Metrics* 11, no. 1 (2013), article 7.

81 Parker and Wang, "Modern Parenthood."

82 Moshe, "Media Time Squeezing."

83 Nielsen, "What's Empowering the New Digital Consumer?," Nielsen Newswire, February 10, 2014; Roberto A. Ferdman, "The Slow Death of the Home-Cooked Meal," *Washington Post*, March 5, 2015.

84 Lee Rainie and Kathryn Zickuhr, "Americans' Views on Mobile Etiquette," Pew Research Center, August 26, 2015, 5.

85 Ibid., 3.

86 My research on MARTA riders aimed to understand how the commute operates as an outlet to culture and conversation. Recruiting survey respondents on MARTA rail lines, I catalogued over 200 examples of mobile media usage in 178 questionnaires. The survey contained 20 questions designed to reveal how mobile device use during the commute differed from home use. Additionally, the survey asked respondents to describe what they use their devices for when on the train and to provide examples of their activities by sending screenshots of their mobile device activities. These screenshots were collected via Twitter, Facebook, email, and the study's official website.

87 Sherry Turkle, "Stop Googling. Let's Talk," *New York Times*, September 26, 2015.

88 Clive Thompson, "Brave New World of Digital Intimacy," *New York Times*, September 5, 2008.

89 Rainie and Zickuhr, "Americans' Views on Mobile Etiquette."

90 Amanda Lenhart, "Teens, Technology and Friendships," Pew Research Center: Internet & Technology, August 6, 2015.

91 Anderson, "Neo-Muzak and the Business of Mood."

92 Sean Ludwig, "Spotify Adds Songza-Like 'Playlists for Every Mood' and Messaging with Friends," *Venture Beat*, August 4, 2013.

93 Rocio Guerrero, interview with author, September 30, 2015.

94 The playlist features the tagline, "Let this eclectic playlist carry you home in style."

95 Anderson, "Neo-Muzak and the Business of Mood."

96 Ibid., 835.

97 Raju Mudhar, "Your TTC Station's Personal iPod Playlist," *Toronto Star*, July 6, 2012.

98 Arianna Bassoli, Julian Moore, and Stefan Agamanolis, "tunA: Socialising Music Sharing on the Move," in *Consuming Music Together: Social and Collaborative Aspects of Music Consumption Technologies*, ed. Kenton O'Hara and Barry Brown (Dordrecht, Netherlands: Springer, 2006), 151–172.

99 Each of these apps allows you to put popular-culture emojis and GIFs into text message conversations. Stories on these companies include Ryan Lawler, "Your iOS GIF Keyboard Is Finally Here, Thanks to Riffsy," *Tech-Crunch*, September 23, 2014; Sarah Perez, "Blippy Returns with a Brand-New GIF Keyboard for iOS 8," *TechCrunch*, November 20, 2014; Darrell

Etherington, "PopKey's Animated GIF Keyboard for iOS 8 Is the One You Should Be Using," *TechCrunch*, October 1, 2014; Sarah Perez, "Kanvas Debuts an iOS Keyboard That Lets You Send Decorated Photos, Stickers and GIFs. Or Even Just Text," *TechCrunch*, November 13, 2014; Megan Rose Dickey, "Giphy Wants to Become a Full-Fledged, GIF-Based Media Company," *TechCrunch*, October 7, 2015.

100 According to Jason Eppink, "GIF" (pronounced with either the hard or soft *g*) stands for "graphics interchange format"; GIFs are "short, silent, looping, untitled moving images" shared in communication with friends or colleagues. Jason Eppink, "A Brief History of the GIF (So Far)," *Journal of Visual Culture* 13, no. 3 (2014): 298–306.

101 Ibid., 298.

102 Ibid., 302.

103 See the following discussions of audience's uses of GIFs: Michael Z. Newman, "Say 'Pulp Fiction' One More Goddamn Time: Quotation Culture and Internet-Age Classic," *New Review of Film and Television Studies* 12, no. 2 (2013): 125–142; Ruth Anna Deller, "Simblr Famous and SimSecret Infamous: Performance, Community Norms, and Shaming among Fans of *The Sims*," in "Performance and Performativity in Fandom," ed. Lucy Bennett and Paul J. Booth, special issue, *Transformative Works and Cultures* 18 (2015); Kayley Thomas, "Revisioning the Smiling Villain: Imagetexts and Intertextual Expression in Representations of the Filmic Loki on Tumblr," in "Appropriating, Interpreting, and Transforming Comic Books," ed. Matthew J. Costello, special issue, *Transformative Works and Cultures* 13 (2013).

104 Klinger, *Beyond the Multiplex*, 181.

105 Ibid., 156.

106 Ibid., 156.

107 Jenkins, *Textual Poachers*.

108 Lawrence Lessig, *Remix: Making Art and Commerce Thrive in the Hybrid Economy* (New York: Penguin, 2008).

109 Graig Uhlin, "Playing in the Gif(t) Economy," *Games and Culture* 9, no. 6 (2014): 525.

110 Alex Reimer, "The NFL's War on GIFs Is a Losing Battle," *Forbes*, October 13, 2015.

111 Eppink, "Brief History of the GIF," 304.

112 Uhlin, "Playing in the Gif(t) Economy," 521.

113 Sarah Perez, "Giphy Expands beyond Messenger with Its New GIF-Sharing App," *TechCrunch*, October 29, 2015.

114 Sarah Perez, "Disney Now Has Its Own GIF App and iOS 8 Keyboard," *TechCrunch*, June 26, 2015; Jon Russell, "Facebook Tests Features That Make Sharing GIFs in Messenger Easier than Ever," *Tech-
Crunch*, July 5, 2015.
115 Sarah Perez, "Hulu Launches Its Own GIF Search Engine," *TechCrunch*,
April 6, 2015.
116 Perez, "Disney Now Has Its Own GIF App."
117 Jonathon Dornbush, "C-3PO Can Now Help Guide Drivers as Waze Navigation Voice," *Entertainment Weekly*, November 23, 2015.
118 Georg Szalai, "AT&T to 'Lead the Evolution of Video' Services after
DirecTV Acquisition, CEO Says," *Hollywood Reporter*, August 12, 2015.
119 Ibid.
120 Klint Finley, "T-Mobile's Unlimited Video Raises Net Neutrality Concerns,"
Wired, November 10, 2015.
121 Szalai, "AT&T to 'Lead the Evolution of Video.'"
122 Finley, "T-Mobile's Unlimited Video."
123 Ibid.

CHAPTER 4. THE WAITING ROOM

1 For the 2016 Super Bowl, CBS president Les Moonves claimed that the network was charging $5 million for a 30-second spot. Claire Groden, "This Is
How Much a 2016 Super Bowl Ad Costs," *Fortune*, August 6, 2015.
2 Stuart Dredge, "Clash of Clans Mobile Game Was Most Popular Super
Bowl Ad in 2015," *Guardian*, February 9, 2015; Joe Lynch, "Super Bowl 2015:
10 Best and 5 Worst Commercials," *Billboard*, February 1, 2015.
3 Nielsen, "The Digital Consumer," February 2014.
4 Anna McCarthy has explained that television is watched in public space
despite the fact that television producers create shows for the domestic
space. McCarthy, *Ambient Television*.
5 Lance Strate, *Amazing Ourselves to Death: Neil Postman's Brave New World
Revisited* (New York: Peter Lang, 2014).
6 C. A. Middleton, "Illusions of Balance and Control in an Always-On Environment: A Case Study of Blackberry Users," in *Mobile Phone Cultures*, ed.
Gerard Goggin (New York: Routledge, 2008).
7 McCarthy, "Television While You Wait," in *Ambient Television*.
8 Bogost, *Persuasive Games*.
9 McCarthy, *Ambient Television*, 201.
10 Ibid., 197.
11 Ibid.

12 Media industries studies combines analysis of media companies, labor practices, and business strategies of the media industries. Mayer, Banks, and Caldwell, *Production Studies*; Jennifer Holt and Alisa Perren, *Media Industries: History, Theory, and Method* (New York: Wiley, 2011).

13 Alison Hashimoto, vice president of programming for Turner Private Networks, explains that audiences have reported having a more positive experience in airports that provide CNN Airport. Alison Hashimoto, interview with author, August 28, 2015.

14 Cara Beardi, "Airport Powerhouses Make Connection: TMI, Carosell Link to Reach Affluent Business Travelers," *Advertising Age*, October 2, 2000; Emily Bryson York, "Starbucks Aims to Build Project Red Community: Will Personalize Holiday Push with Site, In-Store World AIDS Day Event," *Advertising Age*, December 1, 2008.

15 Williams, *Television*.

16 Jeanine Poggi, "Turning Point for Turner?," *Advertising Age*, May 12, 2014.

17 Brian Stelter, "A Struggling CNN Worldwide Is Said to Be Drawn to Jeffrey Zucker," *New York Times*, November 27, 2012.

18 Marisa Guthrie, "Jeff Zucker on His New CNN Job: 'If We Don't Try Something Different, We Won't Succeed,'" *Hollywood Reporter*, November 29, 2012.

19 Tim Goodman, "Hello, I'm Jeff Zucker. You're Fired," *Hollywood Reporter*, January 29, 2013.

20 Brian Steinberg, "Will CNN Replace Piers Morgan with Reality TV?," *Variety*, February 24, 2014.

21 Marisa Guthrie, "CNN's Jeff Zucker: Larry King / Piers Morgan–Style Interview Shows 'No Longer Viable,'" *Hollywood Reporter*, April 10, 2014.

22 Hilary Lewis, "Jeff Zucker, CNN Films Execs Talk News-Doc Interplay, Tease Future Features," *Hollywood Reporter*, November 8, 2014.

23 John T. Caldwell, "Critical Industrial Practice: Branding, Repurposing, and the Migratory Patterns of Industrial Texts," *Television & New Media* 7, no. 2 (2006): 105.

24 Ibid., 106.

25 Hashimoto, interview with author.

26 Dorsey Shaw, "CNN Spent an Insane Amount of Time Covering Missing Flight 370 Wednesday Night," *BuzzFeed News*, March 13, 2014.

27 Tony Maglio, "Malaysia Airlines Flight Crash Gives Cable News Ratings Big Boost," *Wrap*, July 18, 2014.

28 David Carr, "Brash Chef and Big Bet for CNN," *New York Times*, June 3, 2012; Gary Baum, "How Anthony Bourdain Could Save CNN," *Hollywood Reporter*, September 26, 2014.

29 Jesper Juul, *A Casual Revolution: Reinventing Video Games and Their Players* (Cambridge, MA: MIT Press, 2010).

30 Rhiannon Williams, "The Best-Selling iTunes Album of the Year Gives Eddy Cue Goosebumps," *Telegraph*, December 10, 2015.

31 Evans, "Economics of Free Freemium Games."

32 Barry Schwartz, "Waiting, Exchange, and Power: The Distribution of Time in Social Systems," *American Journal of Sociology* (1974): 3.

33 McCarthy, *Ambient Television*, 209.

34 Hashimoto, interview with author.

35 McCarthy, *Ambient Television*, 209.

36 Ian Bogost, "The Rhetoric of Video Games," in *The Ecology of Games: Connecting Youth, Games, and Learning*, ed. Katie Salen (Cambridge, MA: MIT Press, 2008), 119.

37 Ibid., 121.

38 "In-Game Purchases Drive Video Game Growth in 2015," Euromonitor International, Datagraphic Toys and Games, June 27, 2016, www.portal.euromonitor.com.

39 Mike Mason, "Demographic Breakdown of Casual, Mid-Core and Hard-Core Mobile Gamers," *Mobile Games Blog*, Magmic, December 19, 2013, http://developers.magmic.com.

40 Ian Bogost, "Asynchronous Multiplay: Futures for Casual Multiplayer Experience," paper presented at the Other Players Conference on Multiplayer Phenomena, Copenhagen, Denmark, December 2004, 2, http://bogost.com/writing/asynchronous_multiplay_futures/.

41 Evans, "Economics of Free Freemium Games," 8.

42 "Mobile Gaming Revenues Won't Quit Growing," *eMarketer*, November 7, 2014, www.emarketer.com.

43 Bogost, "Rhetoric of Video Games," 120.

44 Evans, "Economics of Free Freemium Games," 5.

45 Ian Paul, "Tasty! Activision Snaps Up Candy Crush Maker King for $5.9 Billion," *PC World*, November 3, 2015.

46 Mason, "Demographic Breakdown."

47 Mike Shields, "Zynga Kills Soaps: Audience Shifts as Viewers Become Gamers," *Adweek*, April 25, 2011.

48 John Ellis, *Visible Fictions: Cinema, Television, Video* (New York: Routledge, 1982), 164.

49 John T. Caldwell, *Televisuality: Style, Crisis, and Authority in American Television* (New Brunswick, NJ: Rutgers University Press, 1995), 25.

50 Ian Bogost, "Cow Clicker: The Making of an Obsession," Ian Bogost's website, July 21, 2010, http://bogost.com.

51 Nicole Laporte, "How Mobile Game Company Seriously Aims to Reverse-Engineer Hollywood," *Fast Company*, July 8, 2015.

52 Ibid.

53 Mike Thompson, "Ranked: Best and Worst Movies Based on Videogames," *Metacritic*, September 8, 2010.

54 Henry Jenkins, *Fans, Bloggers, and Gamers: Exploring Participatory Culture* (New York: NYU Press, 2006), 118.

55 Gray, *Watching with "The Simpsons."*

56 Ibid., 92.

57 Ibid., 2.

58 Ibid.

59 Thomson Financial, "Event Brief of Q3 2016 Electronic Arts Inc Earnings Call—Fall," Event Briefs, Electronic Arts Quarterly Financial Disclosure, January 28, 2016; Thomson Financial, "Q4 2015 Electronic Arts Inc Earnings Call—Final," Event Briefs, Electronic Arts Quarterly Financial Disclosure, May 5, 2015; "Mobile Games Veteran Stuart Duncan Launches icejam(TM), Creates New Era of Free-to-Play Mobile Games Based on Playable Data," *Business Wire*, July 30, 2015.

60 This calculation is based on ratings from TV by the Numbers for total viewers for the weeks of January 11–17, 2016 (2.2 million), January 4–10, 2016 (4.5 million), December 28–January 3, 2016 (2.4 million), December 21–27, 2015 (2.3 million). "Weekly Ratings," TV by the Numbers, accessed February 2, 2016.

61 EA Staff, "'Life-Ruiningly Fun' Comes to iPad, iPhone & iPod Touch with the Launch of *The Simpsons: Tapped Out*," Electronic Arts press release, March 1, 2012.

62 Ibid.

63 Ibid.

64 Joshua Green and Henry Jenkins, "The Moral Economy of Web 2.0: Audience Research and Convergence Culture," in *Media Industries: History, Theory, and Method*, ed. Jennifer Holt and Alisa Perren (New York: Wiley, 2009), 213–225.

65 Green and Jenkins cite several examples of the dangers of angering fans, including Hector Postigo's work on gamer communities that reject video game companies' policing of their modding practices. Ibid., 221–223.

66 Jonathan Gray, "In the Game: The Creative and Textual Constraints of Licensed Videogames," in *Wired TV*, ed. Denise Mann (New Brunswick, NJ: Rutgers University Press, 2014), 53–71.

67 Evans, "Economics of Free Freemium Games," 5.

68 Ibid., 12.

69 *The Simpsons: Tapped Out* forum, "What's the Oddest Place / Time You've Played TSTO?," entries from March 28, 2013, accessed February 22, 2016, http://forum.ea.com.

70 Shira Chess, "Going with the Flo," *Feminist Media Studies* 12, no. 1 (2012): 91.

71 Website observations as of February 23, 2016.

72 Henry Jenkins, *Convergence Culture: Where Old and New Media Collide* (New York: NYU Press, 2006).

73 Jerry Lerma and Terry Hogan, "Guide to Springfield USA: A Highly Detailed Map of the Simpsons' Hometown," 2002, last updated August 18, 2006, http://web.archive.org.

74 Bravewall, comment on "Following the Springfield Guide" thread, July 8, 2013, *The Simpsons: Tapped Out* forum: Springfield Showcase.

75 Emmcee1, comment on "Following the Springfield Guide" thread, July 8, 2013, *The Simpsons: Tapped Out* forum: Springfield Showcase.

76 MrCluth111, comment on "What Have You Done with Rancho Relaxo?" thread, January 28, 2015, *The Simpsons: Tapped Out* forum: Springfield Showcase; DaoudX, comment on "What Have You Done with Rancho Relaxo?" thread, January 28, 2015, *The Simpsons: Tapped Out* forum: Springfield Showcase.

77 Larsyuipo, comment on "Town Design Tips" thread, September 16, 2015, *The Simpsons: Tapped Out* forum: Springfield Showcase.

78 4Junk3000, comment on "Town Design Tips" thread, January 23, 2016, *The Simpsons: Tapped Out* forum: Springfield Showcase.

79 Awez1, comment on "Town Design Tips" thread, September 15, 2015, *The Simpsons: Tapped Out* forum: Springfield Showcase.

80 Gray, *Watching with "The Simpsons,"* 69–70.

81 Bolter and Grusin, *Remediation*.

82 Gray, *Watching with "The Simpsons,"* 73.

83 Ibid., 75.

84 Sam Anderson, "Just One More," *New York Times Magazine*, April 4, 2012.

85 Early television studies work from John Fiske, John Hartley, Horace Newcomb, and Raymond Williams makes the case for the legitimization of television as a field of study. Horace Newcomb, *TV: The Most Popular Art*

(New York: Anchor Books, 1974); Williams, *Television*; John Fiske and John Hartley, *Reading Television* (London: Methuen, 1978).

86 Charlotte Brundson, "Crossroads: Notes on Soap Opera," *Screen* 22, no. 4 (1981): 32–37; Dorothy Hobson, *Crossroads: The Drama of a Soap Opera* (London: Methuen, 1982).

87 Chess, "Going with the Flo."

88 Ibid.

89 Gregg, *Work's Intimacy*, 10.

90 Ibid.

91 Jason Wilson, Chris Chesher, Larissa Hjorth, and Ingrid Richardson, "Distractedly Engaged: Mobile Gaming and Convergent Mobile Media," *Convergence: The International Journal of Research into New Media Technologies* 17, no. 4 (2011): 351–355.

CHAPTER 5. THE "CONNECTED" LIVING ROOM

1 Samsung, "Hi, TV," advertisement, March 1, 2012, available at https://www.youtube.com/watch?v=JV6JLcjVJiA.

2 Samsung, "It's Not TV," advertisement, October 14, 2013, available at https://www.ispot.tv/ad/72Fr/samsung-smart-tv-its-not-tv.

3 David Morley, *Television, Audiences and Cultural Studies* (New York: Routledge, 1992); Silverstone, *Television and Everyday Life*; Ang, *Desperately Seeking the Audience*.

4 This argument is laid out most convincingly in Meehan, "Why We Don't Count."

5 The realization of the surveillance implications are clear in the days after the televisions were introduced at the 2012 Consumer Electronics Show. Michael Learmonth, "Soon Your TV Will Watch You, Too," *Advertising Age*, January 13, 2012.

6 Shane Harris, "Your Samsung Smart TV Is Spying on You, Basically," *The Daily Beast*, February 5, 2015.

7 David Meyer, "Worried about Smart TVs Listening In? Welcome to the Smart Home," *Gigaom*, February 9, 2015.

8 A good example of the discussion about the changes in technology and content is available from Mark Harris, "TV Is Not TV Anymore: A Revolution in How We Watch Was Just the Start. Now Comes the Good Stuff," *New York*, May 21, 2012.

9 Tim Wu, "Niche Is the New Mass," *New Republic*, December 9, 2013.

10 Brian Steinberg, "Is This the Fall TV Advertisers Tune In the Second Screen?," *Variety*, August 22, 2013.

11 Hassoun, "Tracing Attentions," 275. He cites Charles Allen, "Photographing the TV Audience," *Journal of Advertising Research* 5, no. 1 (1965): 2–8.

12 Ethan Tussey, "Connected Viewing on the Second Screen: The Limitations of the Living Room," in *Connected Viewing: Selling, Sharing, and Streaming Media in a Digital Era*, ed. Jennifer Holt and Kevin Sanson (New York: Routledge, 2014), 202–216.

13 Will Brooker, "Living on *Dawson's Creek*: Teen Viewers, Cultural Convergence, and Television Overflow," *International Journal of Cultural Studies* 4, no. 4 (2001): 456–472.

14 Richard Mullins, "Super Bowl Ads Will Blitz Your Phone," *Tampa Tribune*, January 28, 2012.

15 Van Es, "Social TV and the Participation Dilemma."

16 Hye Jin Lee and Mark Andrejevic, "Second-Screen Theory: From the Democratic Surround to the Digital Enclosure," in *Connected Viewing: Selling, Streaming and Sharing Media in the Digital Era*, ed. Jennifer Holt and Kevin Sanson (New York: Routledge, 2014), 53.

17 Van Es, "Social TV and the Participation Dilemma," 115.

18 Elizabeth Evans, "Layering Engagement: The Temporal Dynamics of Transmedia Television," *StoryWorlds: A Journal of Narrative Studies* 7, no. 2 (2015): 119–120.

19 Chris Gaylord, " 'Second Screen' Apps Turn Digital Distractions into TV Companions," *Christian Science Monitor*, April 17, 2012.

20 Marianna Orbist, Regina Bernhaupt, and Manfred Tscheligi, "Interactive TV for the Home: An Ethnographic Study of Users Requirements and Experiences," *International Journal of Human-Computer Interaction* 24, no. 2 (2008): 174–196; Wilson, "In the Living Room."

21 Lora Oehlberg, Nicolas Ducheneaut, James D. Thornton, Robert J. Moore, and Eric Nickell, "Social TV: Designing for Distributed, Sociable Television Viewing," *Proceedings of EuroTV*, 2006, 255.

22 Fabio Giglietto and Donatella Selva, "Second Screen and Participation: A Content Analysis on a Full Season Dataset of Tweets," *Journal of Communication* 64, no. 2 (2014): 260–277.

23 "Multi-Screen Is the Ultimate Screen," Bravo Affluencer, accessed April 13, 2016, www.affluencers.com.

24 John Ellis, *Visible Fictions: Cinema, Television, Video* (New York: Routledge, 1992), 128.

25 Ibid., 112.

26 Lee and Andrejevic, "Second-Screen Theory."

27 Andrea Chen, Mahlet Seyoum, Reginald Panaligan, and Kimberly Wasiljew, "The Role of Digital in TV Research, Fanship and Viewing," Think with Google, April 2014.

28 "Broadcasters Sync Up Second-Screen Efforts," *Broadcasting and Cable*, November 19, 2012.

29 "Second-Screen Green Remains Scarce," *Broadcasting and Cable*, April 15, 2013.

30 Simon Khalaf, "The Cable Industry Faces the Perfect Storm: Apps, App Stores and Apple," *Flurry Insights*, September 10, 2015; Randall Stross, "The Second Screen, Trying to Complement the First," *New York Times*, March 3, 2012.

31 Lee and Andrejevic, "Second-Screen Theory," 52.

32 Jeanine Poggi, "Too Many Apps for That," *Advertising Age*, September 29, 2014.

33 This number is from the digital-media-industry blogger Chuck Parker and Miso CEO Somrat Niyogi, both quoted in Lee and Andrejevic, "Second-Screen Theory," 42.

34 "New Ways to Rethink the Second Screen," *Broadcasting and Cable*, November 4, 2013.

35 Andrew Seroff, interview with author, October 24, 2014.

36 Ibid.; Poggi, "Too Many Apps for That."

37 Sam Thielman, "Twitter Killed All These Second Screen Apps," *Adweek*, September 9, 2013.

38 Donghee Yvette Wohn and E. K. Na, "Tweeting about TV: Sharing Television Viewing Experiences via Social Media Message Streams," *First Monday* 16, no. 3 (2011), http://firstmonday.org.

39 Research by Beverly A. Bondad-Brown et al. confirms that television audiences see Twitter as an additional conduit to entertainment and amusement. Beverly A. Bondad-Brown, Ronald E. Rice, and Katy E. Pearce, "Influences on TV Viewing and Online User-Shared Video Use: Demographics, Generations, Contextual Age, Media Use, Motivations, and Audience Activity," *Journal of Broadcasting & Electronic Media* 56, no. 4 (2012): 471–493.

40 Markus Stauff, "The Second Screen: Convergence as Crisis," *Zeitschrift für Medien- und Kulturforschung* 6 (2015): 127; Evans, "Layering Engagement," 119.

41 Dan Biddle, comments at TV ReTweeted event, Royal Television Society, May 28, 2014, https://rts.org.uk.

42 Research by Anders Olof Larsson shows that people use hashtags when they want to react to a television show and have others see their reaction.

Anders Olof Larsson, "Tweeting the Viewer: Use of Twitter in a Talk Show Context," *Broadcasting & Electronic Media* 57 (2013): 135–152.

43 Bill Heil and Mikolaj Piskorski, "New Twitter Research: Men Follow Men and Nobody Tweets," *Harvard Business Review*, June 1, 2009.

44 Agence France-Presse, "Twitter an Awkward Child as It Turns 10," *Nation: Thailand's Independent Newspaper*, March 18, 2016.

45 Research by Tim Highfield et al. showed that people felt that they were getting an accurate representation of the viewing audience when checking Twitter during the Eurovision song contest. Tim Highfield, Stephen Harrington, and Axel Bruns, "Twitter as a Technology for Audiencing and Fandom: The Eurovision Phenomenon," *Information, Communication & Society* 16, no. 3 (2013): 315–339.

46 Nielsen, "Nielsen Launches Demographics for Nielsen Twitter TV Ratings," Nielsen Press Room, May 19, 2014.

47 Nielsen, "TV Season in Review: Biggest Moments on Twitter," Nielsen Newswire, June 1, 2015.

48 Philip Pond, "Twitter Time: A Temporal Analysis of Tweet Streams during Televised Political Debate," *Television & New Media* 17, no. 2 (2016): 155.

49 Van Dijck, *Culture of Connectivity*, 75.

50 Ibid., 82.

51 Twitter dropped the term "Twitter Amplify" in 2015 as it became a standard part of Twitter's revenue strategies and open to any publisher wishing to make money on its videos. Lauren Johnson, "More Preroll Ads Are Coming to Twitter with Expanded Video Program," *Adweek*, October 8, 2015.

52 Van Dijck, *Culture of Connectivity*, 85.

53 Bill Brioux, "Now You Can Watch 'Desperate Housewives,' 'Grey's Anatomy' in Two Minutes Flat," *Canadian Press*, April 2012.

54 Seth Abramovitch, "Twitter Partners with Viacom for Ad-Supported Highlights," *Hollywood Reporter*, June 19, 2013.

55 Van Dijck, *Culture of Connectivity*, 12.

56 Tanzina Vega, "ESPN to Use Twitter to Send Instant Replays of College Football," *New York Times*, December 14, 2012.

57 Abramovitch, "Twitter Partners with Viacom."

58 Judit Nagy and Anjali Midha, "The Value of Earned Audiences: How Social Interactions Amplify TV Impact," *Journal of Advertising Research* 54, no. 4 (2014): 448–453.

59 Abramovitch, "Twitter Partners with Viacom."

60 Garett Sloane, "Gooooaaalll! Fox Deportes Amplifies on Twitter," *Adweek*, March 14, 2014.

61 Adgully Bureau, "Starsports.com and Vodafone India to Bring 'Twitter Amplify' for Indian Sport Fans," *Adgully*, August 8, 2014.

62 Christopher Heine, "ESPN Re-ups with Twitter Amplify for College Football," *Adweek*, August 29, 2013.

63 Caldwell, "Second-Shift Media Aesthetics."

64 Johnson, "More Preroll Ads Are Coming."

65 Ethan Tussey, "Desktop Day Games: Workspace Media, Multitasking and the Digital Baseball Fan," in *Digital Media Sport: Technology, Power and Culture in the Network Society*, ed. Brett Hutchins and David Rowe (New York: Routledge, 2013), 37–51.

66 Jeanine Poggi, "Marketers Find Strengths, and Limits, to Twitter Amplify," *Advertising Age*, July 16, 2014.

67 Garett Sloane, "NFL Says It's the Champ of Twitter's Amplify Program," *Adweek*, June 29, 2014.

68 Ibid.

69 Tussey, "Desktop Day Games."

70 Abramovitch, "Twitter Partners with Viacom.

71 Mark Andrejevic, "The Work That Affective Economics Does," *Cultural Studies* 25, nos. 4–5 (2011): 604–620.

72 Stuart Kemp, "Viacom International Media Networks Partners with Twitter," *Hollywood Reporter*, October 8, 2013; Todd Spangler, "ABC Signs on to Twitter's Advertising Program, Starting with #Oscars," *Variety*, February 27, 2014.

73 Brian Steinberg, "Fox, American Express Take to Twitter to Promote Sharing of TV-Show Clips," *Variety*, November 14, 2013; Janko Roettgers, "Twitter Does First Season-Long Amplify Ad Deal for 'Pretty Little Liars,'" *Variety*, June 29, 2015.

74 Roettgers, "Twitter Does First Season-Long Amplify Ad Deal."

75 Poggi, "Marketers Find Strengths, and Limits."

76 Ibid.

77 Meehan, "Why We Don't Count."

78 Allie Kosterich and Philip M. Napoli, "Reconfiguring the Audience Commodity: The Institutionalization of Social TV Analytics as Market Information Regime," *Television & New Media* 17, no. 2 (2015): 99–107.

79 Nielsen Twitter TV Rating calculates tweets only three hours before through three hours after the broadcast of a television show.

80 Anthony Ha, "Nielsen's Steve Hasker Says the New Twitter TV Rating Isn't Just for Advertisers," *TechCrunch*, December 17, 2012.

81 Lisa de Moraes, "Full 2014–15 TV Season Series Rankings," *Deadline Hollywood*, May 21, 2015.

82 Nielsen, "TV Season in Review."

83 Ibid.

84 De Moraes, "Full 2014–15 TV Season Series Rankings."

85 Alex Ben Block, "NATPE Keynote: Twitter Execs Say Platform Will Impact TV Ad Rates at Next Upfronts," *Hollywood Reporter*, January 27, 2014.

86 Matthew Pittman and Alec C. Tefertiller, "With or Without You: Connected Viewing and Co-viewing Twitter Activity for Traditional Appointment and Asynchronous Broadcast Television Models," *First Monday* 20, no. 7 (2015), http://firstmonday.org.

87 Nielsen, "Who's Tweeting about TV?," Nielsen Newswire, May 19, 2014.

88 Nielsen, "From Live to 24/7: Extending Twitter TV Engagement beyond the Live Airing," Nielsen Newswire, December 15, 2014.

89 Ibid.

90 Christopher Heine, "5 Things Advertisers Should Know about Twitter's NFL Livestreaming Deal," *Adweek*, April 5, 2016.

91 Todd Spangler, "BBC Creating News Program about Twitter Trends to Be Broadcast via Twitter," *Variety*, October 23, 2013.

92 Sarah Perez, "SEEiT, the Feature That Turns Twitter into a Remote Control for Comcast Subscribers, Rolls Out This Week," *TechCrunch*, November 22, 2013.

93 Shea Bennett, "Have You Seen the Twitter Mirror?," *Adweek*, December 18, 2013; Kayvon Beykpour, "Periscope Broadcasts: Live on Twitter," Twitter, January 12, 2016.

94 Todd Spangler, "Why Twitter's NFL Deal Won't Really Move the Ball," *Variety*, April 7, 2016.

95 Todd Spangler, "Twitter Lands NFL 'Thursday Night Football' Streaming Deal," *Variety*, April 5, 2016.

96 Agence France-Presse, "Twitter an Awkward Child."

97 Lee and Andrejevic, "Second-Screen Theory."

98 "Platform mobility" is a term used by marketing material and detailed in Chuck Tryon's book *On-Demand Culture*.

99 Ibid., 62.

100 Ibid., 64.

101 Ibid., 66.

102 Ibid.

103 Ibid., 72.

104 David Morley, *Television, Audiences and Cultural Studies* (New York: Routledge, 1992), 134, citing James Lull, "How Families Select Television

Programs: A Mass-Observational Study," *Journal of Broadcasting & Electronic Media* 26, no. 4 (1982): 802.

105 Morley, *Television, Audiences and Cultural Studies*, 132.

106 Ibid., 140.

107 Dish Network, "Who Wears the Pants?," advertisement, August 6, 2016, available at https://www.ispot.tv/ad/ATzi/dish-network-hopper-who-wears-the-pants.

108 Wilson, "In the Living Room," 183.

109 Ibid., 184.

110 Ibid.

111 William Uricchio, "Television's Next Generation," in *Television after TV: Essays on a Medium in Transition*, ed. Lynn Spigel and Jan Olsson (Durham, NC: Duke University Press, 2004), 169.

112 Morley, *Television, Audiences and Cultural Studies*, 148.

113 Ibid., 149.

114 Ibid., 145.

115 Susan Kelley, "Gender Equality's Final Frontier: Who Cleans Up," *Cornell Chronicle*, January 22, 2013.

116 Belfast5348, comment on "Sound during Ads," October 25, 2015, Xfinity Website and Mobile App Forum: "I wanted to suggest that you add the toolbar/sound function to ads that run while watching Xfinity on the Internet. I am a football wife and watch online while husband watches TV. The ads do not have a toolbar that allows sound adjustment. I am wearing a headset and the sound goes up to full volume which is dangerous. Listeners should always be able to readjust the sound without exiting the window/tab."

117 Doconnor6408, "Re: Xfinity TV App," February 19, 2016, Xfinity TV App Forum: "Wanted to see if anyone could help me out! New to X1, I tried to put the Xfinity TV app on my Amazon Fire HD to watch local news channels when my spouse is watching something on TV."

118 Carols46, "Can't Stream Live TV," April 2, 2015, Xfinity TV App Forum: "Also wanted to watch Cavs on my computer but 'm using Chrome. Instead of an error code I'm getting a blank screen after it tells me that the program is rated TV-MA (for a basketball game?). I couldn't get A&E live either. Guess live streaming must be broken. I haven't tried the Xfinity app on my Kindle Fire HDX but the Watch TNT app is working so I am at least able to watch (although I was hoping for a bigger screen to watch on). We only have one tv and my husband is using it to play wow!"; TheJessle, "Xfinity TV Online Broken Due to Service Transfer Request?" July 21, 2015, Xfinity

TV App Forum: "On top of all that, I was right. I logged in catch up on some TV while my husband uses the TV in the living room to play video games (we only have 1 set in the house and 1 DVR because this hasn't been an issue for us until right at this very moment)—and the DVR isn't showing up, the internet TV App isn't recognizing this as the home network (even though the website does) and the on demand content isn't even showing up because the new account isn't even active for weeks still."

119 RH2514, "Watching live TV on my laptop," July 28, 2012, Xfinity TV App Forum: "We have X-Finity as of last night. 1 simple question that nobody at Comcast can answer. If my husband is watching a live show at 6 p.m. on the TV in the living room, can I watch a different live TV show on my laptop in the living room?"

120 TheDaveMitchell, "SF Giants," April 22, 2015, Xfinity Website and Mobile App Forum.

121 RayGoQuestions, "Watch live TV on Computer in-home," March 6, 2016, Xfinity Website and Mobile App Forum.

122 QuessP, "Suggestion—Categories for Recordings," February 5, 2016, Xfinity Website and App Forum.

123 Majesty1919, "Re: Preventing others from deleting my shows on DVR," April 1, 2014, Comcast X1 Forum: "Is there a way to password protect the dvr contect. My daughter deletes my shows to make room for her stuff. I want to set up the dvr to require a password to prevent accidental or intentional deletions of material. Thanks Renee."

124 Lisa Guernsey, "Science-Based Advice on Toddler Screen Time," *Slate*, November 13, 2014.

125 cnunes6636, "Re: Need Nicktoons app/offer it as a live stream on xfinity go!," March 20, 2016, Xfinity Website and App Forum.

126 Tiffany_Ivanov, "Can't Download Purchased Movies," March 10, 2016, Xfinity Website and App Forum.

127 Alexandra Samuel, "Happy Mother's Day: Kids' Screen Time Is a Feminist Issue," *JStor Daily*, May 3, 2016.

128 Todd Spangler, "Password Sharing: Are Netflix, HBO Missing $500 Million by Not Cracking Down?," *Variety*, July 15, 2015.

129 Morley, *Family Television*, 11.

130 Bella1213, "Access TV Shows on Laptop," January 26, 2013, Xfinity Website and Mobile App Forum.

131 Tryon, *On-Demand Culture*, 72.

132 Stauff, "Second Screen," 134.

133 Ibid., 135.

134 James Bennett, "'Your Window-on-the-World': The Emergence of Red-Button Interactive Television in the UK," *Convergence: The International Journal of Research into New Media Technologies* 14, no. 2 (2008): 161–182.

135 Daniel Chamberlain, "Scripted Spaces: Television Interfaces and the Non-Places of Asynchronous Entertainment," in *Television as Digital Media*, ed. James Bennett and Niki Strange (Durham, NC: Duke University Press, 2011), 230–254.

136 Daniel Chamberlain, "Television Interfaces," *Journal of Popular Film & Television* 38, no. 2 (2010): 84–88.

137 Comcast Corporation, "Comcast Launches X1—A Next-Generation Cloud-Based Video Platform," *PR Newswire*, August 1, 2013.

138 Karen Orr Vered, "Televisual Aesthetics in Y2K: From Windows on the World to a Windows Interface," *Convergence* 8, no. 3 (2002): 40–60.

139 Wildrisc, "Re: X1–DVR," September 29, 2013, Comcast X1 Forum.

140 Ckpeck, "How do I switch TV the 'Watch TV Live' site changes the channels of?," August 24, 2014, Xfinity Website and App Forum.

141 JPL, "DSL Reports," April 26, 2014, Verizon Fios Forum.

CONCLUSION

1 Rob Kitchin and Martin Dodge, *Code/Space: Software and Everyday Life* (Cambridge, MA: MIT Press, 2011), 221.

2 Ibid., 216.

3 For an example of the ways that the Internet is experienced differently around the world, see Cyrus Farivar, *The Internet of Elsewhere: The Emergent Effects of a Wired World* (New Brunswick, NJ: Rutgers University Press, 2011).

4 Nate Silver, *The Signal and the Noise: Why So Many Predictions Fail but Some Don't* (New York: Penguin, 2012), 162.

5 Kitchin and Dodge, *Code/Space*, 247.

6 Samsung, "Birthday Party," advertisement, August 18, 2016, available at https://www.ispot.tv/ad/ATeV/samsung-family-hub-birthday-ft-kristen-bell-dax-shepard.

7 "Kristen Bell and Dax Shepard Return in Samsung's New Home Appliance Marketing Campaign," *Business Wire*, May 10, 2016.

8 Lynn Spigel, *Welcome to the Dreamhouse: Popular Media and Postwar Suburbs* (Durham, NC: Duke University Press, 2001).

9 This fear is espoused by Philip Howard in *Pax Technica: How the Internet of Things May Set Us Free or Lock Us Up* (New Haven, CT: Yale University Press, 2015).

10 Paul Mozur and Su-Hyun Lee, "Samsung to Recall 2.5 Million Galaxy Note 7s over Battery Fires," *New York Times*, September 2, 2016.

11 Samsung, "Samsung Introduces an Entirely New Category in Refrigeration as Part of Kitchen Appliance Lineup at 2016 CES," press release, Samsung Newsroom, January 5, 2015.

12 Carlos Barreneche, "The Cluster Diagram: A Topological Analysis of Locative Networking," in *Locative Media*, ed. Rowan Wilken and Gerard Goggin (New York: Routledge, 2015).

13 Ibid., 113.

14 Paresh Dave and Meg James, "Viacom, Snapchat Expand Content, Ad Deal," *Los Angeles Times*, February 10, 2016.

15 Katie Rogers, "*X-Men: Apocalypse* Takes over Snapchat Lenses in Film Promotion," *New York Times*, May 24, 2016.

16 Ibid.

17 Mark Andrejevic, "The Work That Affective Economics Does," *Cultural Studies* 25, nos. 4–5 (2011): 604–620.

18 J. Sage Elwell, "The Transmediated Self: Life between the Digital and the Analog," *Convergence: The International Journal of Research into New Media Technologies* 20, no. 2 (2014): 233–249.

19 Reuters, "Pokemon Go Can Boost Health by Making Gamers Exercise, Says GP," *Guardian*, August 10, 2016.

20 "Get Up, Get Out, and Explore!," Pokémon Go webpage, accessed July 11, 2016, www.pokemongo.com.

21 Gabriel Rosenberg, "Pokémon Go Is Catching Us All—In Unexpected Ways," NPR, July 11, 2016.

22 Luke Kawa and Lily Katz, "These Charts Show That Pokemon Go Is Already in Decline," Bloomberg Markets, August 22, 2016.

23 Pokémon Go, "Get Up and Go!," YouTube, July 6, 2016, https://www.youtube.com/watch?v=SWtDeeXtMZM&feature=youtu.be.

24 Karen K. Ho, "Players and Quitters: Who's Still Playing Pokemon Go?," *Globe and Mail*, August 31, 2016.

25 Ibid.

26 Henry Jenkins, *Convergence Culture: Where Old Media and New Media Collide* (New York: NYU Press, 2006), 5.

27 Rupert Murdoch announced his dedication to media franchises in 1988. David S. Vise, "The World According to Rupert Murdoch: How the High-Rolling Billionaire Views the Media, Business and Management," *Washington Post*, August 14, 1988.

28 Jennifer Holt, *Empires of Entertainment: Media Industries and the Politics of Deregulation, 1980–1996* (New Brunswick, NJ: Rutgers University Press, 2011).

29 Justin Wyatt, *High Concept: Movies and Marketing in Hollywood* (Austin: University of Texas Press, 2010).

30 Toby Miller, Nitin Govil, John McMurria, Richard Maxwell, and Ting Wang, *Global Hollywood 2* (London: BFI, 2005).

31 Grainge, *Brand Hollywood.*

32 Axel Bruns, *Blogs, Wikipedia, Second Life, and Beyond: From Production to Produsage* (New York: Peter Lang, 2008); Jenkins, *Convergence Culture.*

33 Turow, *Daily You*; Lotz, *Television Will Be Revolutionized*; Chuck Tryon, *Reinventing Cinema: Movies in the Age of Media Convergence* (New Brunswick, NJ: Rutgers University Press, 2009).

34 Cecilia Kang, "Broadband Providers Will Need Permission to Collect Private Data," *New York Times*, October 27, 2016.

SELECTED BIBLIOGRAPHY

Anderson, Paul Allen. "Neo-Muzak and the Business of Mood." *Critical Inquiry* 41, no. 4 (2015): 811–840.

Ang, Ien. *Desperately Seeking the Audience*. New York: Routledge, 2006.

Augé, Marc. *Non-places: An Introduction to Supermodernity*. Translated by John Howe. London: Verso, 2008.

Benkler, Yochai. *The Wealth of Networks: How Social Production Transforms Markets and Freedom*. New Haven, CT: Yale University Press, 2006.

Berry, Richard. "A Golden Age of Podcasting? Evaluating *Serial* in the Context of Podcast Histories." *Journal of Radio & Audio Media* 22, no. 2 (2015): 170–178.

Boddy, William. *New Media and Popular Imagination*. Oxford: Oxford University Press, 2004.

Bogost, Ian. *Persuasive Games: The Expressive Power of Videogames*. Cambridge, MA: MIT Press, 2007.

Bolter, J. David, and Richard Grusin. *Remediation: Understanding New Media*. Cambridge, MA: MIT Press, 2000.

Browne, Nick. "The Political Economy of the Television (Super) Text." In *American Television: New Directions in History and Theory*, edited by Nick Browne, 69–79. Chur, Switzerland: Harwood, 1994.

Bull, Michael. *Sound Moves: iPod Culture and Urban Experience*. New York: Routledge, 2007.

Caldwell, John T. *Production Culture: Industrial Reflexivity and Critical Practice in Film and Television*. Durham, NC: Duke University Press, 2008.

———. "Second-Shift Media Aesthetics and Transmedia Storytelling." In *New Media: Theories and Practices of Digitextuality*, ed. Anna Everett and John T. Caldwell, 127–144. New York: Routledge, 2003.

Campbell, Scott. "Mobile Communication and Network Privatism." *Review of Communication Research* 3, no. 1 (2015): 1–21.

Castells, Manuel. *The Internet Galaxy: Reflections on the Internet, Business, and Society*. Oxford: Oxford University Press, 2001.

———. *The Rise of the Network Society*. Vol. 1 of *The Information Age: Economy, Society and Culture*. Malden, MA: Blackwell, 1996.

Certeau, Michel de. *The Practice of Everyday Life*. Berkeley: University of California Press, 1984.

Christian, Aymar Jean. "The Web as Television Reimagined? Online Networks and the Pursuit of Legacy Media." *Journal of Communication Inquiry* 36, no. 4 (2012): 340–356.

Couldry, Nick, and Anna McCarthy. Introduction to *MediaSpace: Place, Scale and Culture in a Media Age*, edited by Nick Couldry and Anna McCarthy, 1–18. London: Routledge, 2004.

Dawson, Max. "Little Players, Big Shows: Format, Narration, and Style on Television's New Smaller Screens." *Convergence: The International Journal of Research into New Media Technologies* 13, no. 2 (2007): 231–250.

Du Gay, Paul, Stuart Hall, Linda Janes, Anders Koed Madsen, Hugh Mackay, and Keith Negus. *Doing Cultural Studies: The Story of the Sony Walkman*. Thousand Oaks, CA: Sage, 2013.

Evans, Elizabeth. "The Economics of Free Freemium Games, Branding and the Impatience Economy." *Convergence: The International Journal of Research into New Media Technologies* 22 (2015): 563–580.

———. *Transmedia Television: Audiences, New Media and Daily Life*. New York: Routledge, 2011.

Fiske, John. *Television Culture*. New York: Routledge, 1987.

Galloway, Alexander R. *The Interface Effect*. Cambridge, UK: Polity, 2012.

Goggin, Gerard. *Cell Phone Culture: Mobile Technology in Everyday Life*. New York: Routledge, 2006.

Grainge, Paul. *Brand Hollywood: Selling Entertainment in a Global Media Age*. New York: Routledge, 2007.

Gray, Jonathan. *Show Sold Separately*. New York: NYU Press, 2010.

———. *Watching with "The Simpsons": Television, Parody, and Intertextuality*. New York: Routledge, 2006.

Gregg, Melissa. *Work's Intimacy*. New York: Wiley, 2013.

Hassoun, Dan. "Tracing Attentions: Toward an Analysis of Simultaneous Media Use." *Television and New Media* 15, no. 4 (2014) 271–288.

Hjorth, Larissa, and Ingrid Richardson. *Gaming in Social, Locative and Mobile Media*. Basingstoke, UK: Palgrave Macmillan, 2014.

Hobson, Dorothy. "Soap Operas at Work." In *Remote Control: Television, Audiences, and Cultural Power*, edited by Ellen Seiter, Hans Borchers, Gabriele Kreutzner, and Eva-Maria Warth, 150–167. New York: Routledge, 1989.

Hosokawa, Shuhei. "The Walkman Effect." *Popular Music* 4 (1984): 165–180.

Jenkins, Henry. *Textual Poachers: Television Fans and Participatory Culture*. New York: Routledge, 2012.

Jones, Keith. "Music in Factories: A Twentieth-Century Technique for Control of the Productive Self." *Social & Cultural Geography* 6, no. 5 (2005): 723–744.

Klinger, Barbara. *Beyond the Multiplex: Cinema, New Technologies, and the Home*. Berkeley: University of California Press, 2006.

Kobayashi, Tetsuro, and Jeffrey Boase. "Tele-cocooning: Mobile Texting and Social Scope." *Journal of Computer-Mediated Communication* 19, no. 3 (2014): 681–694.

Lessig, Lawrence. *Free Culture: How Big Media Uses Technology and the Law to Lock Down Culture and Control Creativity*. New York: Penguin, 2004.

Lotz, Amanda D. *The Television Will Be Revolutionized*. New York: NYU Press, 2014.

Manovich, Lev. *The Language of New Media*. Cambridge, MA: MIT Press, 2001.

Marx, Nick. "'The Missing Link Moment': Web Comedy in New Media Industries." *Velvet Light Trap* 68 (2011): 14–23.

Marvin, Carolyn. *When Old Technologies Were New*. New York: Oxford University Press, 1997.

Mayer, Vicki, Miranda J. Banks, and John T. Caldwell. *Production Studies: Cultural Studies of Media Industries*. New York: Routledge, 2009.

McCarthy, Anna. *Ambient Television: Visual Culture and Public Space*. Durham, NC: Duke University Press, 2001.

McClung, Steven, and Kristine Johnson. "Examining the Motives of Podcast Users." *Journal of Radio & Audio Media* 17, no. 1 (2010): 82–95.

Meehan, Eileen, "Why We Don't Count: The Commodity Audience." In *Logics of Television: Essays in Cultural Criticism*, edited by Patricia Mellencamp, 117–137. Bloomington: Indiana University Press, 1990.

Modleski, Tania. "The Rhythms of Reception: Daytime Television and Women's Work." In *Regarding Television: Critical Approaches-an Anthology*, ed. E. Ann Kaplan, 67–74. Lanham, MD: University Publications of America, 1983.

Morley, David. *Family Television: Cultural Power and Domestic Leisure*. New York: Routledge, 1986.

Morse, Margaret. "An Ontology of Everyday Distraction: The Freeway, the Mall, and Television." *Logics of Television: Essays in Cultural Criticism*, edited by Patricia Mellencamp, 193–221. Bloomington: Indiana University Press, 1990.

Moshe, Mira. "Media Time Squeezing: The Privatization of the Media Time Sphere." *Television & New Media* 13 (January 2012): 68–88.

Papacharissi, Zizi. *A Private Sphere: Democracy in a Digital Age*. Malden, MA: Polity, 2010.

Perren, Alisa, and Jennifer Holt, eds. *Media Industries Studies: History, Theory, and Method*. New York: Wiley, 2011.

Radway, Janice A. *Reading the Romance: Women, Patriarchy, and Popular Literature*. Chapel Hill: University of North Carolina Press, 2009.

Ross, Sharon Marie. *Beyond the Box: Television and the Internet*. Malden, MA: Wiley Blackwell, 2011.

Schwartz, Barry. "Waiting, Exchange, and Power: The Distribution of Time in Social Systems." *American Journal of Sociology* 79, no. 4 (1974): 841–870.

Simun, Miriam. "My Music, My World: Using the MP3 Player to Shape Experience in London." *New Media Society* 11, no. 9 (2009): 921–941.

Silverstone, Roger. *Television and Everyday Life*. New York: Routledge, 1994.

Spigel, Lynn. *Make Room for TV: Television and the Family Ideal in Postwar America*. Chicago: University of Chicago Press, 1992.

———. "Portable TV: Studies in Domestic Space Travel." In *Welcome to the Dreamhouse: Popular Media and Postwar Suburbs*, 000–000. Durham, NC: Duke University Press, 2001.

Spigel, Lynn, and Max Dawson. "Television and Digital Media." In *American Thought and Culture in the 21st Century*, ed. Catherine Morley and Martin Halliwell, 275–290. Edinburgh: Edinburgh University Press, 2008.

Souza e Silva, Adriana de. "From Cyber to Hybrid Mobile Technologies as Interfaces of Hybrid Spaces." *Space and Culture* 9, no. 3 (2006): 261–278.

Sterne, Jonathan. *The Audible Past: Cultural Origins of Sound Reproduction*. Durham, NC: Duke University Press, 2003.

Thompson, Kristin. *The Frodo Franchise*. Berkeley: University of California Press, 2007.

Thulin, Samuel. "Mobile Audio Apps, Place and Life beyond Immersive Interactivity." *Mobile Cultures Issue* 6, no. 3 (2012). http://wi.mobilities.ca.

Tobin, Samuel. *Portable Play in Everyday Life: The Nintendo DS*. New York: Palgrave Macmillan, 2013.

Tryon, Chuck. *On-Demand Culture: Digital Delivery and the Future of Movies*. New Brunswick, NJ: Rutgers University Press, 2013.

Turow, Joseph. *The Daily You: How the New Advertising Industry Is Defining Your Identity and Your Worth*. New Haven, CT: Yale University Press, 2012.

Van Dijck, José. *The Culture of Connectivity: A Critical History of Social Media*. New York: Oxford University Press, 2013.

van Es, Karin. "Social TV and the Participation Dilemma in NBC's *The Voice*." *Television & New Media* 17, no. 2 (2016): 108–123.

Williams, Raymond. *Television: Technology and Cultural Form*. New York: Routledge, 1974.

Wilson, Sherryl. "In the Living Room: Second Screens and TV Audiences." *Television & New Media* 17, no. 2 (2016): 174–191.

Zittrain, Jonathan. *The Future of the Internet and How to Stop It*. New Haven, CT: Yale University Press, 2008.

INDEX

ABOUT THE AUTHOR

Ethan Tussey is Assistant Professor of Communication at Georgia State University. He has contributed book chapters on creative labor, online sports viewing, connected viewing, and crowdfunding to multiple anthologies.